Dummies 101®: Microsoft® Outlook™ 97 For Windows®

CHEAT SHEET

The Inbox Toolbar

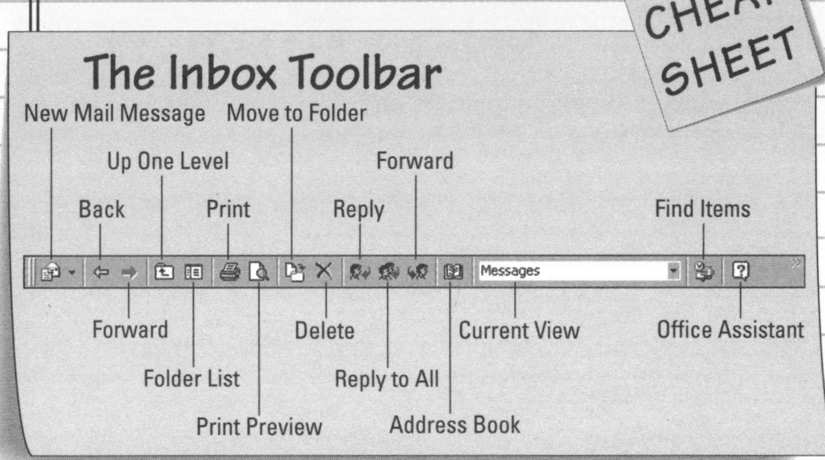

The Message Toolbar

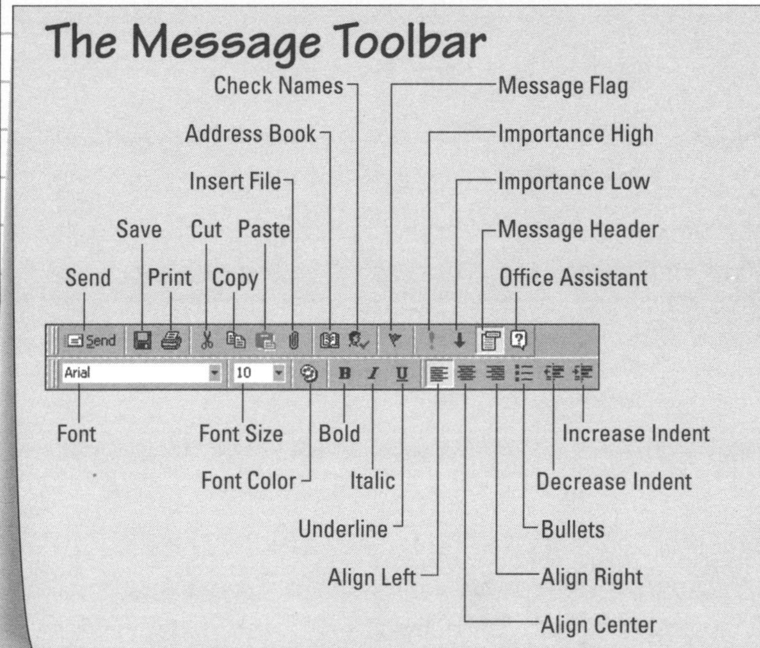

The Tasks Toolbar

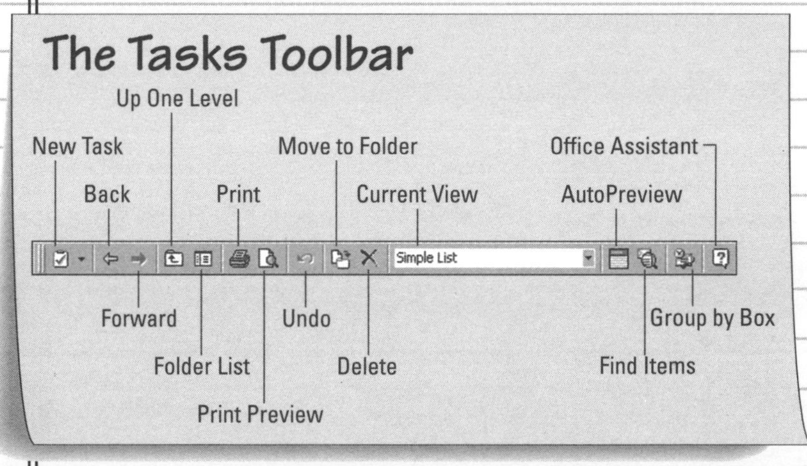

☑ **Progress Check**

Unit 1: Touring Outlook 97 and the Mail Window

- ❑ Lesson 1-1: Starting Outlook from the Desktop
- ❑ Lesson 1-2: Getting around in Outlook
- ❑ Lesson 1-3: Navigating the Mail Window

Unit 2: Writing and Sending Messages

- ❑ Lesson 2-1: Adding an Address to the Address Book
- ❑ Lesson 2-2: Editing and Deleting Addresses
- ❑ Lesson 2-3: Creating Groups of Recipients
- ❑ Lesson 2-4: Composing and Sending an E-mail Message
- ❑ Lesson 2-5: Formatting an E-Mail Message
- ❑ Lesson 2-6: Creating an AutoSignature
- ❑ Lesson 2-7: Attaching a File to an E-Mail Message
- ❑ Lesson 2-8: Setting Message Options

Unit 3: Receiving Messages

- ❑ Lesson 3-1: Understanding the Inbox
- ❑ Lesson 3-2: Reading Messages
- ❑ Lesson 3-3: Responding to Messages
- ❑ Lesson 3-4: Printing Messages

Unit 4: Organizing Your E-Mail

- ❑ Lesson 4-1: Using the Folder List
- ❑ Lesson 4-2: Creating Folders
- ❑ Lesson 4-3: Using Folders to Store E-Mail
- ❑ Lesson 4-4: Sorting E-Mail
- ❑ Lesson 4-5: Viewing Messages that Match Criteria
- ❑ Lesson 4-6: Grouping Messages

Unit 5: Making Appointments

- ❑ Lesson 5-1: Scheduling Appointments
- ❑ Lesson 5-2: Refining Your Reminders
- ❑ Lesson 5-3: Entering Recurring Appointments
- ❑ Lesson 5-4: Creating an Event
- ❑ Lesson 5-5: Setting Up a Meeting
- ❑ Lesson 5-6: Viewing Appointments

Unit 6: Managing Appointments

- ❑ Lesson 6-1: Modifying Appointments
- ❑ Lesson 6-2: Editing Appointments with Drag and Drop
- ❑ Lesson 6-3: Archiving Appointments
- ❑ Lesson 6-4: Printing the Calendar

Unit 7: Tracking Tasks

- ❑ Lesson 7-1: Recording a Task
- ❑ Lesson 7-2: Entering Details about a Task
- ❑ Lesson 7-3: Creating a Recurring Task
- ❑ Lesson 7-4: Editing Tasks
- ❑ Lesson 7-5: Changing Recurring Tasks
- ❑ Lesson 7-6: Charting the Progress of a Task
- ❑ Lesson 7-7: Tracking Tasks as Projects
- ❑ Lesson 7-8: Sorting Tasks
- ❑ Lesson 7-9: Printing Task Reports
- ❑ Lesson 7-10: Handling Task Housekeeping

Unit 8: Setting Up the Contacts Database

- ❑ Lesson 8-1: Entering Contacts
- ❑ Lesson 8-2: Entering Repetitive Contact Information
- ❑ Lesson 8-3: Entering Detailed Contact Information
- ❑ Lesson 8-4: Setting Journal Options
- ❑ Lesson 8-5: Creating a Contact from an E-Mail
- ❑ Lesson 8-6: Importing Your Personal Address Book
- ❑ Lesson 8-7: Importing a Contact List from Another Program
- ❑ Lesson 8-8: Cutomizing the Address Cards View

Unit 9: Using the Contact List

- ❑ Lesson 9-1: Viewing Contacts
- ❑ Lesson 9-2: Modifying Contacts Table Views
- ❑ Lesson 9-3: Doing Real Work from the Contacts Database
- ❑ Lesson 9-4: Recording Automatic Journal Entries
- ❑ Lesson 9-5: Recording Manual Journal Entries
- ❑ Lesson 9-6: Deleting and Restoring Journal Entries
- ❑ Lesson 9-7: Filtering the Contacts Database
- ❑ Lesson 9-8: Printing Contacts
- ❑ Lesson 9-9: Creating an Outlook Address Book
- ❑ Lesson 9-10: Using Word Mail Merge with the Contacts Database

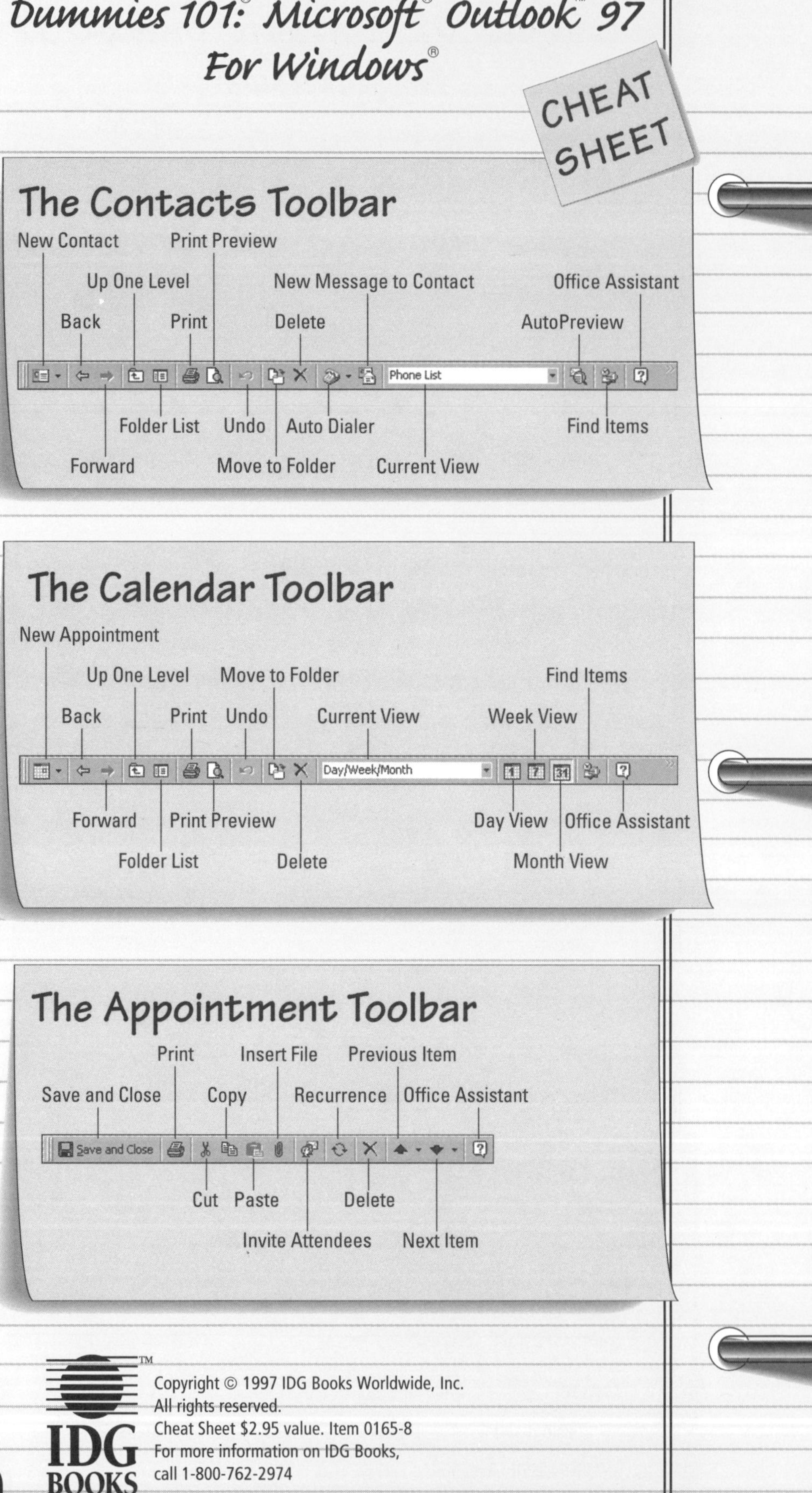

References for the Rest of Us!®

COMPUTER BOOK SERIES FROM IDG

Are you intimidated and confused by computers? Do you find that traditional manuals are overloaded with technical details you'll never use? Do your friends and family always call you to fix simple problems on their PCs? Then the *...For Dummies®* computer book series from IDG Books Worldwide is for you.

...For Dummies books are written for those frustrated computer users who know they aren't really dumb but find that PC hardware, software, and indeed the unique vocabulary of computing make them feel helpless. *...For Dummies* books use a lighthearted approach, a down-to-earth style, and even cartoons and humorous icons to diffuse computer novices' fears and build their confidence. Lighthearted but not lightweight, these books are a perfect survival guide for anyone forced to use a computer.

"I like my copy so much I told friends; now they bought copies."

Irene C., Orwell, Ohio

"Quick, concise, nontechnical, and humorous."

Jay A., Elburn, Illinois

"Thanks, I needed this book. Now I can sleep at night."

Robin F., British Columbia, Canada

Already, hundreds of thousands of satisfied readers agree. They have made *...For Dummies* books the #1 introductory level computer book series and have written asking for more. So, if you're looking for the most fun and easy way to learn about computers, look to *...For Dummies* books to give you a helping hand.

7/96r

Dummies 101®: Microsoft® Outlook™ 97 for Windows®

by Kathy Ivens and Thomas E. Barich

IDG Books Worldwide, Inc.
An International Data Group Company

Foster City, CA ✦ Chicago, IL ✦ Indianapolis, IN ✦ Southlake, TX

Dummies 101®: Microsoft® Outlook™ 97 For Windows®

Published by
IDG Books Worldwide, Inc.
An International Data Group Company
919 E. Hillsdale Blvd.
Suite 400
Foster City, CA 94404
http://www.idgbooks.com (IDG Books Worldwide Web site)
http://www.dummies.com (Dummies Press Web site)

Library of Congress Catalog Card No.: 97-70733

ISBN: 0-7645-0165-8

Printed in the United States of America

10 9 8 7 6 5 4 3 2 1

1M/QW/QV/ZX/IN

Distributed in the United States by IDG Books Worldwide, Inc.

Distributed by Macmillan Canada for Canada; by Transworld Publishers Limited in the United Kingdom and Europe; by WoodsLane Pty. Ltd. for Australia; by WoodsLane Enterprises Ltd. for New Zealand; by Longman Singapore Publishers Ltd. for Singapore, Malaysia, Thailand, and Indonesia; by Simron Pty. Ltd. for South Africa; by Toppan Company Ltd. for Japan; by Distribuidora Cuspide for Argentina; by Livraria Cultura for Brazil; by Ediciencia S.A. for Ecuador; by Addison-Wesley Publishing Company for Korea; by Ediciones ZETA S.C.R. Ltda. for Peru; by WS Computer Publishing Company, Inc., for the Philippines; by Unalis Corporation for Taiwan; by Contemporanea de Ediciones for Venezuela. Authorized Sales Agent: Anthony Rudkin Associates for the Middle East and North Africa.

For general information on IDG Books Worldwide's books in the U.S., please call our Consumer Customer Service department at 800-762-2974. For reseller information, including discounts and premium sales, please call our Reseller Customer Service department at 800-434-3422.

For information on where to purchase IDG Books Worldwide's books outside the U.S., please contact our International Sales department at 415-655-3023 or fax 415-655-3299.

For information on foreign language translations, please contact our Foreign & Subsidiary Rights department at 415-655-3021 or fax 415-655-3281.

For sales inquiries and special prices for bulk quantities, please contact our Sales department at 415-655-3200 or write to the address above.

For information on using IDG Books Worldwide's books in the classroom or for ordering examination copies, please contact our Educational Sales department at 800-434-2086 or fax 817-251-8174.

For press review copies, author interviews, or other publicity information, please contact our Public Relations department at 415-655-3000 or fax 415-655-3299.

For authorization to photocopy items for corporate, personal, or educational use, please contact Copyright Clearance Center, 222 Rosewood Drive, Danvers, MA 01923, or fax 508-750-4470.

About the Authors

Kathy Ivens has written more than two dozen books about computers. She's had a number of other careers during which she learned plenty about a lot of things. As a result, she plays a mean game of trivia.

Thomas E. Barich writes computer books in addition to running a CD production company that builds and designs software CDs. He's had a wide variety of careers and as a result knows just enough to be dangerous about a whole lot of subjects.

ABOUT IDG BOOKS WORLDWIDE

Welcome to the world of IDG Books Worldwide.

IDG Books Worldwide, Inc., is a subsidiary of International Data Group, the world's largest publisher of computer-related information and the leading global provider of information services on information technology. IDG was founded more than 25 years ago and now employs more than 8,500 people worldwide. IDG publishes more than 275 computer publications in over 75 countries (see listing below). More than 60 million people read one or more IDG publications each month.

Launched in 1990, IDG Books Worldwide is today the #1 publisher of best-selling computer books in the United States. We are proud to have received eight awards from the Computer Press Association in recognition of editorial excellence and three from *Computer Currents'* First Annual Readers' Choice Awards. Our best-selling *...For Dummies®* series has more than 30 million copies in print with translations in 30 languages. IDG Books Worldwide, through a joint venture with IDG's Hi-Tech Beijing, became the first U.S. publisher to publish a computer book in the People's Republic of China. In record time, IDG Books Worldwide has become the first choice for millions of readers around the world who want to learn how to better manage their businesses.

Our mission is simple: Every one of our books is designed to bring extra value and skill-building instructions to the reader. Our books are written by experts who understand and care about our readers. The knowledge base of our editorial staff comes from years of experience in publishing, education, and journalism — experience we use to produce books for the '90s. In short, we care about books, so we attract the best people. We devote special attention to details such as audience, interior design, use of icons, and illustrations. And because we use an efficient process of authoring, editing, and desktop publishing our books electronically, we can spend more time ensuring superior content and spend less time on the technicalities of making books.

You can count on our commitment to deliver high-quality books at competitive prices on topics you want to read about. At IDG Books Worldwide, we continue in the IDG tradition of delivering quality for more than 25 years. You'll find no better book on a subject than one from IDG Books Worldwide.

John Kilcullen
CEO
IDG Books Worldwide, Inc.

Steven Berkowitz
President and Publisher
IDG Books Worldwide, Inc.

Eighth Annual Computer Press Awards 1992

Ninth Annual Computer Press Awards 1993

Tenth Annual Computer Press Awards 1994

Eleventh Annual Computer Press Awards 1995

Dedication

Kathy Ivens: To Rich, with deep affection, for knowing when and how to jump in, and for sensing those times when all that's needed is a warm hug.

Thomas E. Barich: To Tom Barich, Sr., who taught me that perseverance pays off. Thanks, Dad.

Authors' Acknowledgments

The authors owe thanks to David Madison of Microsoft Corporation for his support, especially his willingness to answer picayune questions and check up on all the details we insisted we wanted to know about.

We both extend our heartfelt gratitude to all the members of the talented team at IDG Books Worldwide, Inc. Thanks to Senior Acquisitions Editor Jill Pisoni for being supportive and terrific (as she always has been). Special thanks to Mary Goodwin, who skillfully handled the production and development for this book, providing support, feedback, and good conversation throughout the process. We're grateful for the time, attention, and experience she brought to our book.

Technical Editor Michael Zulich checked the technical accuracy of every lesson we wrote so that we wouldn't make fools of ourselves, and Copy Editor Felicity O'Meara made it look as if we are experts in the use of the language.

Publisher's Acknowledgments

We're proud of this book; please send us your comments about it by using the IDG Books Worldwide Registration Card at the back of the book or by e-mailing us at `feedback/dummies@idgbooks.com`. Some of the people who helped bring this book to market include the following:

Acquisitions, Development, and Editorial

Project Editor: Mary Goodwin

Senior Acquisitions Editor: Jill Pisoni

Product Development Director: Mary Bednarek

Media Development Manager: Joyce Pepple

Copy Editor: Felicity O'Meara

Technical Editor: Michael Zulich

Editorial Manager: Mary C. Corder

Editorial Assistants: Chris H. Collins, Steven H. Hayes, Darren Meiss

Production

Project Coordinator: Regina Snyder

Layout and Graphics: Linda M. Boyer, J. Tyler Connor, Dominique DeFelice, Angela F. Hunckler, Brent Savage

Proofreaders: Arielle Carol Mennelle, Nancy L. Reinhardt, Carrie Voorhis, Joel K. Draper, Rachel Garvey, Robert Springer

Indexer: Lynnzee Elze Spense

General and Administrative

IDG Books Worldwide, Inc.: John Kilcullen, CEO; Steven Berkowitz, President and Publisher

Dummies, Inc.: Brenda McLaughlin, Senior Vice President & Group Publisher

Dummies Technology Press & Dummies Editorial: Diane Graves Steele, Vice President and Associate Publisher; Judith A. Taylor, Brand Manager; Kristin A. Cocks, Editorial Director

Dummies Trade Press: Kathleen A. Welton, Vice President & Publisher; Stacy S. Collins, Brand Manager

IDG Books Production for Dummies Press: Beth Jenkins, Production Director; Cindy L. Phipps, Supervisor of Project Coordination, Production Proofreading and Indexing; Kathie S. Schutte, Supervisor of Page Layout; Shelley Lea, Supervisor of Graphics and Design; Debbie J. Gates, Production Systems Specialist; Tony Augsburger, Supervisor of Reprints and Bluelines; Leslie Popplewell, Media Archive Coordinator

Dummies Packaging & Book Design: Patti Sandez, Packaging Specialist; Lance Kayser, Packaging Assistant; Kavish + Kavish, Cover Design

♦

The publisher would like to give special thanks to Patrick J. McGovern,
without whom this book would not have been possible.

♦

ABC 123

Files at a Glance

Here's a list of the files stored on this book's CD-ROM. You'll use these files as you work your way through the book. For more information about using the CD-ROM, please see Appendix B.

Part I

Lesson 2-7 .... Attaching files to a message .... Pest.doc

Part II

Lesson 6-1 .... Attaching files to a meeting form .... TaxRefrm.doc

Part III

Lesson 8-7 .... Importing a contact list .... Governor.mdb

Lesson 9-5 .... Recording manual journal entries .... Tribute.doc

Part III Lab Assignment ...... Recording journal entries .... Activities.doc

Contents at a Glance

Table of Contents

Introduction

Microsoft Outlook 97 is so large and has so many different programs and features, it would take you months to figure the program out on your own. Luckily, you have *Dummies 101: Microsoft Outlook 97 For Windows* so that you won't have to stumble blindly through Outlook, clicking your mouse in an effort to figure out what all those icons and menus mean.

We've already stumbled through Outlook blindly until we figured it out, and now we're giving you the benefit of our experience and new expertise. We're computer propeller heads, and we know how to stumble and grope productively when we come across new software. Besides that, we have friends at Microsoft who guided us. That's why this book has such good stuff in it.

This book is designed to help you get the most out of Outlook in a very short time. By going through all the lessons, you'll gain hands-on experience with all the important features in Outlook.

Who Are You?

This book is for you if you're just beginning to use Outlook. You may be using the program on your home computer or in the office and dialing out through your modem to reach the Internet. Doesn't matter — we also covered all the bases for you if you are connected to a network, and even if you're connected to a network that is running Microsoft Exchange Server as an e-mail system (which changes some of the basic Outlook features).

This book is also for all the software pioneers — and that includes you — because Outlook is a brand new program and there isn't anything else exactly like Outlook in existence. Even if you didn't get your hands on this book the first day Outlook was installed on your computer, and you have already tinkered around with the program a bit, we bet we can still show you a thing or two about some of Outlook's finer features.

Using This Book

The best way to use this book is to start at the beginning and keep going until you get to the end. You don't have to do that in one session, of course. In fact, if you try to go through this book in one day your brain will hurt.

hey, look over here — it's a margin note

As you read each unit, do every exercise in order. If you skip an exercise in any lesson, you won't learn as much because each lesson builds on the things you learn in previous lessons. For example, after we tell you several times exactly which buttons or icons to click in order to perform a task, we assume you've learned how to do that task. Then, in some future lesson, we tell you to perform that same task without giving you the specific keystrokes or mouse clicks.

We made the exercises simple and fun, hoping you won't feel you're back in elementary school (where almost nobody has much fun). By the way, as you read this book, it's okay to laugh out loud when we tell you something amusing. In fact, we'd appreciate it.

Here's how to follow along with the different parts of this book:

- **Units:** The book contains nine units. Each unit starts with an introduction which tells you what you'll learn in the unit and why you would want to learn it. The units contain lessons, which take you step-by-step through the skill we want you to learn.
- **Extra Credit:** Throughout the text, we talk about some topics that are a little more complicated than you may need to know. We put these topics in Extra Credit sidebars, separate from the step-by-step instructions you need to learn how to use Outlook. That way, if you want to read about this extra stuff, you know where to find it. If you could care less about anything except the basics, you can skip the Extra Credit with no penalties. Do not pass Go!
- **Margin Notes:** When we tell you something really important about using Outlook, we put that information in a note in the margin of the book (look right next to this text to see what we're talking about). We also leave you plenty of room in the margins if you want to scribble down a few thoughts as you're working through the book. Unlike your elementary-school text books, we want you to write in the book so that you can remember key points for future reference.
- **Recesses:** At least once in each unit, we include a Recess section to remind you that there is more to life than computers. In the Recess, we encourage you to relax a while before moving on with the rest of the book.
- **Quizzes and Tests:** These may be the only fun quizzes and tests you take in your life. At the end of each unit, we ask you a few simple questions about the unit that may just even make you laugh. If you can't recall the answer to one of the questions, we even use an icon to tell you where to find the answer in the unit. At the end of each part, we want you to review what you've learned in the part by answering a few more questions. Don't worry — if you don't know the answer, you can always look in Appendix A, which contains the answers, for a little help.

We used some conventions throughout this book that you should know about so that they make sense to you when you come across them:

- Whenever we want you to type something, we'll format those characters in a special way. If the instructional step is bold, the stuff we want you to type won't be bold.

- When you have to press more than one key at a time, we show you the names of the keys connected with a plus sign, like this: Ctrl+S. That means you should hold down the first key (Crtl, in this example), press the second key (S), and then release both of the keys at the same time.
- When you should choose a command from the menu bar, we put a little arrow between the different parts of the command, like this: File⇨Open. When you see a command written like that, you should click the first part of the command (File, in this example) on the menu bar and then click the second part (Open) on the menu that appears. See how some of those letters in the menu commands are underlined? The underlining means that those letters are *hot keys* for the command — just press and hold down the Alt key while you press a hot key to access the corresponding menu.

How the Book Is Organized

For your enjoyment, we've divided this book into four action-packed parts:

Part I: Working with E-Mail

Part I talks about e-mail and messages and all the wondrous things you can do with your Outlook e-mail system.

Part II: Staying on Schedule

Part II revels in the Outlook programs that keep you organized, efficient, and on-track. In this part, you learn all about the Outlook calendar and other features that get you where you need to go — on time.

Part III: Managing Your Contacts

In this part, you hear about tracking contacts. *Contacts* are people with whom you are in contact, which probably accounts for the name of the feature. Outlook has all sorts of powerful methods of keeping track of the people you contact, so you know when, why, or how you contact them and what happened. In bureaucratic jargon, this is sometimes called *keeping a paper trail*.

Part IV: Appendixes

Part IV offers two reference chapters. The first one has the answers to the all the quizzes and tests in this book (no fair looking before you answer the test questions). The second appendix is all about the CD that comes with this book, including what's on the CD and how to install it.

Icons Used in This Book

Some special icons pop up throughout this book to draw your attention to important points:

We use the Heads Up icon to warn you when we think you'd better pay close attention to avoid a serious mistake.

The On The Test icon alerts you that the subject under discussion appears on the test.

When you see the On The CD icon in the margin, you need a file from the CD in order to complete this lesson.

We put one of these icons next to any material that isn't really essential to your basic understanding of Outlook.

Using the Dummies 101 CD-ROM

The CD-ROM at the back of this book contains some practice files that you use with the lessons in this book. It also contains a handy installation program that copies the files to your hard drive in a very simple process.

In addition, we offer you some nifty software on the CD that you first have to install before you can use. For example, if you would like to sign up for an Internet e-mail account with AT&T WorldNet Service (you need some kind of access to e-mail in order to work through Part I of the book), the CD contains the AT&T WorldNet software. If you decide to sign up for an account with AT&T WorldNet Service, be sure to use these registration codes: L5SQIM631 if you are an AT&T long-distance residential customer; L5SQIM632 if you use another long-distance phone company.

The CD also contains a program that helps you send and receive material through e-mail more efficiently.

Note: The CD-ROM does not contain Microsoft Outlook 97 software or Windows 95. You must already have these programs installed on your computer in order to follow along with the lessons in this book.

Before installing the CD files and software, check out the following system requirements. If your computer doesn't meet the minimum requirements, you may have trouble using the CD:

- Microsoft Windows 95 and Office 97 installed on your computer

- A 486 or Pentium-equipped PC with CD-ROM drive
- At least 15MB of free hard-disk space if you want to install just the exercise files; at least 33MB if you want to install all the programs
- At least 8MB of RAM installed on your computer
- A modem with a speed of at least 14,400 bps (for sending e-mail)

If you need more information on PC or Windows basics, check out *PCs For Dummies,* 4th Edition, by Dan Gookin, or *Dummies 101: Windows 95,* by Andy Rathbone (both published by IDG Books Worldwide, Inc.). For the details on working with Microsoft Office 97, pick up a copy of *Dummies 101: Microsoft Office 97 For Windows,* by Peter Weverka, also Published by IDG Books.

Just insert the CD in your CD-ROM drive to start installing the exercise files and software. See Appendix B for more details.

If you have problems with the installation process, you can call the IDG Books Worldwide, Inc., Customer Support number: 800-762-2974 (outside the U.S.: 317-596-5261).

With Windows 95 up and running, follow these steps:

1. **Insert the Dummies 101 CD (label side up) into your computer's CD drive and wait about 30 seconds to see whether AutoPlay starts the CD for you.**

   Be careful to touch only the edges of the CD. The CD drive is the one that pops out with a circular drawer.

   If your computer has the Windows CD AutoPlay feature, the CD Installer should begin automatically. If nothing seems to happen after a minute or so, go to Step 2. If you see the CD installer window, you are ready to install the exercise files (see "Installing the exercise files" in Appendix B for the details).

2. **If the installation program doesn't start automatically, click the Start button and click Run.**

3. **In the dialog box that appears, type** d:\seticon.exe **(if your CD drive is not drive D, substitute the appropriate letter for D) and click OK.**

   A message informs you that the program is about to install the icons.

4. **Click OK in the message window.**

   After a moment, a program group called Dummies 101 appears on the Start menu, along with an icon that runs the CD installer. Then another message appears, asking whether you want to use the CD now.

5. **Click Yes to use the CD now or click No if you want to use the CD later.**

   If you click No, you can start the CD simply by clicking the Dummies 101 - Outlook 97 For Windows CD icon in the Dummies 101 program group (on the Start menu).

After installing the files . . .

The installation process puts the files in the following location:

Exercise files: C:\Outlook101

You don't have to do anything with the files yet — the book tells you when you need to open the first file.

Note: The files are meant to accompany the book's lessons. If you open a file prematurely, you may accidentally make changes to the file, which may prevent you from following along with the steps in the lessons. So please don't try to open or view a file until you've reached the point in the lessons where we explain how to open the file.

Store the CD where it will be free from harm so that you can reinstall a file in case the one that's installed on your computer gets messed up.

What's Next?

We hope you're excited to get started using Outlook. After you work through the lessons and exercises in this book, don't be surprised if people start to call you or stop by your office to ask you questions about using Outlook. Just be ready if your boss decides to visit to see why you've become so popular around the office.

Part I

Working with E-Mail

In this part . . .

Before you dive into learning about e-mail, we start you off with a quick tour of Outlook. Unless you understand how Outlook works and where to find the necessary tools to accomplish your tasks, mastering e-mail will be quite difficult. After you're familiar with the parts that make up Outlook and how to maneuver through them, you can move on to tackle e-mail.

E-mail, e-mail, e-mail. It's all you hear about these days, but what the heck is it, really, and why would you want to use it? E-mail is fast becoming one of the major vehicles of electronically written communication. For cost and convenience, e-mail has no match. Unlike the telephone, e-mail doesn't have any additional cost beyond your initial connection fee, regardless of whether you are sending a message to a co-worker in the next office or someone halfway around the globe. Sending and reading e-mail at your convenience, regardless of time zones or work hours, gives you flexibility offered by no other means of communication. The ease with which you can save and keep track of messages practically eliminates misunderstandings and memory lapses that often create unpleasant situations.

So, without further ado, turn on your computer, grab your mouse, and get ready to take a tour of Outlook and harness the power of its e-mail features.

Unit 1

Touring Outlook 97 and the Mail Window

Objectives for This Unit

- ✓ Starting Outlook from the desktop
- ✓ Understanding basic Outlook features
- ✓ Getting around in Outlook
- ✓ Navigating the Mail window

Prerequisites

- Turning on your computer
- Having Outlook installed on your computer

Outlook can take care of all your e-mail, scheduling, contact-management needs, and more, all in one place. Outlook makes getting and staying organized easy. After you get acquainted with Outlook, you'll find that reading and writing e-mail, making appointments, and locating phone numbers and addresses when you need them is a breeze.

Opening Outlook for the first time can be a little daunting. However, after you recognize Outlook's main parts and can find your way around, you'll feel right at home. Unit 1 takes you on a tour of Outlook and familiarizes you with the program's basic features. After your whirlwind tour of Outlook, you'll take a closer look at the Mail window.

Starting Outlook from the Desktop — Lesson 1-1

Before you can wander around in Outlook, you need to get the program up and running, which is the subject of this lesson. So strap yourself in — you're about to fire up the program!

Before you can start Outlook, you need to check that your computer has what it takes to run the program. If the following systems are go, then you can start working with Outlook:

- Windows 95 is loaded on your machine. Outlook can't run under older versions of Windows.
- Outlook must already be installed on your computer. The program currently comes bundled as part of the Microsoft Office 97 Suite. Therefore, if you have Office 97 on your machine, you should also have Outlook.

To start Outlook and begin the tour follow these steps:

☑ Progress Check

If you can do the following, you've mastered this lesson:

- ❑ Open Outlook by double-clicking the Microsoft Outlook icon.
- ❑ Open and view the Outlook main window.
- ❑ Get help from Outlook when you need it.

1. **Locate the Microsoft Outlook icon on your Windows 95 Desktop.**

   Outlook automatically places an Outlook icon on your desktop during installation. If you can't find the Outlook icon on your desktop, Outlook may not be installed on your computer.

   If you have other programs open that obscure the icon, reduce them to buttons on the Taskbar by clicking the *Minimize button* in the upper right corner of each program window.

2. **Double-click the Microsoft Outlook icon.**

   If double-clicking is not your cup of tea, you can click the Microsoft Outlook icon once to highlight it, and then press the Enter key to open Outlook.

   The Microsoft Outlook 97 *splash screen* appears, followed by the Outlook Inbox window, as seen in Figure 1-1. Each time you load Outlook it immediately takes you to the Inbox window. The splash screen is a temporary window that flashes basic program information while the program is loading; the splash screen disappears after the program is running.

   As shown in Figure 1-2, Outlook provides you with immediate assistance in the form of the Office Assistant. The animated helpmate, which can be accessed by clicking the Office Assistant button in the toolbar, offers a variety of help options, including the following:

   - **Context sensitive help:** No matter where you are, click on the Outlook Assistant button in the toolbar to get help on the current window and features.
   - **Outlook Wizard help:** Outlook Wizards are sets of dialog boxes that walk you through a particular task, such as creating a letter or importing a file. The Office Assistant automatically provides you with help each time you start an Outlook Wizard.
   - **Tips:** Brief productivity hints for Outlook are available when the yellow light bulb appears in the Outlook Assistant.
   - **User questions:** The Outlook Assistant provides answers to questions posed by the user.

3. Click OK in the Outlook Assistant dialog box to close the Office Assistant.

   You can prevent the Outlook Assistant from appearing each time you open Outlook by clicking Show these choices at start up to remove the check mark in front of the Office Assistant option.

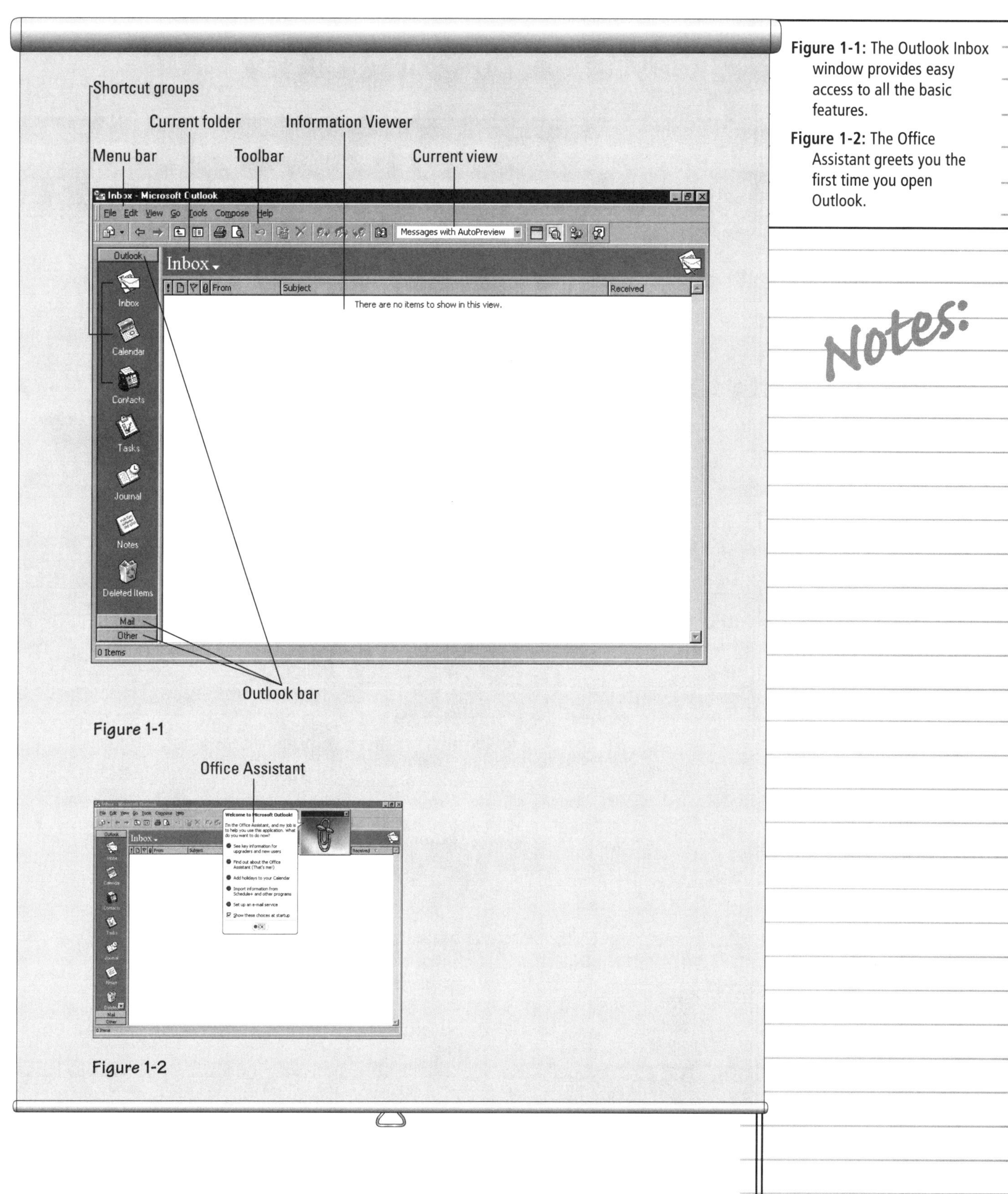

Figure 1-1

Figure 1-2

Figure 1-1: The Outlook Inbox window provides easy access to all the basic features.

Figure 1-2: The Office Assistant greets you the first time you open Outlook.

Lesson 1-2 Getting around in Outlook

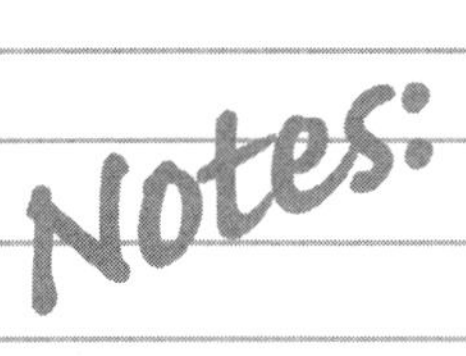

Outlook collects and stores individual pieces of information, such as e-mail messages, contact names and phone numbers, individual appointments, tasks, and more. To manage the information effectively, Outlook provides quick storage, easy retrieval, and flexibility in viewing all the bits and pieces that make up your hectic workday.

Outlook manages all this information with brilliant simplicity. The program creates a series of folders where it stores these various sets of data. These folders include the following:

- **Inbox folder:** Stores incoming e-mail and provides the tools to create and send e-mail.
- **Calendar folder:** Contains everything you need to schedule and track appointments.
- **Contacts folder:** Handles all your contact information, including name, addresses, phone numbers, and more.
- **Tasks folder:** Offers a turbo-powered personal to-do list.
- **Journal folder:** Tracks everything from phone calls to Office 97 documents.
- **Notes folder:** Features electronic sticky notes to organize every scrap of information that doesn't have a home.
- **Deleted Items folder:** Retains deleted information in case you change your mind about getting rid of it.

Each folder has a different set of viewing options that allows you to manipulate and view your information in a variety of ways. The various features in the Outlook window allow you to access all of this information.

The Outlook window is well-organized and easy to use after you understand the basics. In addition to the menu bar and the toolbar, which are standard Windows 95 components, the Outlook window contains the following three unique elements:

- The Outlook bar
- The Information Viewer
- The Folder list

heads up

If you need some help working with Windows 95, pick up a copy of *Dummies 101: Windows 95,* by Andy Rathbone, published by IDG Books Worldwide, Inc.

on the test

The Outlook bar, which you find on the left-hand side of the Outlook window, offers three groups of *shortcuts,* Outlook, Mail, and Other, which offer quick access to Outlook's main features. To the right of the Outlook bar you find the Information Viewer, a large window in which items from the selected folder are displayed. The Folder list is a drop-down list of your existing folders. You activate the Folder list by clicking the current folder name on the banner just above the Information Viewer. You can use these three items to help navigate Outlook.

To see how the Outlook bar, the Information Viewer, and the Folder list help you get around in Outlook, follow these steps:

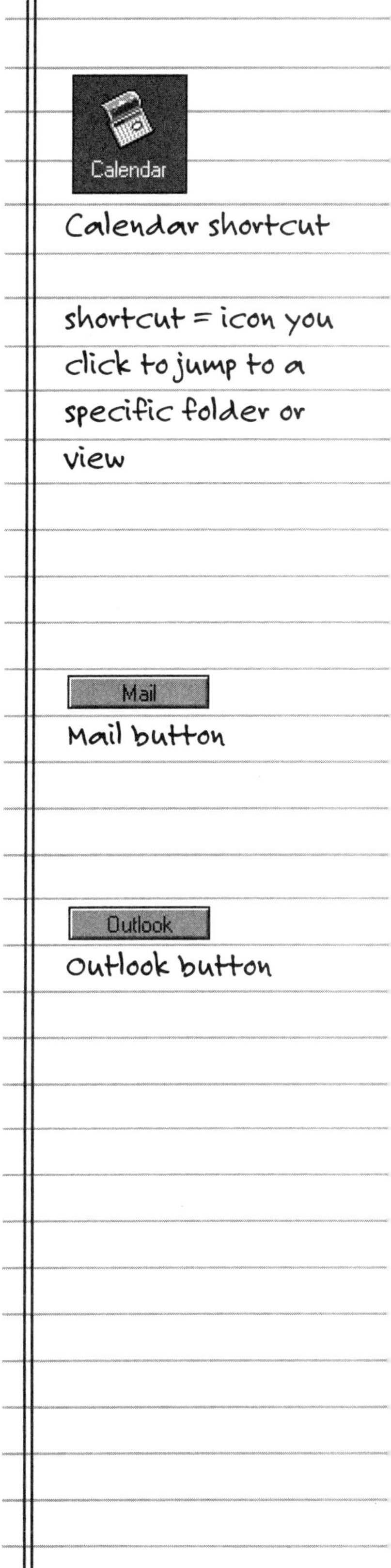

1. **Move your mouse pointer to the Calendar shortcut in the Outlook bar and click it to move to the Outlook Calendar.**

   This simple action causes many things to happen. The most obvious change is that the Information Viewer now displays the Day/Week/Month view of the Calendar folder. This view includes a daily appointment calendar, two small monthly calendars, and a TaskPad, which allows you to maintain a to-do list.

   In addition to changing the view, clicking the Calendar shortcut causes both the menu bar and the toolbar to change to reflect the options that are specific to the Calendar view.

2. **Click the Inbox shortcut in the Outlook bar to move to the Inbox.**

   You move to the *Messages with AutoPreview* view of the Inbox folder. Note the different options in the menu bar and the toolbar.

3. **Move the mouse pointer back to the Outlook bar and click the Mail button.**

   on the test

   Immediately, the Mail button slides up, bringing with it the Mail shortcut group, which contains shortcuts to the main e-mail folders: Inbox, Sent Items, Outbox, and Deleted Items. Unless you have used Outlook for e-mail prior to starting this session, these e-mail folders are empty at this point. Have no fear — as soon as you get to Unit 2, you can start filling these folders up.

4. **Click the Outlook button, which is just above the Mail button in the Outlook bar.**

   Returning to the Outlook group of shortcuts gives you access to the major Outlook features. Note that even though you change shortcut groups, the Information Viewer does not change unless you click one of the shortcuts or select a different folder from the Folder list. This allows you to search through the other shortcut groups without losing your original place.

5. **Move your mouse pointer to the current folder name, which in this case is Inbox, located in the banner above the Information Viewer.**

   As you move the mouse pointer over the current folder name it becomes a button. By the way, after you start working with Outlook, you may notice that the folder name you see in the banner above the Information Viewer changes depending on the last shortcut you clicked.

6. **Click the folder name/button to open the Folder list.**

   A drop-down list appears with a map of all your existing folders. If the only folder you see is Personal Folders, click the small plus sign (+) to the left to expand the subfolders contained in Personal Folders. Notice that each of the shortcuts on the Outlook bar has a corresponding folder in the Folder list.

☑ Progress Check

If you can do the following, you've mastered this lesson:

- ❑ Open a folder by clicking a shortcut.
- ❑ Change the shortcut group by clicking a group button.
- ❑ Open the Folder list by clicking the current folder name.

7 Click the Tasks folder.

Just like clicking a shortcut, clicking a folder in the Folder list immediately takes you to that folder, which in this case is Tasks. The Simple List view of the Tasks folder is opened in the Information Viewer. This lets you see all your tasks in list form, by task subject and due date.

Congratulations, you've just completed your quick tour of the main features in Outlook. Now that you've got a handle on Outlook basics, you're ready to move on to the Outlook e-mail feature.

Recess

Feel like you've been around the world and back? You have seen quite a bit already in Unit 1. Feel free to kick back, take a rest, and go out for a walk. Then come back and delve into the next lesson, which explores the Outlook Mail window.

Lesson 1-3 Navigating the Mail Window

Now that you understand the basic Outlook components, you can take a look at the Outlook e-mail feature. E-mail is by far the most popular and useful electronic communication tool available today. If you use nothing else in Outlook, you will be amply rewarded by mastering and using the Outlook e-mail feature. The basic e-mail folders included with Outlook are:

- **Inbox:** Stores the messages you receive.
- **Sent Items:** Stores copies of messages you've sent (great for reference at a later date).
- **Outbox:** Temporarily stores messages that you have written, but have not yet sent.
- **Deleted Items:** Temporarily stores messages you don't want anymore (junk e-mail, for example), but haven't yet purged from your computer forever.

Now, without further ado, we are pleased to present the Mail window, up close and personal:

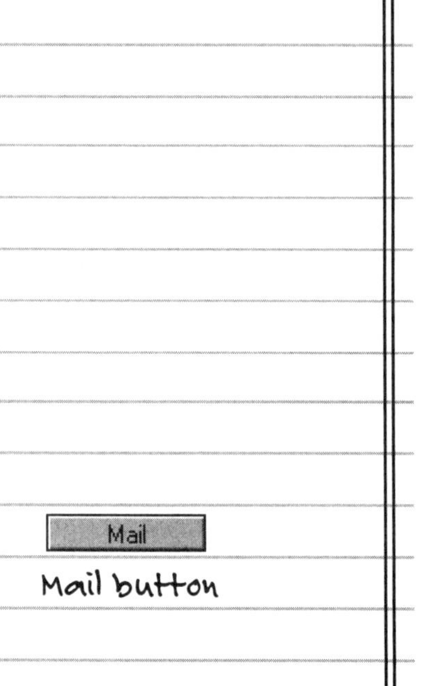

Mail button

1 Click the Mail button in the Outlook bar.

The Mail shortcuts appear with a shortcut for each of the basic mail folders.

2 Click the Inbox shortcut to open the Inbox folder.

Unless you have been using Outlook e-mail prior to this lesson, your Inbox should be empty. When you receive e-mail messages, you open the Inbox to read your mail. Outlook displays your messages along with relevant information, if available, in each of the columns across the top of the Information Viewer window.

3 Click the Sent Items shortcut in the Outlook bar.

Although the Information Viewer remains empty, notice that the view has changed and the last column heading has changed from Received to Sent.

4 Click the Outbox and Deleted Items shortcuts in the Outlook bar.

Don't worry if you don't understand all the buttons and gadgets in each view. We just want you to get a sneak peek at each of the windows that pops up. Make sure to notice the differences in each view — you'll soon be working with each of these views, and it will help if you feel comfortable with them.

If you plan to march ahead into Unit 2 (after working through the Unit 1 Quiz and Exercise, of course), leave Outlook up and running. If you plan to be away from your computer awhile, you may want to close Outlook (choose File➪Exit) and turn your computer off.

☑ Progress Check

If you can do the following, you've mastered this lesson:

- ❑ Bring up the Mail group of shortcuts in the Outlook bar.
- ❑ Visit each of the folders within the Mail window.

Unit 1 Quiz

Take this fun quiz to see how much you've learned in Unit 1. You can find the answers in Appendix A.

1. **How do you start Outlook?**

   A. Get your next-door neighbor to help push your computer.

   B. Double-click the Outlook shortcut on the desktop.

   C. Call AAA and ask for their computer department.

   D. Click the Start button and hope for the best.

   E. I'm sorry, could you repeat the question?

2. **What is the quickest way to open a folder?**

   A. With a sharp instrument.

   B. By holding both ends tightly and pulling vigorously.

   C. Click a shortcut for the folder in the Outlook bar.

   D. Close your eyes, place your hand on the computer monitor palm down, and use the Vulcan mind meld.

   E. What's wrong with opening folders slowly?

3. **What does the Information Viewer contain?**

   A. The crossword puzzle from last week's *New York Times*.

   B. Embarrassing baby pictures of you when you first learned to ride a bike.

   C. Helpful household hints.

   D. The contents of the currently selected folder.

   E. Beats me! I can't see a thing without my glasses.

Notes:

4. **Where do you store messages that you receive?**

   A. In a shoebox under the bed.

   B. Don't tell me, I know they're here somewhere.

   C. In the Inbox folder.

   D. With your favorite recipes.

   E. I don't know. Nobody ever writes to me.

Unit 1 Exercise

1. Start Outlook.
2. Open the Notes folder in the Outlook bar.
3. Use the Folder list to open the Calendar folder.
4. Open the group of shortcuts named Other.
5. Live it up a little now that you're an Outlook maven.

Unit 2

Writing and Sending Messages

Objectives for This Unit

- ✓ Adding addresses to the Address Book
- ✓ Filling out the Message form
- ✓ Formatting an e-mail message
- ✓ Sending an e-mail message
- ✓ Attaching files to an e-mail message

Prerequisites

- Opening the Mail group of shortcuts (Lesson 1-2)
- Using a shortcut to open a folder (Lesson 1-2)
- Recognizing and locating the Outlook bar and the Information Viewer (Lesson 1-2)

- Pest.doc

After you get comfortable using e-mail, you may wonder how you ever got along without it. Its ease of use and effectiveness (when used properly) are unmatched by most other means of communication. Whether you use e-mail to transact business or merely to stay in touch with family and friends, you'll find e-mail an invaluable tool. Among other things, you can use e-mail to:

- Set up meetings and appointments.
- E-mail one person or a hundred people with the same amount of effort.
- Transmit pictures and documents around the world instantaneously.
- Obtain technical support from hardware and software vendors.
- Trade gossip, recipes, and war stories with your best friend across the country.

Of course, this list just shows the tip of the iceberg. After you start using e-mail, you'll discover a multitude of uses that make e-mail truly indispensable.

Lesson 2-1

Adding an Address to the Address Book

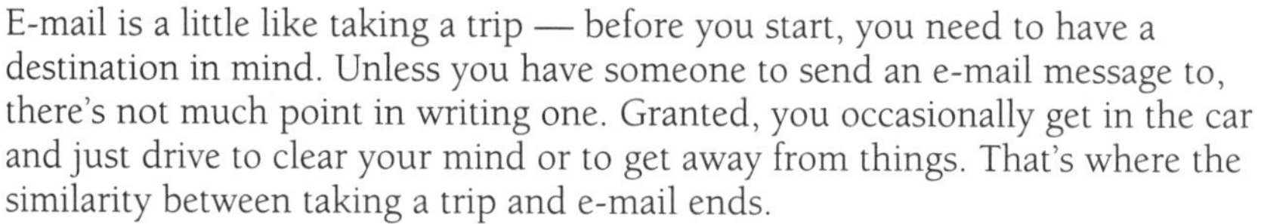
E-mail is a little like taking a trip — before you start, you need to have a destination in mind. Unless you have someone to send an e-mail message to, there's not much point in writing one. Granted, you occasionally get in the car and just drive to clear your mind or to get away from things. That's where the similarity between taking a trip and e-mail ends.

Aimless e-mail has neither the romance nor the therapeutic effect of driving off into the sunset. Therefore the first thing you must do before composing your first e-mail message is record an e-mail address, and what better place to record it than in an address book? Pretty neat the way that works, isn't it? To get started, follow these steps:

Address Book button

1. **Click the Address Book button on the toolbar.**

   The Address Book window opens, and you're ready to put e-mail addresses in it. After you open the Address Book, be sure that the Personal Address Book is listed in the box labeled Show Names. If another address book is listed in that box, click the arrow to the right of the box and select the Personal Address Book from the drop-down list that appears.

2. **Choose File⇨New Entry from the Address Book menu bar.**

   The New Entry dialog box appears (see Figure 2-1), and you see a list of the types of e-mail addresses available for your Outlook system.

   The choices vary depending on whether you are part of a network mail system (and the options selected by the network administrator). You may see two choices or you may see five choices. However, Other Address will always appear as an option. For this lesson, we continue with the Other Address option because we know you will see it listed as an option no matter what kind of system you have.

   heads up

   If you aren't sure which option you should choose, consult the person at your company who is responsible for maintaining the computers in the office.

3. **Select Other Address and click the OK button.**

   Now you're getting somewhere. A New Other Address Properties dialog box appears asking you for information about the new e-mail address.

   You are now about to add your first entry to the Address Book. We've always found that it pays to start at the top when you want to get something done. Someday you may want to express your opinion or demand action on an issue you think is important. Therefore, the first entry in your Address Book is going to be the address of the president of the United States.

4. **In the Display name text box, type** William R. Clinton **and then press the Tab key to move to the next field.**

   The display name just identifies the recipient in your Address Book. In this case, you're using the e-mail recipient's full name as the display name. When you enter your mother's e-mail address you can probably use the display name Mom. The purpose of this field is to enter information you'll recognize when

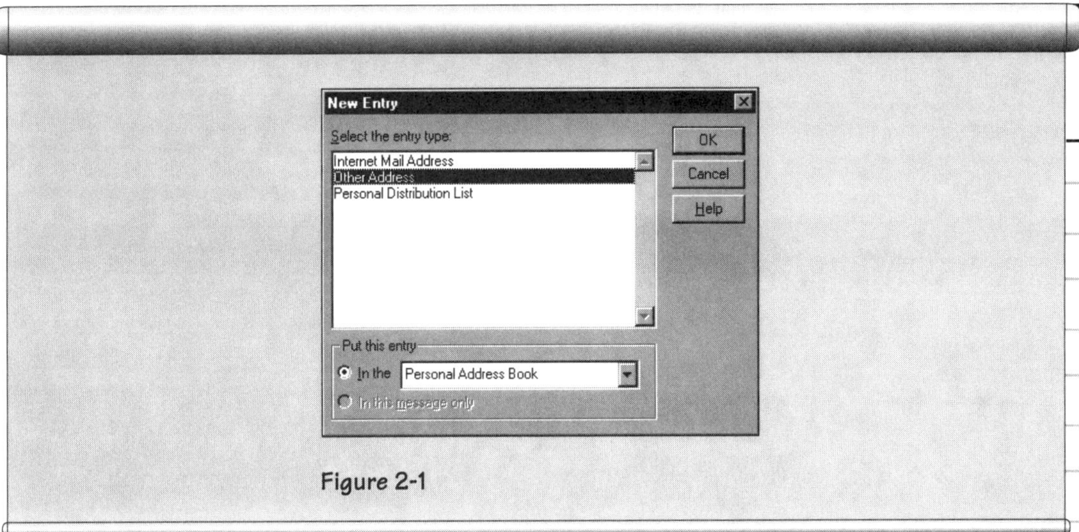

Figure 2-1: The New Entry dialog box may display different choices.

Notes:

you want to find the recipient on your list. There's nothing official or technically important about this field; it's strictly for your comfort as you look at your Address Book.

Tip: Although you may be tempted to use nicknames for people, we recommend that you use full names most of the time; a year down the road you may not easily remember who "Pinky" is.

5. **Type** president@whitehouse.gov **in the E-mail address text box and then press the Tab key to move to the next field.**

   You type the recipient's official, technically correct e-mail address into the E-mail address text box. Notice that this entire e-mail address appears in lowercase letters. Only rarely do you see uppercase letters in an e-mail address. When in doubt, drop to lowercase!

6. **Type** Internet **in the E-mail type field.**

   The E-mail type field lets you tell Outlook what kind of e-mail account your recipient uses. Depending on what kind of account the person has, you may type Internet, CompuServe, AOL, or something else in this box. The data you enter in this field is not used by the e-mail software; it is informational only. You can leave it blank if you don't want to mess with it.

7. **Click the checkbox next to Always send to this recipient in Microsoft Exchange rich-text format.**

   Clicking the checkbox turns this option off (the box should be empty now). You can only check this option when you know that your recipient can read messages in *rich text format* (RTF). RTF enables you to format your messages with cool stuff like bold and italic type. Unfortunately, not everyone uses Outlook, so some poor souls can't read your messages if you check this option. It's safe to send RTF messages to anyone using Outlook or Microsoft Exchange, but if you aren't sure that your recipient uses these programs, you'd better turn off this option.

That's all there is to entering an address in the Address Book. The entry has all the necessary information and should look like Figure 2-2.

Figure 2-2: Setting up a new address is a breeze.

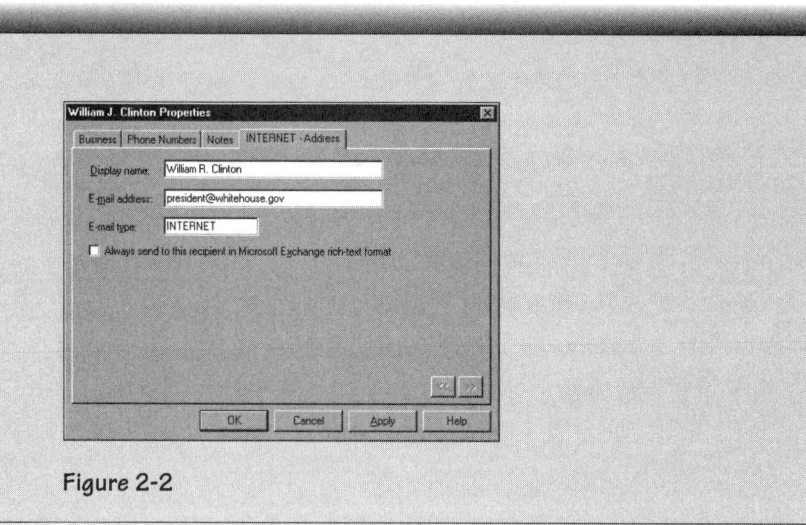

Notes:

8 Click OK to return to the Address Book dialog box.

You now see your new entry for the president listed in your Address Book. Congratulations, you should be proud of yourself.

In case you're wondering why you skipped over the other three tabs in the New Other Address Properties dialog box, the reason is twofold. At this point, we don't want to complicate matters by asking you to enter additional information, such as street addresses and phone numbers. More important, Outlook has an excellent contact manager in which you can record detailed information about anyone you regularly communicate with, so you don't need to waste time and energy entering that data here. We discuss the Outlook contact-management options in Unit 9. For now, we want you to concentrate on e-mail.

You need several entries in your Address Book to complete all the lessons in this unit, so you need to add a couple more addresses. Start by entering your own address.

Tip: Some people send copies of e-mail to themselves so they know when their e-mail system delivered the e-mail, providing good insurance that the other recipients received the message, too.

9 Choose File⇨New Entry from the Address Book menu bar.

If you know that your e-mail address is an Internet address, choose Internet Address as the address type instead of Other Address. You only have to fill in the display name and the exact e-mail address, and you won't see a field for Address Type because you've already announced that the address type is Internet address. In fact, any time you enter additional e-mail addresses, choose the correct address type instead of Other Address (if you see it on the listing of available types).

10 Follow Steps 4 through 6, substituting your own name and e-mail address.

For your own entry, don't deselect the RTF option as you did in Step 7, because you do want to see the formatting if you send yourself a message.

11 **Now create another new entry. To keep things in the family, add the vice president's e-mail address, using the following information:**

Display name: Al Gore

E-mail address: vice.president@whitehouse.gov

E-mail type: Internet

12 **Because the state of the government and the country depends upon the leaders of both parties, include Newt Gingrich in your Address Book by typing the following information:**

Display name: Newt Gingrich

E-mail address: georgia6@hr.house.gov

E-mail type: Internet

13 **Choose File⇨Close from the menu bar to leave the Address Book and return to Outlook.**

Understanding e-mail addresses

Your e-mail address may take any of several forms. If you're working on a network, your network administrator has probably given you your e-mail address (if not, ask for it), which may look different depending on the type of e-mail used at your company.

We want to show you a few sample e-mail addresses by using George Goodworker, who works at the Goodgadgets Company, as an example. You shouldn't care about what each part of these addresses stands for — right now, we just want you to see what different addresses look like so that you know what to expect when you start writing and receiving lots of e-mail. If you can't resist the temptation to dissect the various parts of e-mail addresses, we suggest you take a look at Chapter 3 of *Internet E-Mail For Dummies,* by John R. Levine, Carol Baroudi, Margaret Levine Young, and Arnold Reinhold, published by IDG Books Worldwide, Inc., for the details.

If the administrators at the Goodgadgets Company installed cc:Mail (a popular e-mail system), then Georgie (you can call him Georgie if you wish — he won't mind) has an e-mail address something like `Goodworker,George at Goodgadgets`. If Goodgadgets has an Internet account, Georgie may have an address like `ggoodworker@goodgadgets.com`. As a Microsoft Mail user (another popular e-mail system), you can reach Georgie at `Goodgadgets/Accounting/George` (assuming Georgie works in the accounting department).

If you don't work on a network and you use a modem to dial out to a service that gets you into an Internet mailbox, you have an e-mail address from that service. Perhaps your name is `bettyboop@musicnet.net`.

No matter what the e-mail address looks like, typing it correctly into the Address Book is very important. Be sure to type the address exactly as it's given to you by the recipient.

☑ Progress Check

If you can do the following, you've mastered this lesson:

- ❑ Open the Address Book.
- ❑ Enter a recipient's information in the Address Book.

Lesson 2-2 Editing and Deleting Addresses

Notes:

When someone's e-mail information changes (perhaps someone in your Address Book changes jobs and has a new e-mail address at the new company), or on that rare occasion when you make a mistake, you may need to edit an entry in your Address Book.

You also may find, after a while, that you never send e-mail to some recipients in your address book and you're sure you never will. In that case, you should delete the listing. We'll talk about both of these tasks in this lesson.

Editing e-mail addresses

How many of you noticed that Mr. Clinton's middle initial is wrong in Lesson 2-1? That's right — someone led you astray (okay, *we* did). The man's name is William *J.* Clinton, not William *R.* Clinton. Quite convenient, wouldn't you say? A perfect opportunity to edit an address.

1. **Open the Address Book by clicking the Address Book button.**
2. **Double-click William R. Clinton.**

   The William R. Clinton Properties dialog box appears, with the Display name, William R. Clinton, highlighted. If you wanted to replace the name entirely you could type right over the existing name. In this case, however, you only want to change one letter.
3. **Position your mouse pointer just to the left of the R and click, which places the blinking cursor on the left side of the R.**

   If you have misplaced the blinking cursor, or find it difficult to position it exactly where you want it, click anywhere and then use the arrow keys on the keyboard to move the cursor left or right as necessary to position it just to the left of the R.
4. **Press the Delete key to remove the R.**
5. **Type the letter J (don't forget to capitalize it).**
6. **Click OK to save your changes and return to the Address Book.**

   Mission accomplished. The entry in the Address Book now says William J. Clinton. Of course, if you wanted to edit the official e-mail address or the address type, you would simply click in the appropriate field and type the new information as you have just done in Steps 3 through 6.

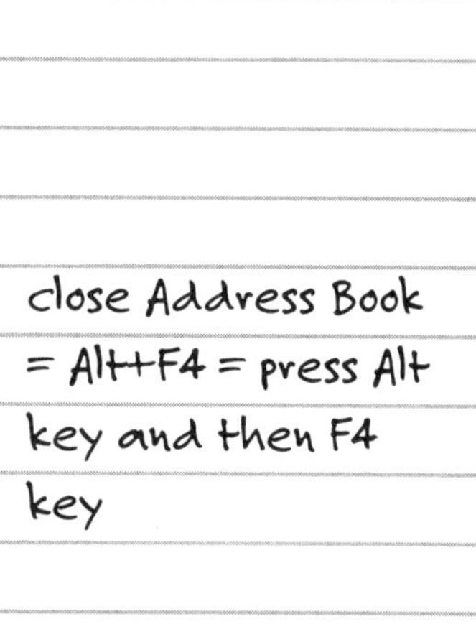

7. **Choose File⇨Close from the menu bar to shut down the Address Book and return to Outlook.**

   You can also close the Address Book by pressing the Alt key and then the F4 key. Experiment with both ways of closing the Address Book and decide which way you like the best.

Deleting e-mail addresses

on the test

When an entry in the address book has outlived its usefulness, you can follow these steps to delete it from your Address Book:

1. **Open the Address Book by clicking the Address Book button.**
2. **Highlight the entry for your own name by clicking it.**
3. **Press the Delete key.**

   A message appears asking if you really, really want to delete this address. Deleting an entry in the Address Book is a permanent action. If you accidentally delete the wrong entry, you will have to reenter all the information. Therefore, Outlook requires you to confirm your decision to delete the selected address.
4. **Click No.**

   For this exercise, you choose No because we don't really want to delete this entry — we just want you to learn how to do it. If you really wanted to delete the entry *and* you were sure it was the right entry, you would click Yes.
5. **Close the Address Book by pressing Alt+F4.**

☑ Progress Check

If you can do the following, you've mastered this lesson:

- ❑ Change information in an Address Book entry.
- ❑ Delete an Address Book entry.
- ❑ Remember the president's middle initial.

Creating Groups of Recipients

Lesson 2-3

Frequently, you find yourself communicating information to the same group of people on a regular basis. For example, when you are part of a team assigned to the same project, you often have to distribute reports, notices, meeting requests, and other information to all members of the team. The good news is that Outlook provides an easy way to do this. You can create a group of recipients, formally known as a *Personal Distribution List*. By creating a group of recipients, you eliminate the need to select individual members from your Address Book as recipients every time you want to send them all a message. Instead, you can choose the group, and all members who are part of the group automatically receive a copy of the message.

Personal Distribution List sends message to many people at one time

You should now have four addresses in your Address Book: yourself, Al Gore, Newt Gingrich, and William J. Clinton. The number of people you can include in a Personal Distribution List is limited only by the number of entries in your Address Book. Now that you have a quorum, so to speak, it's time to create a group.

1. **If your Address Book is not open, open it by clicking the Address Book button.**
2. **Choose File⇨New Entry from the menu bar.**

Figure 2-3: Give it a name, add some members, and voilà! You have a Personal Distribution List.

Figure 2-4: We're sure Newt won't mind moving to the right, but how about Al and Bill?

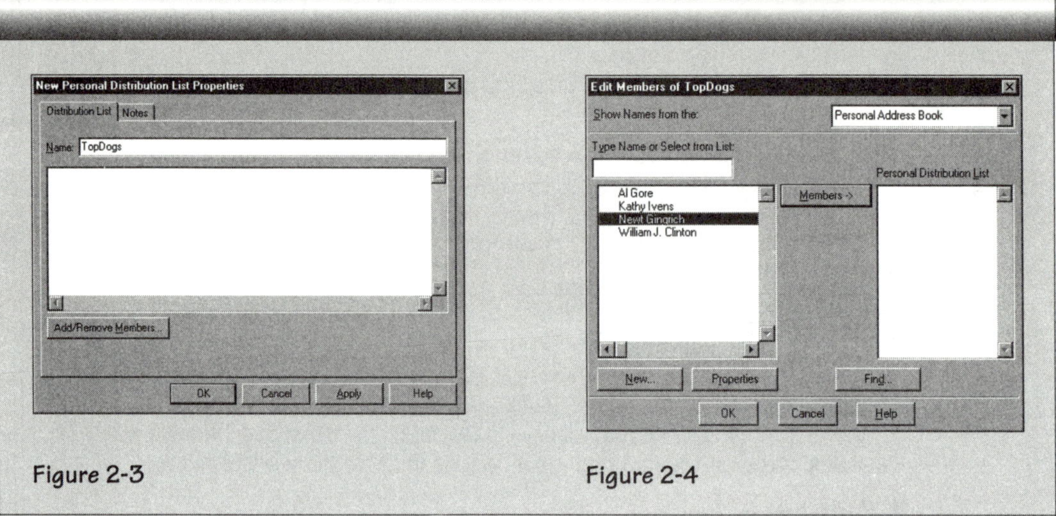

Figure 2-3

Figure 2-4

select multiple contiguous names = highlight first name, hold Shift key, and then highlight last name

3. **Click Personal Distribution List in the New Entry list and then click OK.**

   The New Personal Distribution List Properties dialog box appears so you can name your Personal Distribution List and determine its members (see Figure 2-3).

   Tip: Be sure to give the group a name that reminds you of the group's purpose and membership. It won't do any good if you can't remember which Personal Distribution List to send information to.

4. **Type the group name,** TopDogs**, in the Name text box.**

5. **Click the Add/Remove Members button.**

   The Edit Members of TopDogs dialog box that pops up contains all the names currently in your Address Book (see Figure 2-4). From here, you choose the individuals to populate your group. You see a column of Address Book entries on the left and a blank column labeled Personal Distribution List, on the right. To include members in the TopDogs group, we're going to add their names to the Personal Distribution list on the right.

6. **Click Newt Gingrich in the Address Book entries list and then click the Members button to add him to the Personal Distribution List.**

   Congratulations! Newt Gingrich is now in your Personal Distribution List.

   Suppose you wanted to add half of Congress to a Personal Distribution List? It would take you half the day to select all the names, one by one, and add them to the group. You may be glad to hear that you can add several names to the group in one fell swoop. It's quite simple — you just select multiple names and transfer them to the Personal Distribution List all at once.

7. **Click Al Gore, hold down the Ctrl key, move your mouse pointer to William J. Clinton, and then click again.**

   Al Gore and William J. Clinton should be highlighted in the left column.

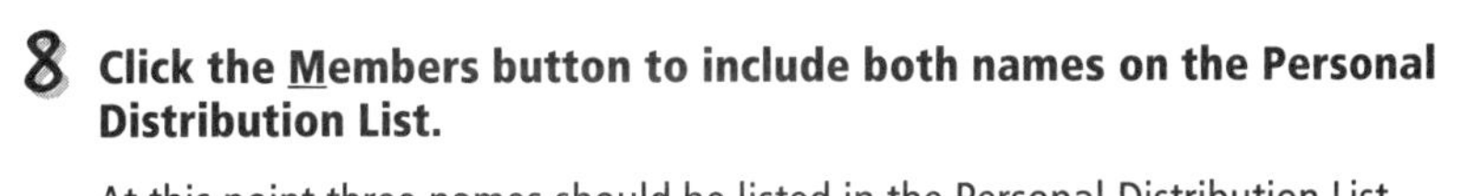

8 Click the Members button to include both names on the Personal Distribution List.

At this point three names should be listed in the Personal Distribution List column, separated by semicolons. Notice that all three names are underlined, which indicates that they are in your address book.

Incidentally, if you type fast and you have so many entries in your address book that it's time-consuming to scroll through the list, you could type the names directly into the right pane of the Edit Members dialog box, separating each name with a semicolon.

9 Click OK to return to the New Personal Distribution List Properties dialog box.

The three TopDogs are now included in the group. If you had typed the names directly into the list, Outlook displays an error message if any of the names are not part of your address book.

heads up

When the next election comes around, you may find a new cast of dogs for the TopDogs group. In that case, you may need to remove some names from the group. To remove a member from a Personal Distribution List, click Add/RemoveMembers in the Edit Members of TopDogs dialog box. Then in the Personal Distribution List, highlight the name(s) to remove and press the Delete key.

10 Click OK again to return to the Address Book dialog box.

Your TopDogs group now appears in the Address Book. To make it easy to pick out, the group's listing appears in boldface and is preceded by a small icon.

11 Close the Address Book by pressing Alt+F4.

☑ Progress Check

If you can do the following, you've mastered this lesson:

- ❑ Create a Personal Distribution List.
- ❑ Add and remove members from a Personal Distribution List.

Composing and Sending an E-Mail Message

Lesson 2-4

Now that you have several entries in your Address Book, including a Personal Distribution List, you are ready to create your first e-mail message. An e-mail message has four basic components:

- To
- Cc
- Subject
- Message body

Some of the components are optional, others are not. You can't send an e-mail message without someone to send it to. Therefore, you must enter a valid e-mail address in the To (recipient) field. The Cc field is where you put the e-mail addresses of individuals to whom you wish to send copies of the message. You're probably asking, "Why not just include them in the To line?"

Notes:

New Mail Message button

Bcc = Blind carbon copy = Bcc recipient's name is hidden from all other recipients

Often you will send a message that is specifically directed to an individual or group, but you also may want someone other than the recipient(s) to receive the message. In some cases, it is simply a courtesy to keep a third party informed. Sometimes it's prudent to let others know what's happening, in the event that they have some valuable input. Finally, there are times when you just need to make sure that all your bases are covered and that no one can claim ignorance in case a problem arises.

on the test

Although the Subject field is technically optional, it should never be left blank. If you deal with a large amount of e-mail, it is nice to be able to figure out which e-mail is important and which can wait until a more convenient time. One of the primary ways to make such a determination is to look at the Subject field. The explanatory text in the Subject field gives the recipient a clue about the contents of the message.

You may think that the body of the message is the one thing that is not optional. In reality, however, it is. There are times when all you want to do is send a file to someone and have no need to communicate anything at all (you will learn all about sending files in Lesson 2-7). In that case, you can fill out the other fields, attach a file, and send the e-mail without typing a single word in the body. It is generally more cordial, however, to add a quick note like "Here's the file I promised."

Now that you understand the basic components of an e-mail message, it's time to move from theory to practice. To compose an e-mail message, follow these steps:

1. **Click the New Mail Message button on the toolbar to open a new Mail Message form (see Figure 2-5).**

   Check out the menus and the tools, many of which are unique to the Message form. Also notice that the Formatting toolbar is unavailable (grayed out). As soon as you enter text in the body of the message, the Formatting toolbar springs to life (until then, there is nothing to format).

2. **Click the To button to open your Address Book.**

   The Select Names dialog box that opens is different from the Address Book dialog box you opened earlier while entering addresses. The Select Names dialog box lists the entries in your Address Book and provides several options, including placing the highlighted name in the To field, the Cc field, or the Bcc field (see Figure 2-6). The Bcc (blind carbon copy) field enables you to send a copy of an e-mail to someone without having that recipient's name appear on the message.

heads up

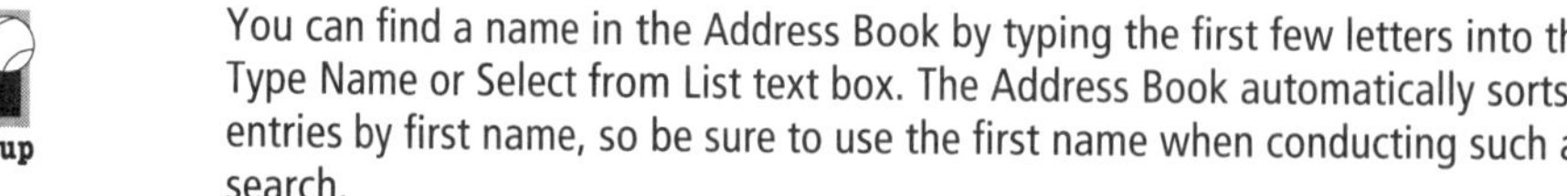
You can find a name in the Address Book by typing the first few letters into the Type Name or Select from List text box. The Address Book automatically sorts entries by first name, so be sure to use the first name when conducting such a search.

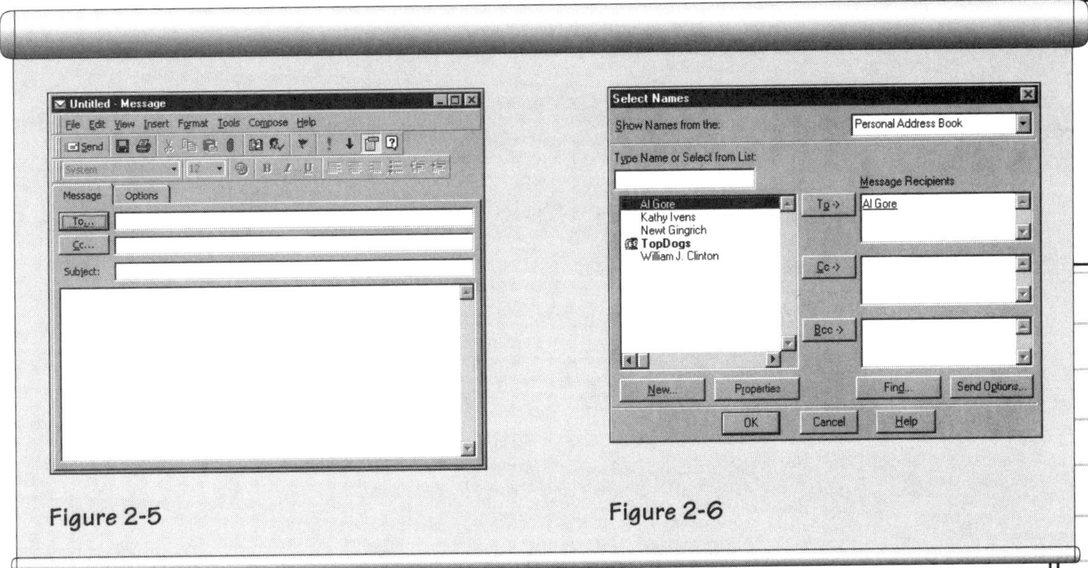

Figure 2-5

Figure 2-6

Figure 2-5: The Message form is like a mini word processor with its own menu bar and toolbars.

Figure 2-6: Add recipients with the Select Names dialog box.

3 Double-click Al Gore.

As soon as you double-click the name, it appears in the To box on the right. It is underlined, indicating that it is a valid e-mail address. Keep in mind that a valid e-mail address is merely one that follows e-mail address conventions. The fact that it is valid does not necessarily mean that it's the correct address for the intended recipient.

4 Click OK to return to the Message form. Then click the Cc button.

You should send Al's boss a copy of your e-mail. It's a good idea to let him know how you feel about Al's work.

5 In the Select Names dialog box double-click William J. Clinton.

This time the name appears in the Cc box to the right. Since you clicked the Cc button in the Message form, Outlook knew that your next selection belonged in the Cc box. Rather than returning to the Message form each time you want to add a recipient, you can make your selections all at once, by highlighting a name and clicking the appropriate button (To, Cc, Bcc).

While you're at it, you may as well send Newt a copy, just to keep him informed. However, Al and Bill might not appreciate it, so you should send Newt a blind carbon copy.

6 Click Newt Gingrich once to highlight the name. Then click the Bcc button to send him a blind carbon copy.

Now your Select Names dialog box should have one name in each of the three boxes to the right.

Figure 2-7: The text you enter in the message text box is the heart of an e-mail message.

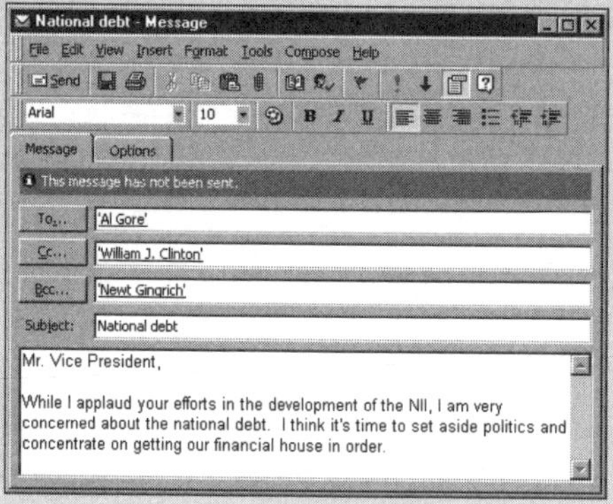

Figure 2-7

Notes:

7 Click OK to return to the Message form.

In addition to having Al Gore in the To field and William J. Clinton in the Cc field, a new field has been added, Bcc, and in it you find Newt Gingrich.

heads up

If you change your mind about a recipient selection, you can eliminate it by highlighting the address in any of the recipient fields and pressing the Delete key. This works in the Select Names dialog box and the New Message form.

8 Move your mouse pointer to the Subject text box and click to place the cursor in the box.

9 Type National debt **as the subject of your message and press the Tab key to move to the message text box.**

The Subject text should be a brief phrase describing the contents of the message.

10 Type your message, indicating your own feelings about the national debt (you don't have to enter the message that appears in Figure 2-7).

11 Click the Send button on the Message window Standard toolbar.

Send

Send button

Your message moves to the Outbox, which is a holding area for outgoing messages. Depending upon your setup, the message may immediately be pulled from the Outbox by the network mailbox courier, or it may sit there waiting for the next time you use the modem to dial out to your Internet service provider. After the message is sent from the Outbox, a copy of it stays in the Sent Messages folder so you can refer to it if you need to at a later date.

extra credit

Peeking inside the Outbox

The Outbox holds your e-mail after you compose it. The Outbox is simple and efficient, just like the mailbox at the corner. If fact, the Outbox and the mailbox are similar in a number of ways. With your corner mailbox, you drop your mail into it and eventually somebody shows up and unlocks the mailbox and takes the contents (including your letter) to a post office. The post office sorts the mail and then ships each piece of mail to a post office near the recipient, and that post office sends a delivery person out to put the mail in the recipient's mailbox.

E-mail works exactly the same way. What differs is the timing with which all this happens. There are people who send e-mail and never see anything in the Outbox (although they know the message was sent because a copy is in the Sent Items folder). But how did it get in and out of the Outbox so fast? There are two ways to send messages through the Outbox so fast that if you blink, you miss it.

The first way is to be connected (with your modem) to your Internet e-mail provider service when you compose the message and click the Send button. Because you're connected, it's sent to the e-mail server (the post office). If you are not already connected, and instead you dial into your Internet service provider later, the Outbox fills up and then is emptied when you make a connection.

The second way is to work at a computer that's connected to a network and the e-mail system on the network is configured to grab anything in your Outbox immediately and bring it back to the server (the post office). In effect, when you click the Send button you set off a bell at the post office (on the server) that says "Send somebody to pick up some mail, please" and the server obeys with the kind of lightning speed you could only get from a computer.

☑ Progress Check

If you can do the following, you've mastered this lesson:

- ❑ Open a new Message form.
- ❑ Add a recipient to the new message.
- ❑ Address a copy to someone other than the primary recipient.
- ❑ Send the message.

Recess

If you've reached this point, and your computer is still in one piece and your sanity intact, you deserve a break. Remember: To exit Outlook, choose File⇨Exit. When you are ready to go on to Lesson 2-5, reopen Outlook using the technique you learned in Unit 1.

Formatting an E-Mail Message

Lesson 2-5

Whether you are writing an e-mail note, a love note, or a book, your choice of words and your style are the primary vehicle for communicating your thoughts. However, like a stew without spices, even a well-written document can sometimes be bland. The judicious use of formatting can often ***drive*** your point home to the reader. Overdo it, **and** you **will** simply ***drive*** your reader *away*!

add flair to messages with formatting

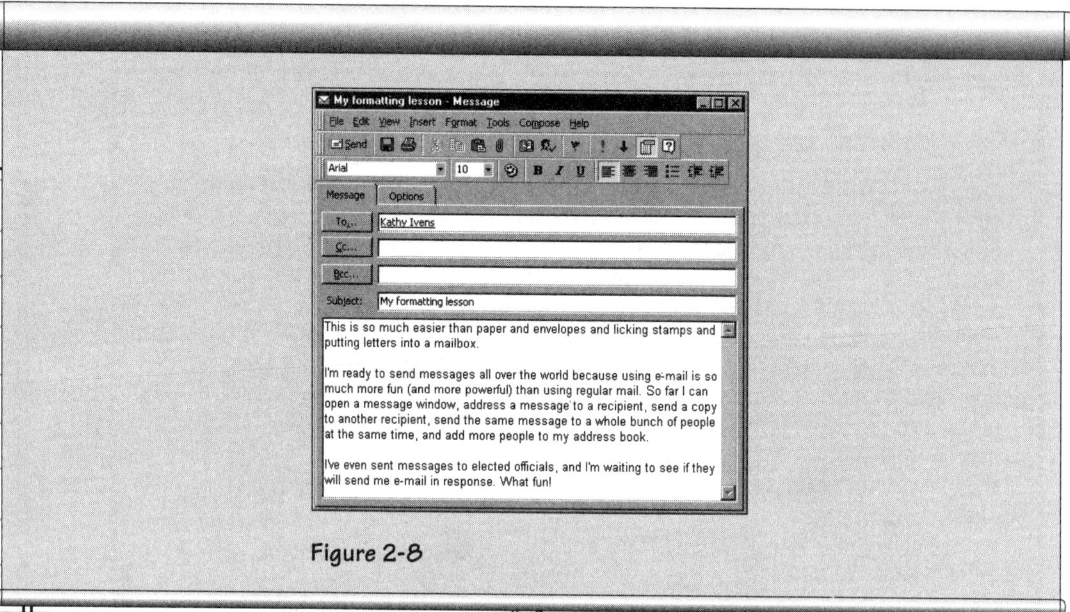

Figure 2-8: Send yourself an e-mail message so you can experiment with its appearance.

Notes:

Formatting is more than just type style (bold, italics, and underlining). Formatting also includes:

- Font
- Font size
- Font color
- Text alignment
- Bulleted lists

Experience, as you well know (how many times did Mom remind you?), is the best teacher. So, follow the steps you learned in the last lesson to open a new e-mail Message window. This time you're going to send yourself e-mail. Ready? Is a Message window open? Then have a go at it by following these steps:

1. **Click the To button and double-click your name when the Select Names dialog box displays.**

   Your name appears in the Message Recipients box. Click OK to return to the Message window.

2. **Click in the Subject field and type** My formatting lesson**.**

3. **Move your cursor to the message body. Write yourself a three paragraph long note explaining to yourself the things you already know how to do with e-mail.**

   If you can't think of a thing to say, you can use the text shown in Figure 2-8.

   After you enter the text, you can format it. To accomplish this, you'll select portions of the text and change the appearance. Start by changing the font for the first paragraph.

4 **To select (highlight) the first paragraph, place the cursor at the beginning of the paragraph; then hold down the Shift and Ctrl keys and press the down arrow.**

5 **Click the down arrow to the right of the Font selection list on the Formatting toolbar.**

When you open the Font selection list, the name of the current font is highlighted. If you know the name of the font you want to use, you can type the first letter(s) of the font name to bring it up quickly.

6 **Type** b **to bring up the fonts that begin with the letter b.**

Notice that Outlook ignores case when searching drop-down lists.

7 **Click Book Antiqua.**

The highlighted text is now in the Book Antiqua font.

8 **On the Formatting toolbar, click the down arrow in the Font Size drop-down list.**

Each of the numbers on the list represents a *point size* of the font. Don't worry about knowing what a point size is; just remember that the larger the number, the larger the text appears.

9 **Click the number 14 to change the size of the font from 10 points to 14 points.**

10 **Move your mouse pointer to the end of the message.**

11 **Hold down the left mouse button and drag the pointer across the last two words (What fun!) to highlight them.**

12 **On the Formatting toolbar, click the Font Color button (it looks like an artist's palette).**

13 **Move your mouse pointer to the red square in the palette and click.**

Nothing appears to happen until you remove the highlighting by clicking anywhere in the message body. You can then see that the text is red.

14 **Drag the mouse to highlight the next-to-last sentence (the one preceding the text that is now red).**

15 **Click the Bold button on the Formatting toolbar.**

Click anywhere in the message to remove the highlighting and notice the text is bold.

Use the same method to select additional words or sentences and format them as Italic or Underlined, using the buttons on the toolbar.

We aren't going to discuss text alignment and bulleted lists here, but you can, if you wish, take a moment to experiment with these options by highlighting text and clicking the appropriate buttons on the toolbar.

16 **Send the message.**

The next time you receive mail, this message arrives in your Inbox. Open it up and marvel at your artistic prowess.

☑ Progress Check

If you can do the following, you've mastered this lesson:

- ❑ Select text to be formatted.
- ❑ Change the font, font size, and font color of selected text.
- ❑ Alter the style of selected text.

Lesson 2-6 Creating an AutoSignature

AutoSignature tells recipients something about you

An *AutoSignature* is a clever shortcut you can use to automate the process of signing your e-mail. People use AutoSignatures for all kinds of things. You can add some pizzazz to your signature with the addition of a clever quote in your AutoSignature, or you can put information about yourself or your company into your signature. To explore the glory of the AutoSignature, follow these steps:

1. **From the Message menu bar, choose Tools⇨AutoSignature to open the AutoSignature dialog box, as shown in Figure 2-9.**

2. **Select Add this signature to the end of new messages by clicking the check box near the upper left corner of the dialog box.**

   This activates a second check box located beneath the text entry box. If you wish to use a different closing for replies or forwarded messages (as opposed to e-mail you compose as an original message) you can leave this box checked.

3. **Tab to the text entry box and enter your personalized signature.**

   Type your name. Then press Enter and type whatever you wish to say about yourself or your company. In Figure 2-9, I typed **It's not an empty nest until they get their stuff out of the basement.**

4. **To change the font, font size, or style, just highlight the text, click the Font button, and format your text the way you want it.**

5. **Click OK.**

   After you create an AutoSignature, the signature is automatically attached to each new message you write.

To use AutoSignature properly, you must include a blank line or two following the last line of your message. Outlook attaches the AutoSignature to the end of the message, and entering blank lines ensures separation between the message and the AutoSignature.

☑ Progress Check

If you can do the following, you've mastered this lesson:

- ❑ Create an AutoSignature.
- ❑ Format your AutoSignature.

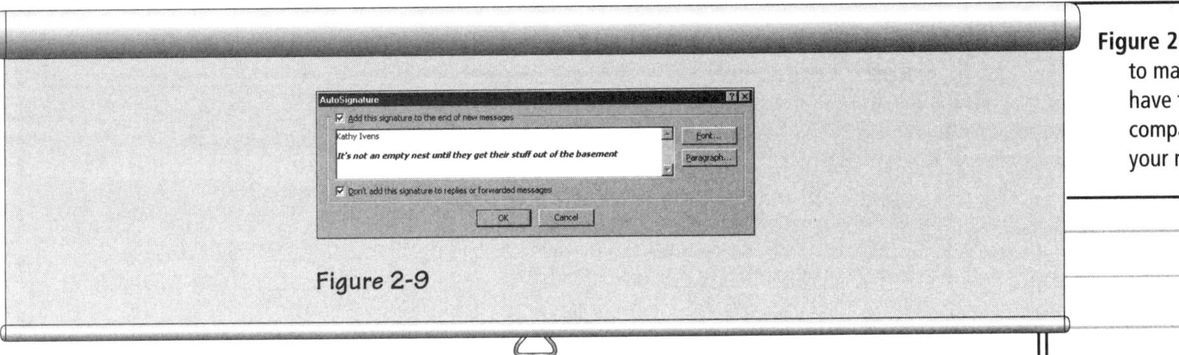

Figure 2-9: Use AutoSignature to make a statement, to have fun, or to include your company title with your name.

Attaching a File to an E-Mail Message

Lesson 2-7

Sometimes there is information in a file (such as a word processing document) that you want to pass along with your e-mail message. If the file is large or formatted for presentation (or both), you don't want to enter the entire contents into your e-mail message (by cutting and pasting). Instead, you can *attach* it to your message, which lets the recipient open the file on his or her own machine, formatting and all.

For the recipient to read your attachment, he or she must have the software that created the file you want to attach. You may have to make a phone call to see if your recipient has the software they need to read the attached file.

1. **Open a new Message window and address the message to yourself.**

   If you have a listing for a coworker or friend in your address book, you can use that address instead of sending this message and attachment to yourself.

2. **In the Subject field enter** For Your Amusement**.**

   The attachment we're sending is a funny document that floated around the Internet some time ago and may still be wending its way through cyberspace.

3. **In the message text box, enter** I thought you might enjoy the attached document.

4. **Click the Insert File button (which looks like a paper clip) on the Formatting toolbar.**

   This opens a dialog box that enables you to locate and select the file to attach (insert). Depending on where you installed the CD files, you may have to click the Look in list box and change the drive and directory where the file can be found.

5. **Double-click the file named Pest.doc.**

   An icon with the filename appears in the message at the point where your cursor was last positioned.

6. **Send the message.**

   The attachment travels along with the message.

☑ Progress Check

If you can do the following, you've mastered this lesson:

- ☐ Attach a file to an e-mail message.
- ☐ Annoy people to distraction.

Notes:

Minding your e-mail manners

If Emily Post were still writing about good manners, especially as they apply in the fine art of writing letters, she'd have to keep up with the times and explain the proper way to compose e-mail. Because Emily can't help you, we'll give you a few e-mail etiquette tips to help you out of trouble.

First of all, you need to remember that there's no such thing as absolute privacy when it comes to e-mail. If you send e-mail, assume other people can (and might) read it. E-mail is much less private and secure than *snail mail* (mail sent through the United States Postal Service). Okay, that's not exactly etiquette, but it's important enough to mention.

If you're responding to a question, either repeat the question's subject matter in your answer, or copy the original question and paste it into your message, then answer it. There is nothing more annoying than receiving e-mail that says, "I'll take Choice Number 3," when you don't remember what Choice Number 3 is. (Wait! There is one that's more annoying — getting e-mail that says simply "yes," "no," or "OK".)

Using uppercase letters IS SHOUTING so don't do it unless you really are angry and are shouting at your recipient.

People who use e-mail tend to work faster and take shortcuts; perhaps it's something about using advanced technology that makes us lose our ability to write long flowing statements. As a result, a number of abbreviations have cropped up and are now considered acceptable in e-mail messages:

btw = by the way

imho = in my humble opinion

imo = in my opinion (if you're not humble)

<grin> or <g> = the preceding statement is a joke

Don't count too much on the <grin> or <smile> technique, though — for example, it's not effective when you precede it with "You're the most obnoxious person I've ever met."

You can also use *emoticons*, the e-mail term for symbols that describe an emotion:

:) = smiling

:(= frowning

:D or :P = sticking your tongue out

Lesson 2-8 Setting Message Options

You can set a few e-mail options to make your messages more efficient. To learn about these different options, follow these steps:

1. **Open a New Message window.**

2. **Click the Options tab on the window to move to the Options window, which looks like Figure 2-10.**

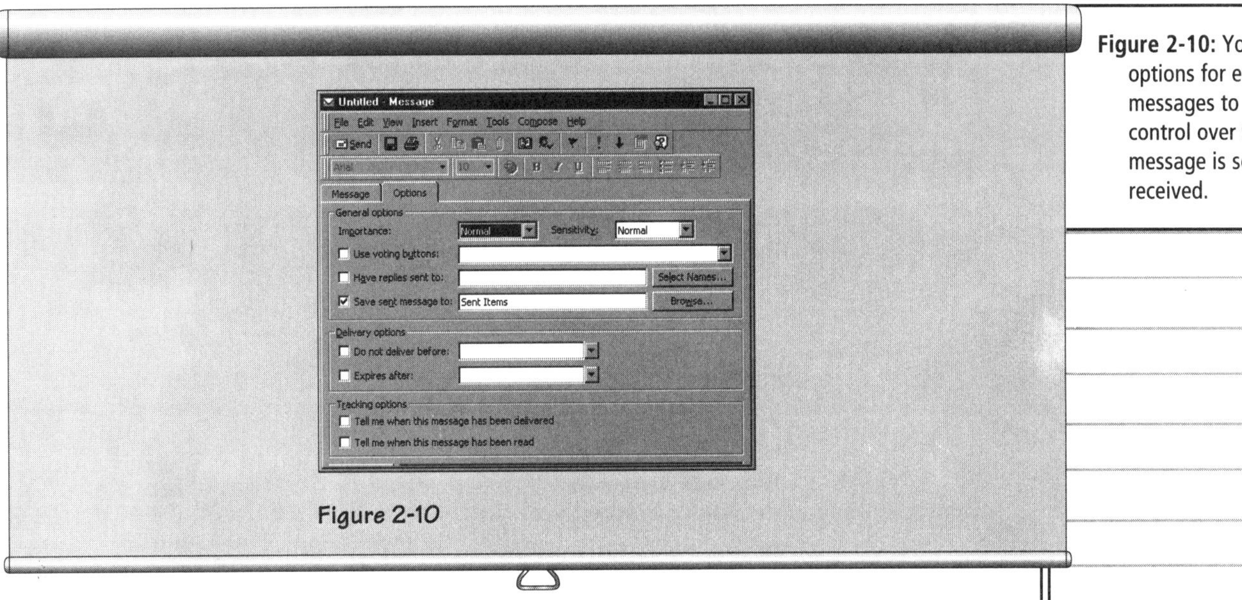

Figure 2-10

Figure 2-10: You can use options for e-mail messages to gain some control over the way the message is sent and/or received.

3 **To tell the recipient that the message contents are extremely urgent, click the arrow to the right of the Importance field and choose High to raise the priority of this message (the choices are High, Normal, and Low).**

When the recipient receives the message, a red exclamation point next to the message indicates that you've pronounced this e-mail very important. You can save some time by clicking the High Priority button on the toolbar while you're working in the Message window. That way, you don't even have to move to the options page.

You could also choose low priority, indicating that the message can wait (messages with interoffice gossip are good candidates for low priority status).

Most of the time, you won't mark an e-mail message for a priority status, because a status of Normal is the default, and most of your messages fall into that category.

4 **To tell the recipient that this message is extremely private, click the arrow to the right of the Sensitivity drop-down list to see the Sensitivity options. Then choose the appropriate description.**

The choices are Normal, Personal, Private, and Confidential, and as with the priority setting, you'll skip this field most of the time because Normal is the default setting.

The remaining options on the options page are useful only if you are working on a network with e-mail software installed to support the options. Check with your system administrator to learn which options are available and how to use them.

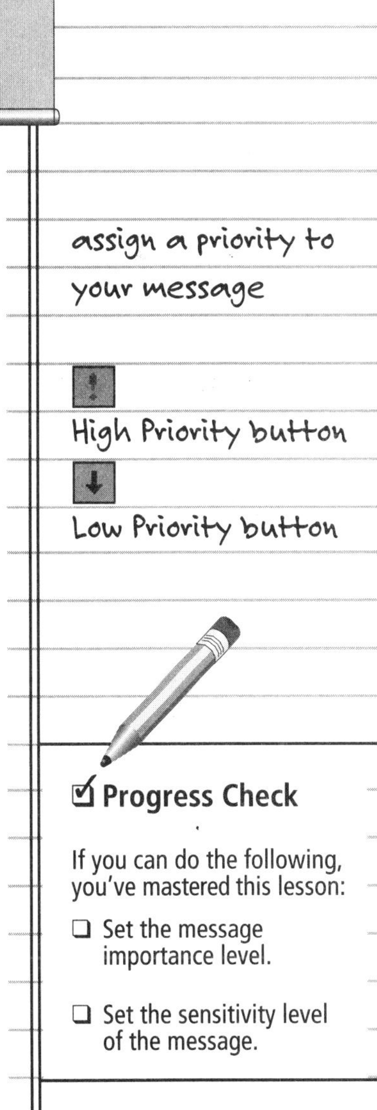

assign a priority to your message

High Priority button

Low Priority button

Progress Check

If you can do the following, you've mastered this lesson:

- ❑ Set the message importance level.
- ❑ Set the sensitivity level of the message.

Unit 2 Quiz

Notes:

The Unit 2 Quiz checks to see how well you followed along with the lessons in this unit. Take the Quiz and then turn to Appendix A to see how many answers you got right.

1. **How do you add an address to the Address Book?**

   A. With a ballpoint pen.

   B. Get a blank Rolodex card, fill it out, and file it alphabetically.

   C. Click the Address Book icon in the toolbar.

   D. Scribble it on a cocktail napkin and take care of it later.

2. **How do you delete an Address Book entry?**

   A. With your rubber eraser.

   B. Tear out the page.

   C. What's an Address Book entry?

   D. Open the Address Book, highlight the entry, and press the delete key.

3. **What is a Personal Distribution List?**

   A. A euphemism for a will.

   B. My holiday gift list.

   C. A group of e-mail recipients.

   D. A list of where your body parts are now, relative to their original location.

4. **How do you change the color of text in your message?**

   A. A little paint usually does the trick.

   B. Highlight the text, click the Color icon, and select a color.

   C. Fiddle with the knobs on the back of the computer.

   D. Take off your sunglasses.

5. **How do you attach a file to an e-mail message?**

   A. Use a stapler.

   B. Scotch tape.

   C. Click the Insert File button and select the file to attach.

   D. With the shiny side down.

Unit 2 Exercise

1. Add a friend's e-mail address to the Address Book.
2. Create a message with every fifth word formatted differently (but don't send it to anyone because it will look like a ransom note).
3. Create a Personal Distribution List called Friends and add three people you know who have e-mail addresses.
4. Send a note to each of those people.

Unit 3

Receiving Messages

Objectives for This Unit

- ✓ Understanding the Inbox
- ✓ Reading messages
- ✓ Marking messages
- ✓ Deleting messages
- ✓ Dealing with attachments to messages
- ✓ Responding to messages
- ✓ Printing messages

Prerequisites

- Starting Outlook (Lesson 1-1)
- Viewing the Inbox (Lesson 1-2)
- Composing and sending e-mail (Lesson 2-5)

The fun part of using e-mail is receiving mail. When new messages appear, there's always the chance that you're going to find out some exciting news or read some interesting information. Of course, most of the time the messages are filled with rather mundane facts about office procedures or notifications of meetings — important information, but not so much fun. Every once in a while, though, you may get a message that has a funny story or some other amusing text, and it's a nice break in your day.

When you receive e-mail, the messages go to your Inbox, which looks like Figure 3-1. In this unit, you learn what to do with your e-mail after it lands in your Inbox.

Figure 3-1: The Outlook Inbox provides lots of information about your messages.

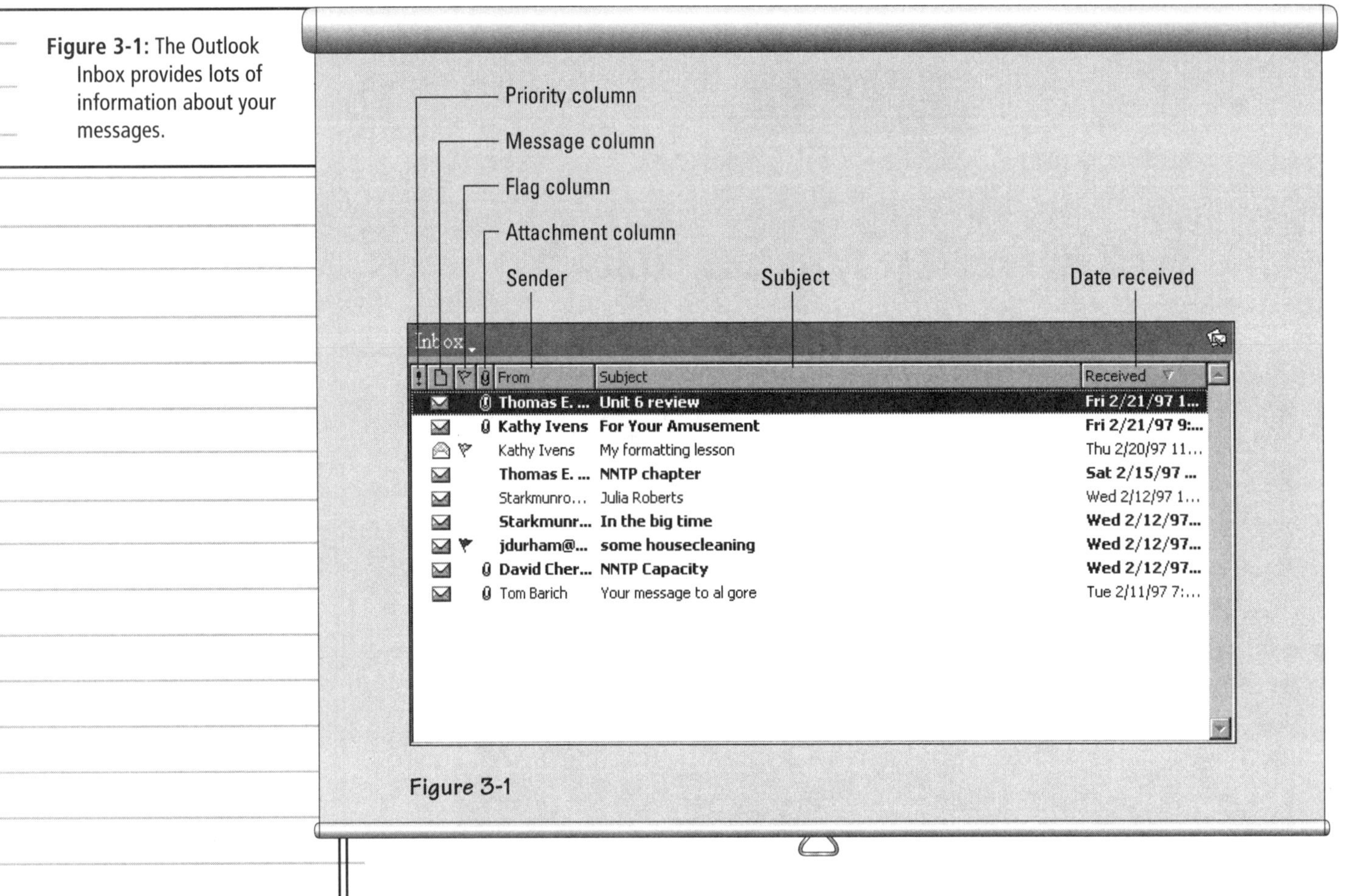

Lesson 3-1 Understanding the Inbox

Inbox = Outlook message center

The Inbox is your message center. The Inbox, which is an Outlook folder, holds the e-mail you've received. E-mail that's picked up from a remote e-mail service (through your modem) or delivered from your network post office is automatically placed in the Inbox for you.

The Inbox can also help you keep your e-mail organized. If you receive lots of e-mail, looking at a long list of messages can be overwhelming. You have to find a way to set some priorities about what to read immediately and what can wait until later. After all, that report you're working on is due in a few minutes, and if you stop to read every message in your Inbox, you may miss your deadline. On the other hand, there may be information in one of the messages that you need for the report.

The trick is to arrange your messages so that you can decide what's important enough to open right away. That's where the Inbox steps in to help you stay on track. Using the Inbox, you can view your e-mail in a variety of different ways that can help you find just the information you need to see.

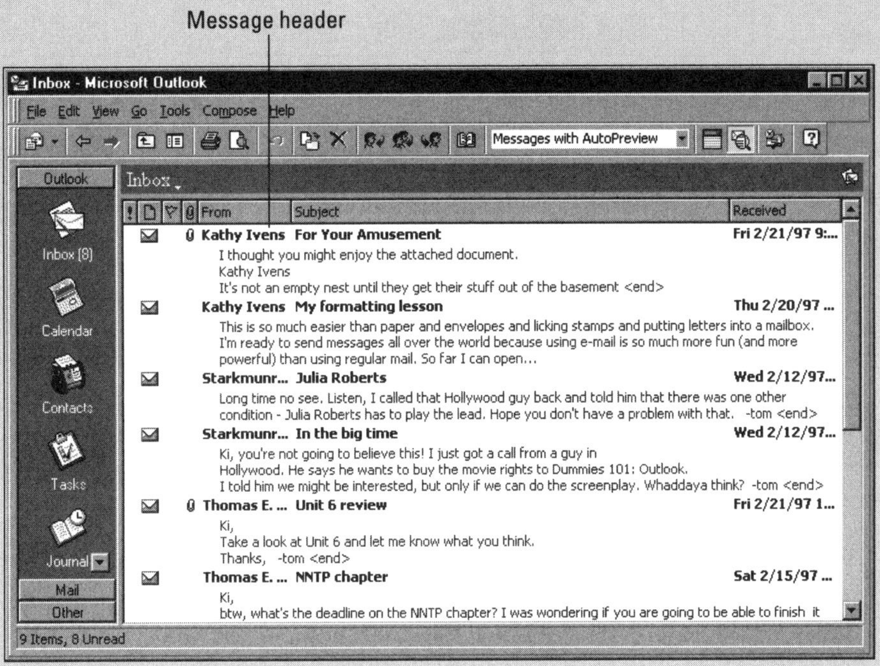

Message header

Figure 3-2

Figure 3-2: You can see some of the text for each unread message in your Inbox.

Notes:

To view information about the messages in your Inbox, follow these steps:

1. **Click the Inbox icon on the Outlook bar.**

   The Inbox displays a list of your received messages. Messages in bold type are the ones you haven't yet read.

   Outlook, by default, shows your unread messages with *AutoPreview* turned on, which means you see a few lines of the text in addition to the message *header* (see Figure 3-2).

Inbox icon

on the test

2. **Click the arrow to the right of the Current view box (which currently says Messages with AutoPreview) and choose Messages from the drop-down list.**

   If you have a lot of messages, it's easier to see all of them if you list them without any text showing. The messages now appear with only the headers, which means more messages can be seen at a time (see Figure 3-3).

   Outlook automatically arranges your messages to show the latest ones first, which is indicated by the little downward-pointing arrow in the Received column header. In fact, this little arrow follows each of the column headers around, depending on which column header you sort your mail by. Just wait and see.

message header = sender's name, subject, and date received

Figure 3-3: The more messages you can see, the easier it is to decide how to deal with them.

Notes:

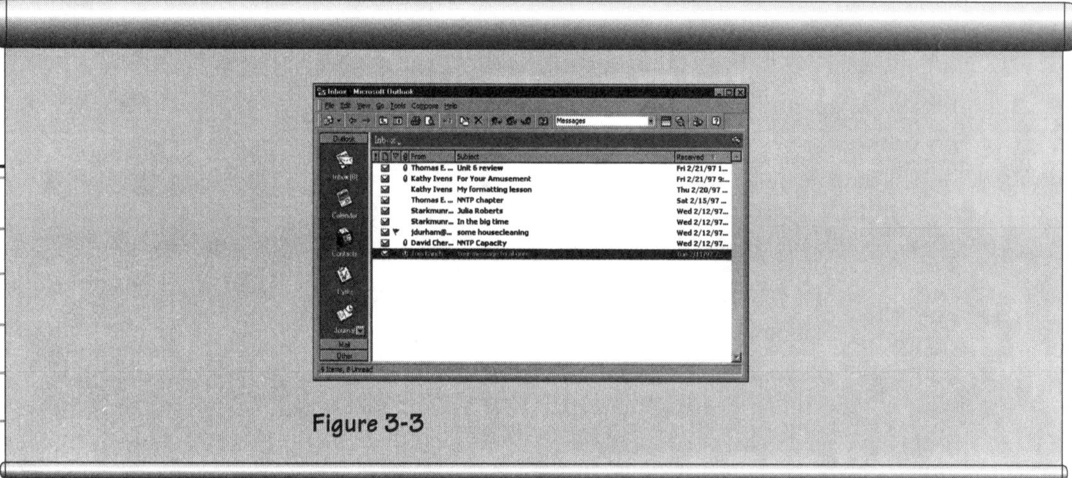

Sometimes, however, you may want to see which messages have been sitting in your Inbox the longest (consequently, who's been waiting the longest for an answer).

3 **To arrange the messages from the oldest to the newest, click the Received column header.**

The oldest messages are now at the top, and the message that arrived last is at the bottom. The little arrow next to the Received column header has hopped around and is pointing up.

If there are old messages displayed in bold text, you'd better think of a good excuse, because whoever it is you're ignoring may be getting a little testy.

Each time you click the Received column header, you switch the listing of e-mail in your Inbox between ascending and descending chronological order. But what if you just need to see messages sent from a particular person — say, your boss? Then you need to sort your messages by sender.

4 **To sort the messages by sender, click the From column header.**

The listing is arranged so that all the messages are sorted by the sender, and the senders are in alphabetical order. (You can click the From column header again to reverse the order.) Now you can head right for the section of messages from your boss or your mother. Notice that the little arrow has jumped over to the From column header.

If your boss has asked you to present for him at your company's next convention, you may want to just see messages from your boss about the convention. In that case, you can sort your messages by subject.

5 **Click the column header called Subject. The messages are listed alphabetically according to the text in the Subject field.**

Arranging messages by subject makes it easy to find all the messages about a project you're working on (or maybe you just want to group all your lunch invitations together). That nimble little arrow has hopped over to the Subject column header.

6 Click any of the icon columns to arrange the messages so that any mail with the corresponding icons attached is shown at the top of the window.

This is a good way to spotlight messages that have high priority, or have attachments (depending on which icon column is important to you at the moment).

7 Click the arrow next to the Current View box on the toolbar to see the available choices; then select the one that matches the view you need.

It's common to change the view in order to look for certain types of messages, and you'll find that your choice of a view depends on what's important today. If you're expecting an important message from your boss, sort the messages by sender. If you are awaiting an important attachment, sort by the attachment column.

Messages
Messages with AutoPreview
By Message Flag
Last Seven Days
Flagged for Next Seven Days
By Conversation Topic
By Sender
Unread Messages
Sent To
Message Timeline

choices in the Current view drop-down list

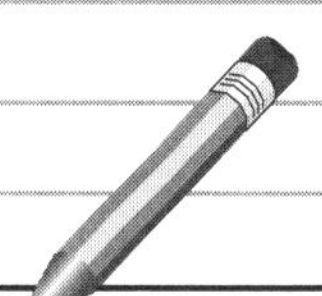

Understanding the Inbox icons

When you look at the Inbox, you see several columns to the left of the From column (see Figure 3-1 for the column names). Those columns occasionally contain icons, and that means that the message has some special attributes. Here are some of the important icon messages:

- Priority Column:
  - Red exclamation point = high priority
  - Blue arrow pointing downward = low priority
  - No icon = normal priority
- Message Icon Column:
  - Closed envelope = unread message
  - Open envelope = read message
- Flag Column
  - Flag = marked for follow-up action
- Attachment Column:
  - Paper clip = attachment

When you view your Inbox, understanding the icons should make it easier to decide which messages you want to open first.

☑ Progress Check

If you can do the following, you've mastered this lesson:

- ❑ Open the Inbox.
- ❑ Sort your messages by the column headings.
- ❑ Arrange the message listing according to a variety of viewing choices.

Reading Messages — Lesson 3-2

Now that you've viewed the list of messages in your Inbox, it's time to read your mail. You may have decided that you'll read some of the messages (the ones that seem to warrant instant attention) and let the rest wait until you're not so busy, or maybe you want to read every message you have. Of course, if your Inbox doesn't have lots of unread messages, you're spared the agony of these decisions.

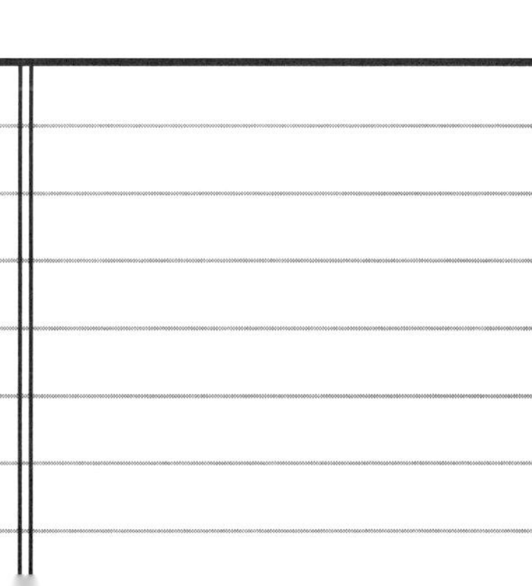

Figure 3-4: Open the Message window to read the text of the message.

Notes:

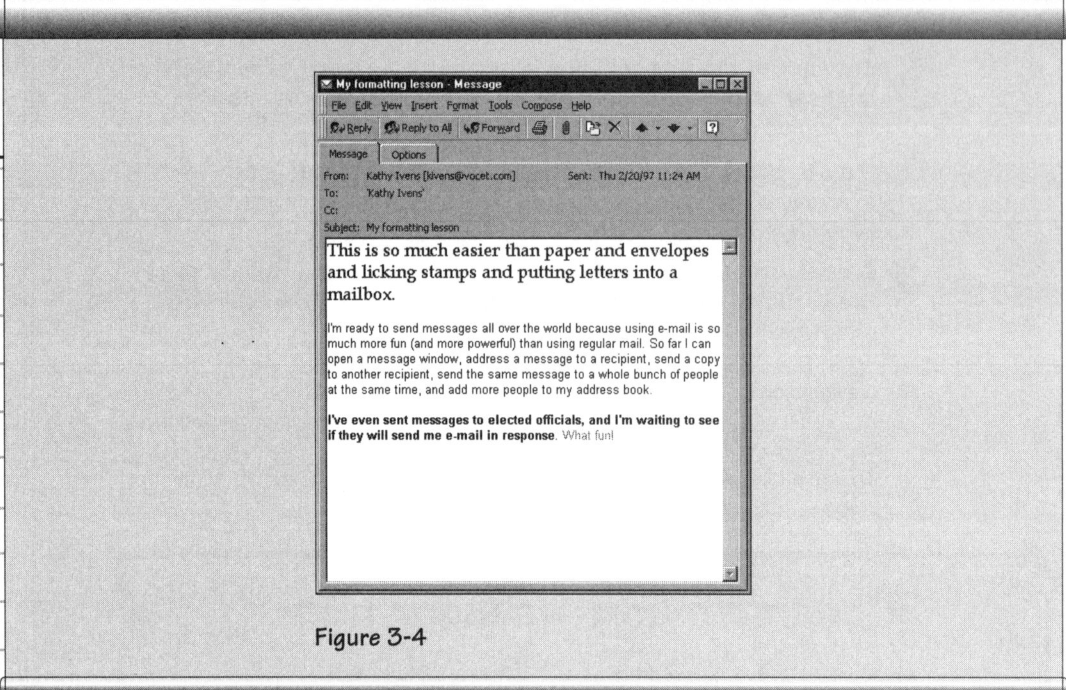

Figure 3-4

While reading a message, you can mark it for special actions (such as reminding yourself that you have to perform some task or otherwise follow up on the message contents) before you close it. You can also mark messages for deletion after you've read them, and we'll discuss those actions in this lesson.

When you receive a message with an attachment, you need to take some special steps to open the attachment. We'll also cover reading attachments in this lesson.

Reading, marking, and deleting messages

In this exercise, you open and read the first message you mailed yourself in Lesson 2-5. To read your message, follow these steps:

1. **From the Inbox listing, double-click the message you sent to yourself that has the Subject My formatting lesson.**

   The message opens in its own window (see Figure 3-4).

2. **Adjust the size of your window so that you can see all of the text.**

   If all the text doesn't fit in the window (your Message window may be smaller than the one in Figure 3-4), you can use the scroll bar to see the rest of the text, or enlarge the window by clicking the Maximize button in the upper right corner of the window.

   You can also adjust the size of the window by moving your pointer to an edge of the window until it turns into a double-headed arrow. Then hold down the left mouse button and drag in the appropriate direction to enlarge the window.

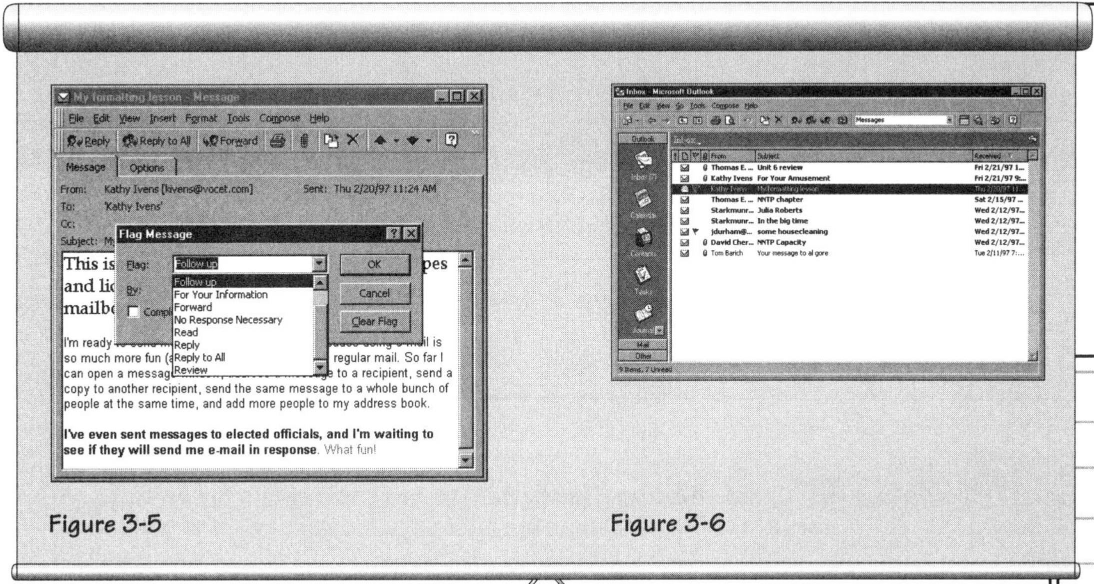

Figure 3-5

Figure 3-6

Figure 3-5: You can flag a message to remind yourself if your message needs some special treatment or follow up action.

Figure 3-6: An icon is in the Flag column to indicate the message needs some special attention.

This message requires your immediate attention, so you'll want to mark it as such in the next step. After all, you don't want to forget to review how much fun you've had with this book so far.

on the test

3 **Choose Edit➪Message Flag to flag your message for special attention.**

The Flag Message dialog box appears so you can mark this message for special treatment. Click the arrow to the right of the Flag field to see the choices for marking the message (see Figure 3-5) and then select one. You don't have to use any of the predefined flag messages; you can enter your own message.

4 **Select a flag message from the drop-down list or enter a brief message of your own in the Flag field and then click OK.**

5 **Close the message by pressing Alt+F4.**

In the Inbox window, the listing for this message now displays an opened envelope to indicate that you've read the message and a red flag to show that you've marked it for special attention (see Figure 3-6).

When you complete the follow-up action you indicated with a flag, right-click the listing for this message and choose Flag Complete from the menu. The flag stays in the Flag column, but it is no longer red. You can choose Clear Message Flag from the right-click menu if you want to get rid of the flag entirely.

You can also choose Clear Message Flag from the right-click menu if you want to get rid of the flag icon regardless of whether you followed up or not.

If you don't remember the action attached to the flag, open the message and choose Edit➪Message Flag to read your entry.

You can also flag a message from the right-click menu. Use this menu if you just want a visual reminder to follow up on the message without going through the steps involved in creating a flag with detailed information.

Figure 3-7: The Deleted Items folder displays everything you've deleted from all the features in Outlook.

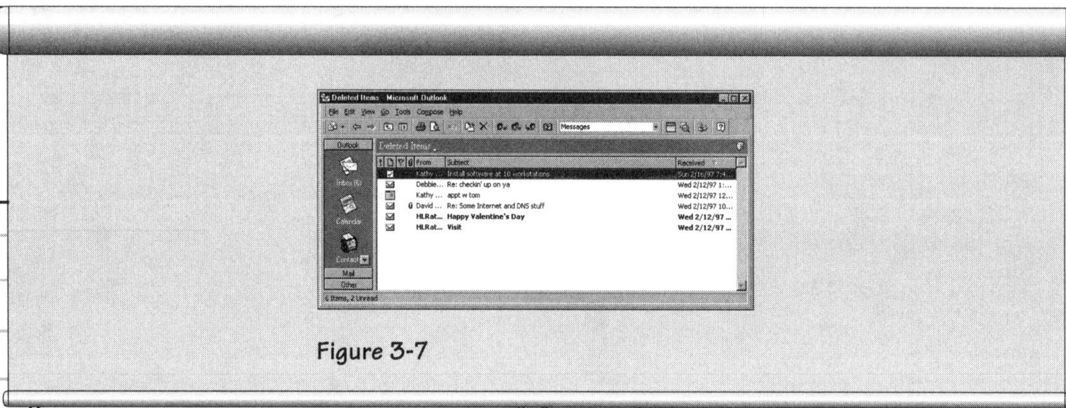

Delete button

Deleted Items folder icon

the Delete Confirmation dialog box

6. **To delete this message after you've read it (while the message is open), click the Delete button on the Message window toolbar. To delete a closed message from the Inbox listing, click it to highlight it and then press the Delete key.**

   When you delete a message, it moves to the Deleted Items folder.

7. **If you made a mistake by deleting the message, click the Deleted Items icon on the Outlook bar and then find the message and double-click its listing to open it so you can read it again.**

   You can rescue deleted items by moving them to other folders. Detailed information about manipulating items and folders is in Unit 4.

8. **To delete a message permanently, move to the Deleted Items folder by clicking its icon on the Outlook bar.**

   The Deleted Items folder holds items from all the Outlook folders, so eventually (after you've completed this book) you may see items other than e-mail messages when the folder window opens (see Figure 3-7). For now, we just want you to concentrate on deleted e-mail, which has a little envelope icon in front of it.

9. **Click the item you want to delete and then press Delete or click the Delete button on the toolbar.**

   Because this is a permanent, irreversible deletion, you have to confirm your intentions with Outlook. Choose Yes to delete the item forever.

Handling attachments

Messages that have attachments display a paper clip icon in the attachment column. When you open a message with an attachment, you must handle the attachment separately from the message text in order to read the attachment. To learn how to do this, follow these steps:

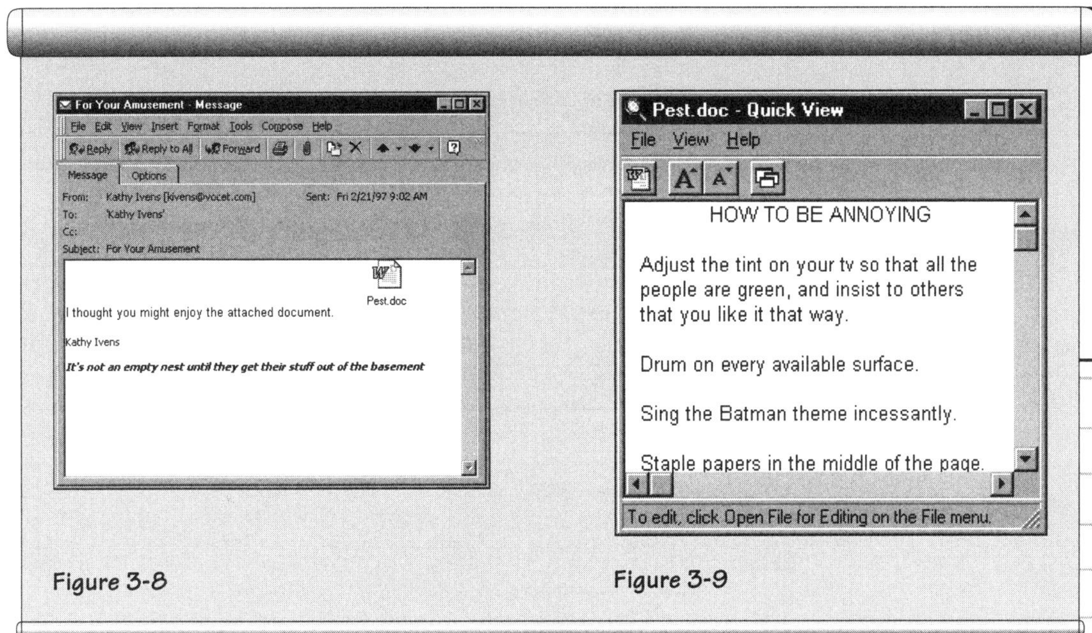

Figure 3-8: An attachment appears as an icon within a message because it's not part of the message text — it's a separate entity.

Figure 3-9: A quick peek into the attachment gives you information about the contents of the file.

Notes:

1 Open the message with the subject For Your Amusement by double-clicking it in the Inbox.

When the Message window opens, you see the text and you also see an icon representing the attachment with the name of the file beneath the icon (see Figure 3-8). Most of the time the attachment icon indicates the software that created the attached file. In this case, the attachment is declaring itself a Microsoft Word document.

2 To get a quick look at the contents of an attachment, right-click its icon and choose Quick View from the menu.

Quick View is a special Windows viewing program that lets you peek into the contents of a file (see Figure 3-9). There is a Quick View program available for many types of files, including word processing files, video files, audio files, and so on.

If the menu that appears when you right-click the attachment icon does not have Quick View as a menu choice, that means the Quick View software wasn't installed. See your Windows documentation (or ask your system administrator) to install the Quick View features into Windows.

on the test

3 To open the attachment, double-click its icon.

You must have the software that created the file if you want to open it (or software that can interpret and convert the file to its own format, although that rarely works well). If there is no software in your computer that can handle the file, you receive an error message.

Figure 3-10: Double-clicking this attachment icon opens Microsoft Word with the attached file in the software window.

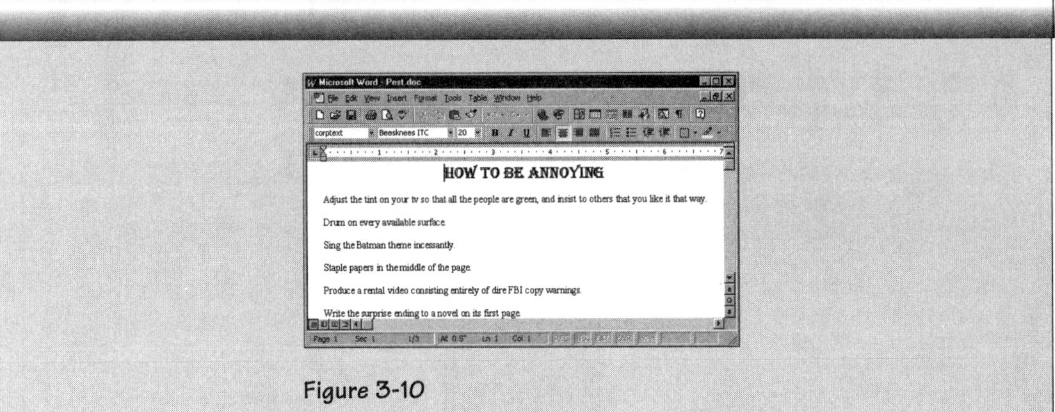

Because Outlook comes with the Microsoft Office 97 Suite, chances are that you have the Microsoft Word program you need to open this attachment. After you double-click the icon, the software launches (opens) and displays the attached file in the software window (see Figure 3-10). You can manipulate the file by using the features in the software application (edit it, change the attributes of the text, and do anything you would do with one of your own documents in this software).

4 **To save the attachment, choose File⇨Save As from the software menu bar. Then choose a location for this file.**

Because the file already has a name, choosing Save instead of Save As keeps the file in the folder where your e-mail attachments are placed. That is usually not convenient, and you probably want to save it to a folder where you keep other similar documents. For example, if the attachment is a word processing file, you might save it with your other word processing files. In a like manner, you would want to save an attachment that is a spreadsheet with your Excel files (assuming you use Excel).

If you wish, because you're using Save As, you can also change the name of the file while you're saving it.

5 **To save the attachment from the Message window (without opening its associated software), right-click the attachment's icon and choose Save As from the menu. Then choose a location from the Save As dialog box.**

6 **To print the attachment, right-click the attachment's icon and choose Print from the menu.**

The associated software opens (in this case Microsoft Word) and automatically issues the command to print. You don't have to use any commands in the software to make this happen — it's all on autopilot. After the file goes to the printer, the software automatically closes. It's magic!

You can also print the attachment if you open it (double-click it, which opens the software with the file ready for editing, viewing, printing, or anything else you want to do with it). Just use the appropriate commands for this software to print the file, or click the appropriate button on the software toolbar.

heads up

If you are comfortable with Windows Explorer, you can also move the attachment by right-clicking its icon and choosing Copy or Cut. You then open Explorer and choose Paste to paste the file in a folder of your choice.

extra credit

Handling compressed files

Sometimes an attachment arrives as a compressed file. This means that the file has been treated with a special software program that takes all the blank spaces out of the file and compresses the data. You can think of it as taking all the air out of a container and shrinking the container to the size needed to hold the items placed in the container.

Sometimes the data in a compressed file is actually several compressed files all crammed together. This is a great way to send someone four files in one fell swoop.

Compressing a file means that the data is transferred much faster, because the size of the data is so much smaller. Anyone who receives a compressed file from you (instead of a big, uncompressed file) will think you are really considerate and e-mail savvy.

When you receive a compressed file, you first need to uncompress the file before you can read it. Many compressed attachments have the file extension .zip (the extension is the part of the file name that comes after the period), which means that the file has been compressed with a popular program called WinZip. In order to read a file with the .zip extension, you need to have WinZip on your computer. Lucky for you, WinZip comes on the CD at the back of this book. To learn all about WinZip and its many amazing features, turn to Appendix B of this book.

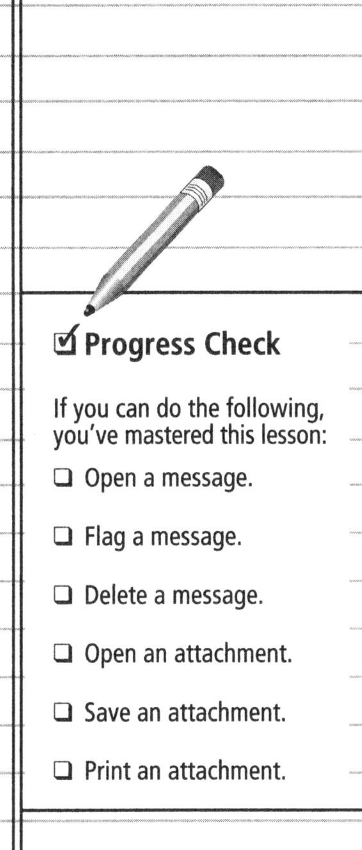

☑ Progress Check

If you can do the following, you've mastered this lesson:

- ❑ Open a message.
- ❑ Flag a message.
- ❑ Delete a message.
- ❑ Open an attachment.
- ❑ Save an attachment.
- ❑ Print an attachment.

Responding to Messages

Lesson 3-3

Because you are a polite and considerate person, you'll want to reply to messages. Even if you're not polite and considerate, some messages demand action because of their contents. Sometimes replying to the sender isn't enough — there might be other people who should see the message or see your reply (or both).

You have plenty of choices when you want to respond to an e-mail message, and we'll discuss them in this lesson.

Notes:

Reply

Reply button

Replying to the sender

The most common response to an e-mail message is a simple reply. You read the message and then you reply to the sender. For this exercise, you will reply to the message you sent yourself about formatting.

1. **From the Inbox window, double-click the message with the subject My formatting lesson.**

2. **To reply to this message, click the Reply button on the toolbar.**

   A Message window opens (see Figure 3-11) so you can compose a reply to the message.

3. **If you don't want to retain the original text in your reply, press Ctrl+A to select all of the text. Then press Delete.**

   The original text is displayed in the window by default, because it's sometimes a helpful reminder for the recipient about his or her original message. Receiving a reply message that says something like "I don't agree with your second point" is incredibly annoying to anyone without total recall or a photographic memory.

   If you are going to refer directly to a specific point in the original message, it's a good idea to leave it in the reply. You can delete any part of the message you wish by highlighting the text you want to get rid of and pressing Delete.

4. **Type** I think the font size for the first sentence is a little too large — it seems as if the message is shouting at me. **in the Message window.**

   The text you enter is blue, as a reminder that you are composing a reply instead of a new message. (The text won't appear blue to the recipient; this is just a convenience for you while you enter your reply.)

   If you did not delete the original text, you'll notice that as you enter text, the original text moves downward to make room for your new messsage.

5. **You can change the text in the Subject field if you wish. Press Alt+J to move to the Subject field, or click anywhere in the field, and then delete the existing text and replace it with text of your choice.**

   It's usually not a good idea to change the text in the Subject field when you reply to a message, in order to make all the messages on this subject easy to find. When messages go back and forth on a single subject, it's referred to as a *thread*, as in a thread of conversation.

   Of course, if you clicked the Reply button as a convenient way to start a message to this sender (instead of going through all the steps to compose a new message) and you have no intention of discussing the original subject, you should change the text in the subject field to reflect your new topic of conversation.

6. **You could send copies of this reply to additional recipients if you think they might be interested in this subject. Click the Cc button and add recipients as you learned to do in Unit 2.**

   If you add recipients to a reply, it's a good idea to leave the original message in the message text box so they can understand your response.

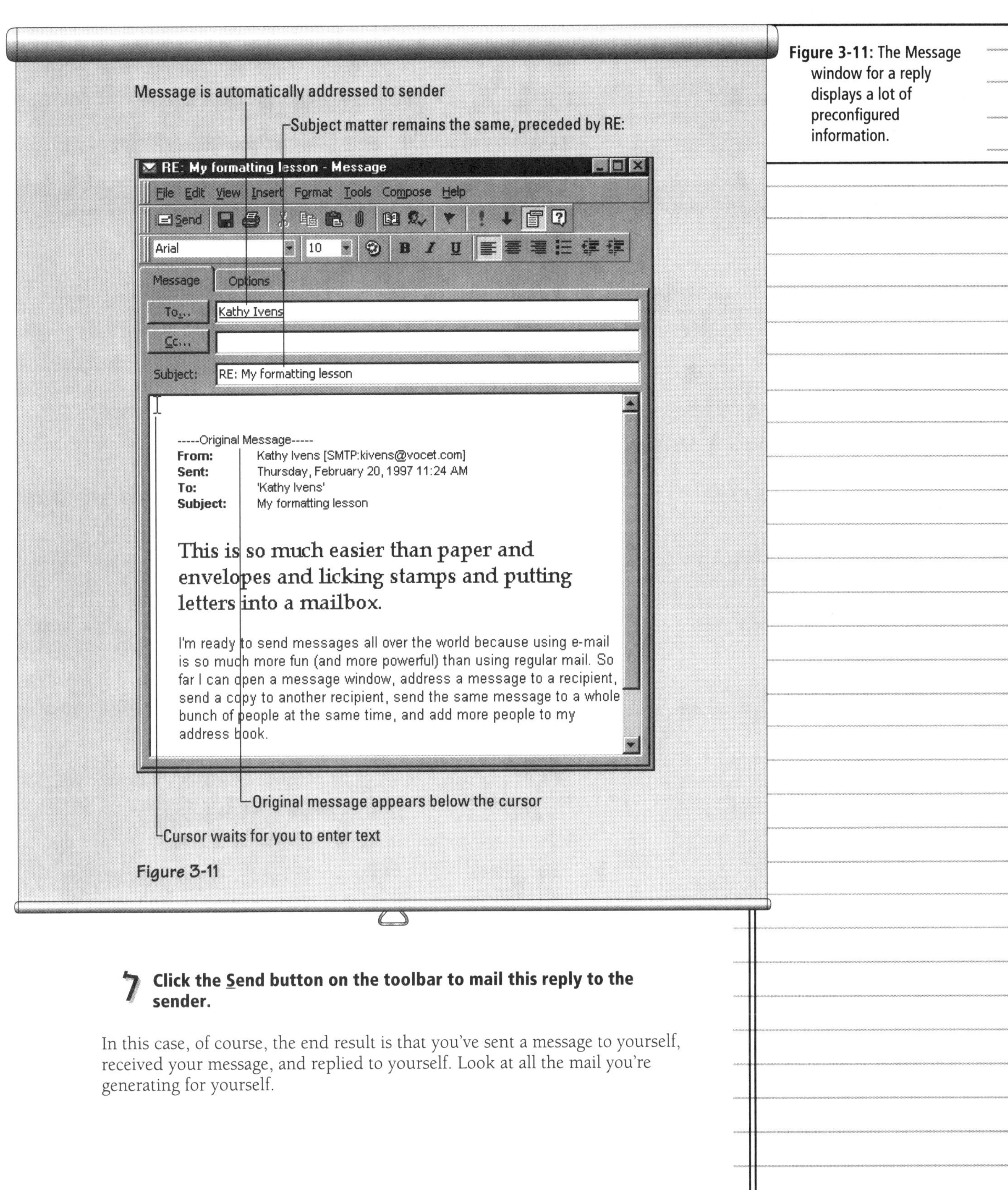

Figure 3-11

Figure 3-11: The Message window for a reply displays a lot of preconfigured information.

7 Click the Send button on the toolbar to mail this reply to the sender.

In this case, of course, the end result is that you've sent a message to yourself, received your message, and replied to yourself. Look at all the mail you're generating for yourself.

Figure 3-12: The names of all direct recipients and copied recipients are shown in the original Message window.

Figure 3-13: The original recipients automatically become the recipients for your reply.

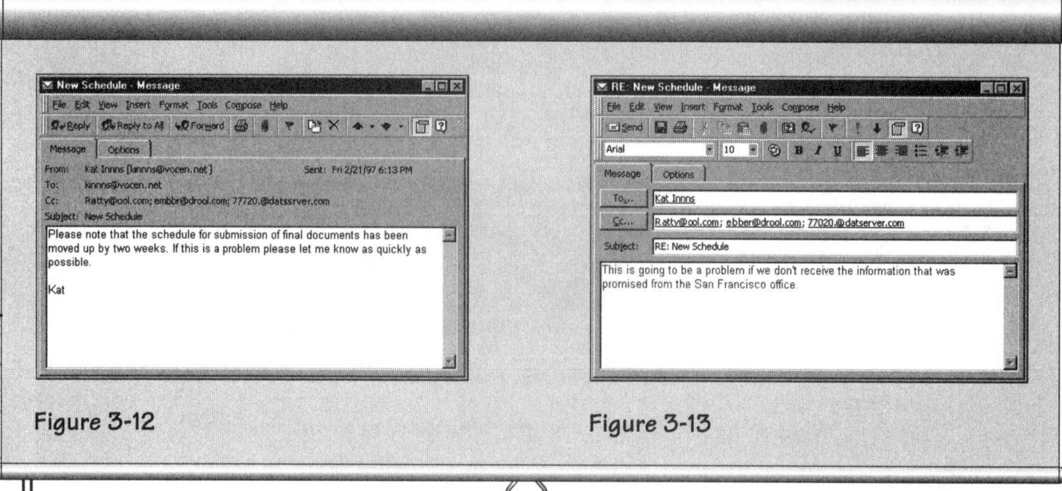

Figure 3-12

Figure 3-13

Notes:

Replying to everyone

If the message you receive is addressed to you and there are other recipients of the e-mail, you can choose to reply to everybody who received this message. This is useful when you are part of a distribution list, especially if all the people on that list are participating in a project. The information in your reply may be important to everyone.

If you have a message in your Inbox that fits this description, you may want to use it to complete this exercise. If not, follow along as we demonstrate this task (we, of course, have mail that went to multiple recipients in our mailbox).

on the test

1. **Open a message that was addressed to other recipients in addition to yourself.**

   It doesn't matter whether the mail was addressed to you, or you are the recipient of a copy of a message that was sent to another person. When the Message window opens, you can see the names of all the recipients (except for those folks who received blind copies). Figure 3-12 shows a Message window for a message addressed to one person and copied to three additional people.

2. **Click the Reply to All button on the toolbar to open a reply Message window.**

   The Message window displays with the sender's name in the To field and the names of the original recipients of copies in the Cc field (see Figure 3-13).

Reply to All button

3. **Enter the text of your reply in the message text box.**

   You can move right to the message text box because you don't want to change the text in the subject field.

4. **To remove a recipient, put your cursor to the left of the name and use the Delete key to delete the name.**

   You can also drag the mouse to highlight the name and then press Delete. Don't forget to delete the semicolon after the name.

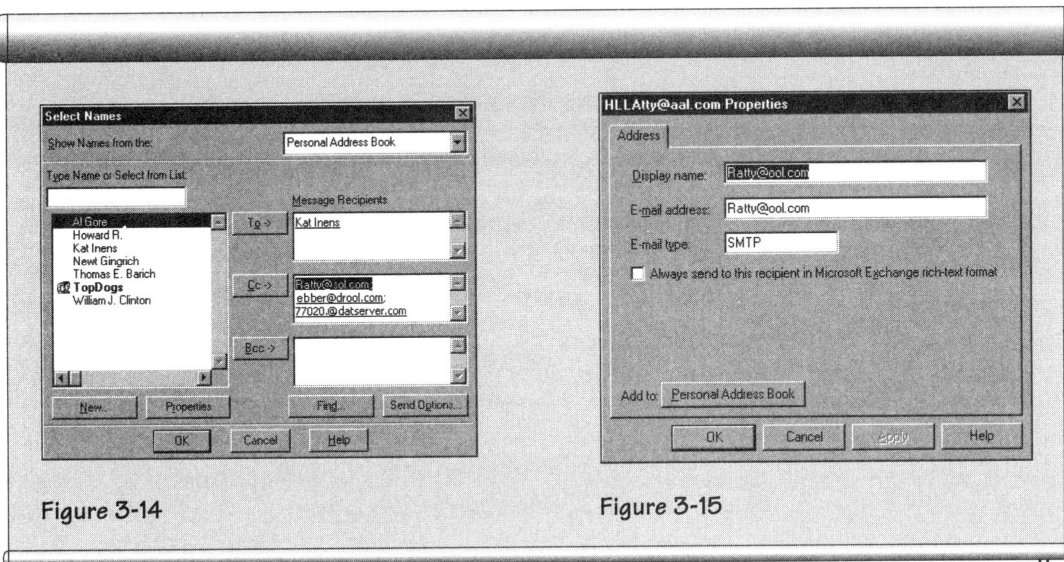

Figure 3-14

Figure 3-15

Figure 3-14: The recipient information for this message is already filled in for you.

Figure 3-15: You have the information you need to make this recipient a member of your own Address Book.

5 **To add a recipient, click the To button or the Cc button and follow the steps you learned in Unit 2 to add the new recipient.**

6 **To add a recipient of a copy to your own Personal Address book, click the Cc button.**

Sometimes you'll find that the additional recipients of messages you receive are not in your address book. In case you ever want to send these people e-mail, you should add them to your address book.

When the Select Names dialog box opens, the names of the recipients are displayed in the appropriate boxes (see Figure 3-14).

7 **Drag the mouse to select (highlight) the name you want to add to your address book.**

8 **Click the Properties button.**

Information about this recipient appears in the Properties dialog box (see Figure 3-15).

9 **Change the Display name to a real name instead of the e-mail address.**

10 **Change the E-mail type to match the type for this recipient.**

If the type is SMTP, you should change it to Internet. It's too complicated to explain why the SMTP type appears, just trust us that it means messages to this recipient will be delivered over the Internet. If the type matches your network mail system, you don't have to change it.

11 **Click the Personal Address Book button.**

The name is now in your address book.

12 **Click OK to return to the Select Names dialog box. Then repeat the process to add any additional names to your Personal Address Book.**

Figure 3-16: When you forward a message to someone else, Outlook automatically displays all the information about the message sender as well as the original text.

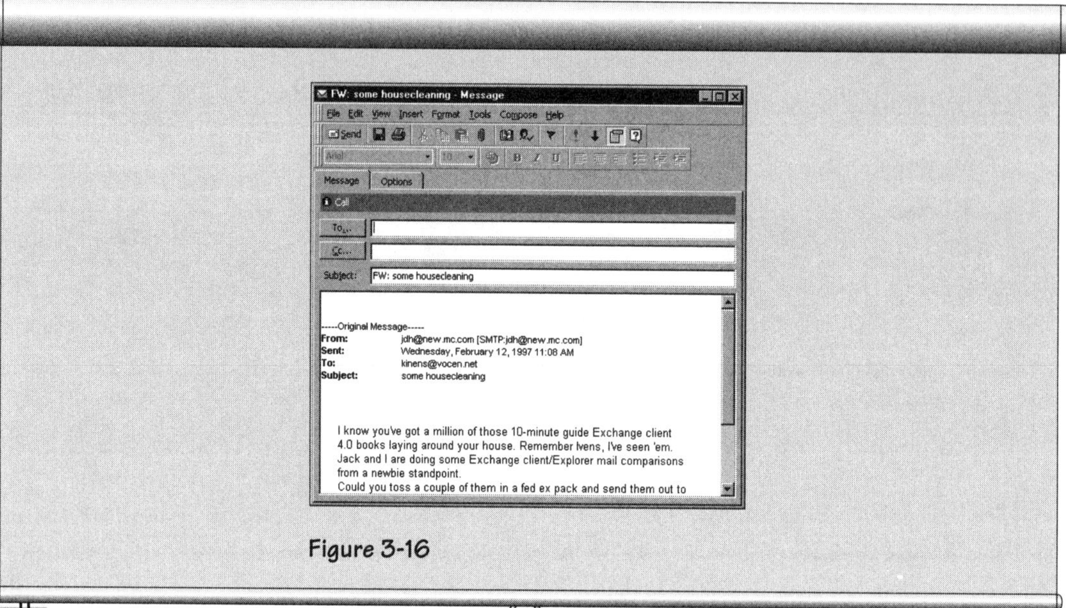

Figure 3-16

13 **Click OK when you are finished adding names. You return to the Message window. Click Send to mail this reply to all the recipients of the original message.**

Notice that the names you added to your address book are changed in the Message window so that instead of the e-mail address, you see the display name you created.

After you send your reply, the original message appears. Press Alt+F4 to close the message. When you return to the Inbox window, you might want to click the Address Book button on the toolbar and peek at the contents, just to prove to yourself that those names were added. Don't worry, we won't be insulted — we figured you'd check.

Forwarding a message

If you receive a message you think someone else should see, you don't have to create a whole new message in order to transmit the information. Any message you receive can be *forwarded* to someone else. To forward a message, take these steps:

1 **Open the message you sent to yourself about formatting e-mail and then click the Forward button on the toolbar.**

A Message window opens with the header and text of the original message displayed in the text box (Figure 3-16). Notice that Subject field displays FW: followed by the original subject text, indicating a forwarded message.

Forward button

2 Click To, which opens the Select Names dialog box. Select a recipient and click OK.

You can, of course, select multiple recipients for the To field or add recipients to the Cc field.

3 If you wish, move to the message text box and enter a note such as I'm forwarding this because I think it is of interest to you.

It's not strictly necessary to add a note, because the FW in the Subject field indicates that you are forwarding a message. It is, however, a gracious and polite protocol to personalize this message by adding a few words.

4 Delete any text or header information you think is unnecessary.

If the original message had several topics, it's only necessary to send the text that relates to the topic you feel the recipient is interested in.

5 Click Send to forward this message. Then close the original message.

Forwarding e-mail is a commonplace activity because it's so convenient and easy to pass information on in this manner. Forwarding saves you untold hours of typing.

☑ Progress Check

If you can do the following, you've mastered this lesson:

- ❑ Send a reply to someone who sent you a message.
- ❑ Send a reply to everyone who received the same message you received.
- ❑ Forward a received message to someone else.

Printing Messages

Lesson 3-4

Even though we'd all like to believe that using computers results in a paperless office, it hasn't and it won't. Offices still have filing cabinets, and there are rules and protocols in most offices about keeping the files in those cabinets up-to-date. That means that eventually you will need to print some of your e-mail messages.

Also, you'll find that sometimes you want to print a message so that you can take the information in it with you when you leave the office. For example, a message about a social engagement should return home with you so you can post it on the refrigerator. Or perhaps you received a humorous message you want to share with others, and if you don't print it you won't remember the punch line (there's nothing more annoying than having someone tell a joke and then forget the punch line).

You can use two methods to print a message: quick printing from the message listing in the Inbox, and formatted printing from the Message window so you can exercise some control over the print job. We'll go over both of these methods in this lesson.

Figure 3-17: You can see a preview of the way a printed document will look.

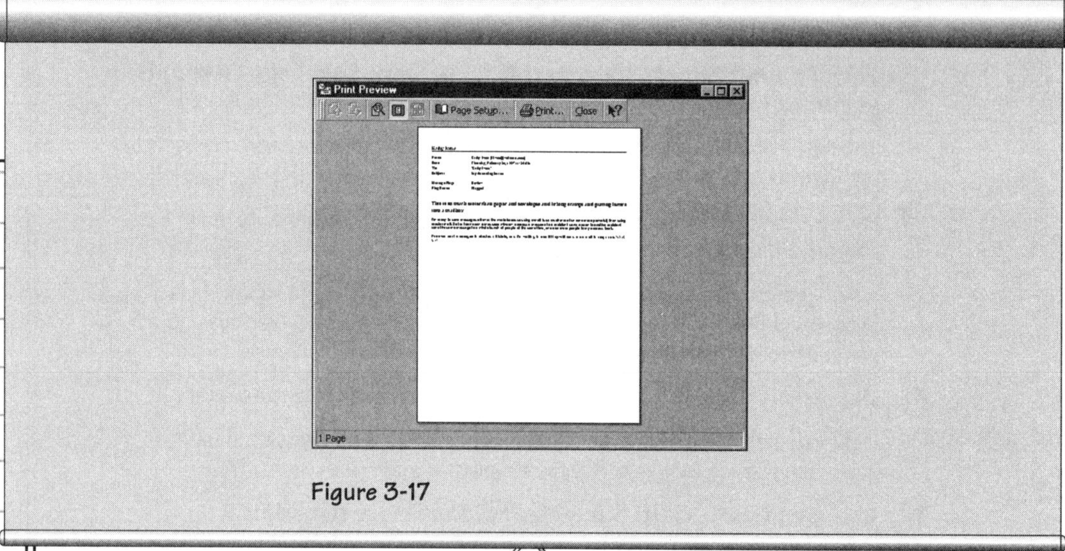

Figure 3-17

Notes:

Printing from the message listing

If you want a quick hard-copy of a message, follow these steps:

1. **Go to the Inbox folder to see the list of messages.**
2. **Click the message you need to print.**

   The message is highlighted.

3. **Click the Print button on the toolbar.**

   The message prints.

Print button

That was certainly easy! Notice that the printed copy of the message has the header information at the top of the page. If there is a flag attached to the message, information about the flag is shown below the header.

Previewing and adjusting the print job

Before you print an e-mail message, you can see what it will look like by printing it to the screen first, as a preview of the print job. Then you can make adjustments before you really print the message. To see a preview of your message, follow these steps:

1. **Open the message you sent yourself that has the Subject My formatting lesson.**
2. **Choose File➪Print Preview to display the message on the screen exactly the way it will look when you print it.**

   The Print Preview window opens, displaying a full-page view of the message (see Figure 3-17).

The Print Preview feature is a good way to get a quick idea of the way the printed message will look, and there are some things you can do if the layout needs minor adjustments. For example, if the message is spilling over onto a second page, but there are only one or two lines on the second page, you can adjust the page margins to fit the message onto one page.

3. **To change the layout, click the Page Setup button and then click the Paper tab of the Page Setup dialog box.**

   The Page Setup section of the dialog box displays information about the paper available in your printer. The printing margins are preset for a half-inch on all sides. If you change the margins to a smaller measurement, the extra line or two from the next page will move back to the first page.

   Most laser printers are incapable of printing all the way to the edge of the paper, so you can't adjust margins any closer than about a third of an inch. This is because the outside edges of the paper are grabbed by an arm in the printer in order to drag and guide the paper through the printer.

4. **Adjust the margins by entering new values in any or all of the margin fields.**

5. **Change the paper by selecting a Type and Size that's available in your printer. Then move to the Paper source field to choose the tray that holds this paper.**

   If your printer has legal-length paper in a separate tray, you can print the message on that paper. If no legal tray appears on the list, your printer doesn't have one and you can't use this solution for creating enough room to hold the contents on one page.

   In that case, check to see if the Paper source field includes an option for manual feed after you select legal paper. If it does, choose that option. When you print the message you'll have to go to the printer and insert the paper in the manual feed tray.

6. **Click OK to return to the Print Preview window.**

7. **Click the Print button on the Print Preview window.**

   The Print dialog box displays so you can select any options you wish. This is the standard Windows Print dialog box, so you can specify the number of copies you want to print, or the specific pages you want to print.

8. **If you have multiple printers available, select the printer you want to use.**

   If you change printers, it may affect the page setup options you chose. Click the Page Setup button in the Print dialog box to review your page setup and make any necessary changes.

9. **Click OK to print the message.**

You can also edit the message to make it fit on the smallest number of pages. If the message covers multiple topics, eliminate the text that is not relevant to the reason you need to print a hard copy. If the formatting of the message includes multiple blank lines between paragraphs, eliminate the extra lines.

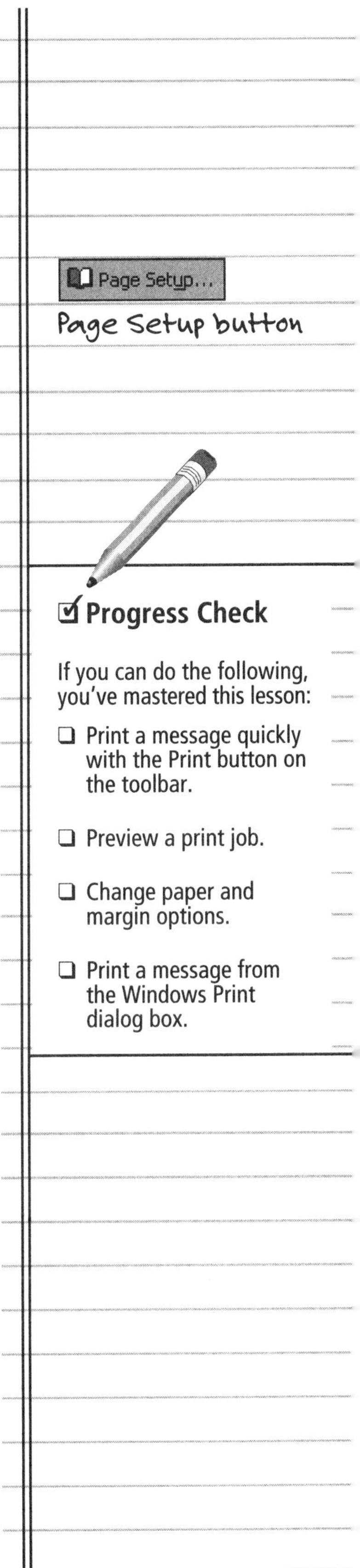

Recess

Unit 3 covered a lot of material — now you deserve a rest. Take a break. Put your feet up. If you're working in an office, close the door first. If you work in a cubbyhole instead of an office with a door, find the biggest person in the office and ask him or her to stand in your cubbyhole doorway to block the view. Or leave the office (just yell "Break time!" as you exit) and go outside and walk around the block. If there are vendors selling junk (merchandise or food), buy something useless. Then come back, all refreshed and ready for your test. Oh, right — did we mention that the next thing you have to do is take a quiz?

Unit 3 Quiz

For each of the following questions, circle the letter of the correct answer. Watch out for sneaky tricks like multiple correct answers — we're pretty devious. You can find the answers in Appendix A.

1. **What happens when you use AutoPreview?**

   A. Your car starts itself ten minutes before you have to leave for work.

   B. You can tell who is sending you a message before you collect your e-mail.

   C. The first few lines of unread messages appear in the Inbox.

   D. Outlook reads your mind and inserts text for you whenever you compose a message.

   E. Used car salesmen become totally honest with you.

2. **What does flagging a message mean?**

   A. The message has a flag icon to remind you that it needs further attention.

   B. The message is longer than six pages.

   C. The message prints with a mark in the corner indicating where to attach it to a flagpole.

   D. The message can safely be ignored.

   E. The message text is red, white, and blue.

Notes:

3. **A red exclamation point displayed to the left of the message means:**

   A. The message contains language unsuitable for children under 14.

   B. The message contains single declarative sentences instead of paragraphs.

   C. The message is important and has a high priority.

   D Delete this message immediately.

   E. The message is written in Serbo-Croatian.

4. **Choosing Reply to All means:**

   A. Your e-mail is sent to everyone in your address book.

   B. Your e-mail is sent to the printer, where 200 copies are made, all of which are posted in the hallways and bathrooms.

   C. Everyone who got a copy of the original message gets a copy of your reply to the message.

   D. Everyone who got a copy of the original message gets all the e-mail you compose for the next 48 hours.

   E. Whenever anyone speaks to anyone else in the office, you have an irresistible urge to reply.

5. **To open an attachment:**

   A. Take it to the cafeteria and ask the cook for a can opener.

   B. Print the message and cut a neat circle where the attachment icon was.

   C. Double-click the attachment icon.

   D. Single-click the attachment icon and press the Delete key.

   E. Print the message and draw hinges on the right edge of the attachment icon, then draw a doorknob on the left edge. Open the icon.

Unit 3 Exercise

1. Open a received message.
2. Flag it for follow-up.
3. Reply to the sender to tell him or her that you have flagged the message.
4. Print the message.

Unit 4

Organizing Your E-Mail

Objectives for This Unit

- ✓ Using folders
- ✓ Managing e-mail messages
- ✓ Grouping and sorting messages
- ✓ Printing messages

Prerequisites

- Using the Outlook bar (Lesson 1-1)
- Using the Inbox (Lesson 2-1)

We've covered a lot of territory in our travels through the e-mail features in Outlook. As you worked, the Outlook bar was staring you in the face. All those buttons and icons (which we'll explain and use in other units) represent different parts of Outlook.

Those Outlook bar icons represent something above and beyond the different parts of Outlook. Most of them represent folders, similar to the folders in your file cabinets. Each folder holds items, also similar to the folders in your file cabinets. For example, the Inbox you've been working with is a folder, and it contains the messages you see listed in the Inbox window. When you sent e-mail, you learned about the Outbox (which is a folder, too) and the Sent Items folder (which is, of course, also a folder).

Using the Folder List

Lesson 4-1

You can use the folders in Outlook just as you use the folders in your file cabinets. You can put additional folders into Outlook and you can move items

Figure 4-1: When you display the Folder list, you have an additional section (pane) in your Outlook window.

Figure 4-2: Exchange Server users deserve equal time.

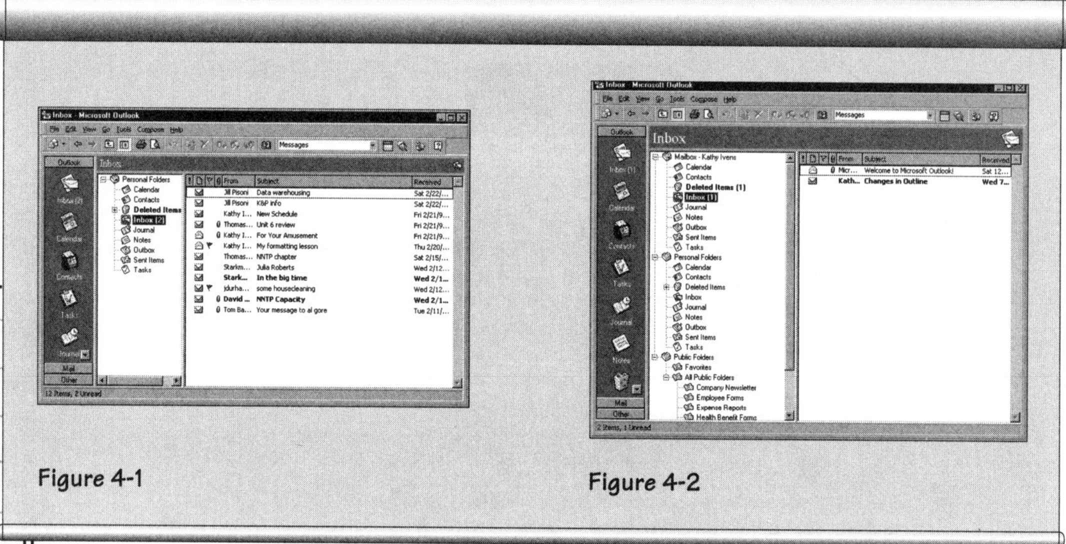

from one folder to another. This gives you the same organizational control over Outlook that you have over the files in your filing cabinets. You can make the folders visible and handy while you work in Outlook by taking these steps:

1. **Start Outlook.**

   When the Outlook window opens, the Inbox appears. To the left of the Inbox is the Outlook bar, holding icons for all the other Outlook programs and features.

on the test

Folder list button

2. **To display the folders, click the Folder list button on the toolbar (to the left of the Print button).**

   Wow! Your Outlook window certainly changed. A graphical representation of the folders in your Outlook system appears in a new pane. The contents of the highlighted folder are shown in the rightmost pane. Your window should look like the window in Figure 4-1.

   Each item in the Folder list is part of your Personal Folders container. Notice that the individual folders are slightly indented when compared to the top folder (the Personal Folders container). The display is similar to an outline, with each level indented. Later, as we add subfolders to existing folders, the outline will indent another level. This is called a *hierarchical display.*

heads up

   If you're using Outlook as part of your company's Microsoft Exchange Server e-mail program, your folders include three containers (Mailbox, Personal Folders, and Public Folders) instead of just one Personal Folders container. Figure 4-2 shows a typical Outlook window for an Exchange Server user. We're pointing this out so you don't get confused (and also so you don't feel left out if you use Exchange Server). Notice that your Personal Folders section matches the setup for Outlook users who are not connected to Exchange Server.

3. **To display the e-mail that you've sent to recipients, click the Sent Items folder.**

   When the folders are not displayed, you have to scroll through the Outlook bar to find the Sent Items icon in order to see the e-mail you've shipped. Using the folder view is much easier because everything is neatly arranged and easy to get to.

You can, of course, move to any Outlook folder in the same manner. Go ahead and try (we'll wait). Click a few folders and see how quick and easy it is to move from feature to feature (easier than using the Outlook bar, we think).

4 To remove the folder display, click the Folder list button again.

The Folder list button is a *toggle.* Each time you click it you reverse the current state, turning it off and on with each click.

One reason to turn off the folder display is to see more information about the contents of the folder. The Folder list takes up quite a bit of room, so all the columns in the contents pane grow narrower. This sometimes results in some very abbreviated data that could be hard to figure out.

Outlook remembers whether the Folder list was on the window when you closed Outlook, and opens next time with the Folder list in the same state.

on the test

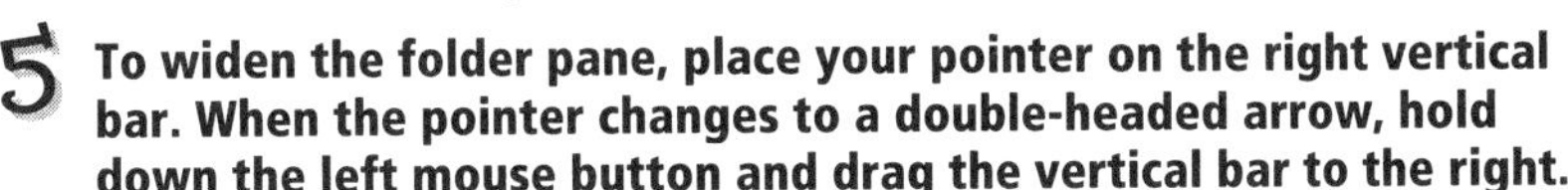

5 To widen the folder pane, place your pointer on the right vertical bar. When the pointer changes to a double-headed arrow, hold down the left mouse button and drag the vertical bar to the right.

Sometimes it's necessary to widen the folder pane in order to see the full names of all the folders.

As you perform your daily work in Outlook, you'll be able to judge for yourself when it's a good idea to see the Folder list and when it's not. For example, when you're looking at your Inbox and you've just received a great deal of mail, it's a good idea to eliminate the Folder list so you can see more details about the messages listed in the Inbox.

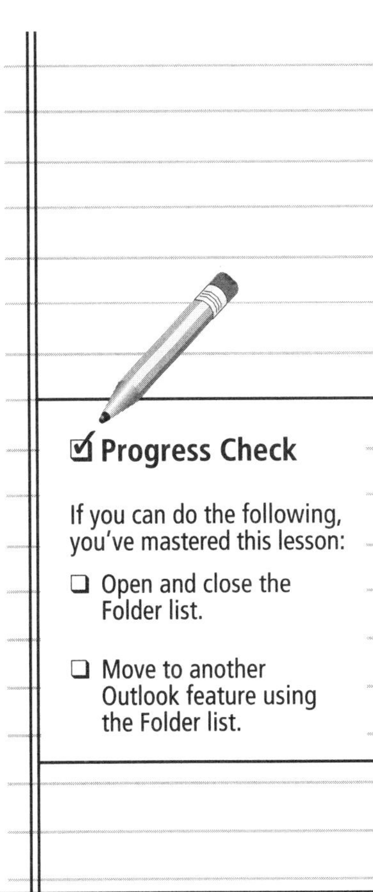

☑ Progress Check

If you can do the following, you've mastered this lesson:

- ❑ Open and close the Folder list.
- ❑ Move to another Outlook feature using the Folder list.

Creating Folders

Lesson 4-2

The folders that are built into Outlook divide the various Outlook features and programs in a neat and logical way. The mail folders are especially useful, making it easy to find and identify received mail and sent mail.

However, as you continue to send and receive e-mail, you may find that you need a way to organize all those messages so that you can find them and refer to them. You could print every message and make neat piles on your desk, creating a pile for each subject. Of course, your desk would be pretty messy. In fact, you'd probably discover that your desk wasn't large enough for the task and you'd begin using the floor space around your desk.

folders keep messages organized

The sensible way organize your e-mail is to follow the same pattern that Outlook uses — create and use folders to organize your e-mail messages.

on the test

Before we begin, we should discuss the concept of folders and subfolders. Then you can make informed decisions when you use the information you learn in this Unit. Remember that we referred to the folders in your Outlook system as hierarchical, like an outline. Each level of folders is a different part of the hierarchy, or a different level of the outline. Incidentally, the computer jargon for the relationship between folders and subfolders is *parent-child*. (Throw this terminology around the next time the system administrator is hanging around your desk).

Notes:

You already have two levels of folders in your Outlook system:

- The top level is a folder called Personal Folders, and the only items within it are the other folders that are preconfigured by Outlook. Think of this as a physical file cabinet. This is the parent folder for all the Outlook folders (which are all children).
- The second-level folders are those preconfigured folders, such as the Inbox and the Sent Items folder. Think of these as hanging file folders (the kind of folders that hold manila folders).

You can create a third level of folders (think of them as manila folders), using a second-level folder as the container. These children have second-level folders as parents (making the Personal Folders container a grandparent). That means that an Outlook folder can be both a child and a parent.

For this exercise, we'll create two new folders. First we'll create a folder to hold the personal e-mail messages you receive from your friends and relatives. Then we'll create a folder to hold all the e-mail messages you've sent to your boss (some people call this creating a paper trail; it's often a good idea to document your correspondence to supervisory personnel).

To create a new folder for personal mail (because this is for mail you've received, it makes sense to create this folder as a subfolder of the Inbox), follow these steps:

1. **Go to the Inbox window.**

   If you were working in another part of Outlook, click the Inbox icon on the Outlook bar or, if the Folder list is showing, click the Inbox folder.

2. **If you do not see the Folder list, click the Folder list button and then click the Inbox folder to highlight it.**

3. **Choose File⇨Folder⇨Create Subfolder or right-click the Inbox folder and choose Create Subfolder.**

   The Create New Folder dialog box appears, as seen in Figure 4-3.

4. **Type** Personal Mail **in the Name field.**

5. **Press Tab to move to the Folder contains field, which displays Mail Items as the preselected item type.**

   Outlook knew that this folder would contain mail items because you started this task while the Inbox was highlighted. The other choices for this field are for other Outlook features, such as Tasks, Contacts, and so on.

6. **Press Alt+D to move to the Description field (or click anywhere in the Description field). Type** Personal e-mail received.

   Notice we skipped over the entry box named Make this folder a subfolder of because the Inbox folder was already selected. If a different folder had been highlighted, we would have clicked the Inbox folder to highlight it instead.

7. **Select Create a shortcut to this folder in the Outlook bar.**

   If this choice has a check mark next to it, it is already selected. If there is no check mark, click the box to insert a check mark. This puts an icon for your folder directly into the Outlook bar, so you can move to this new folder quickly

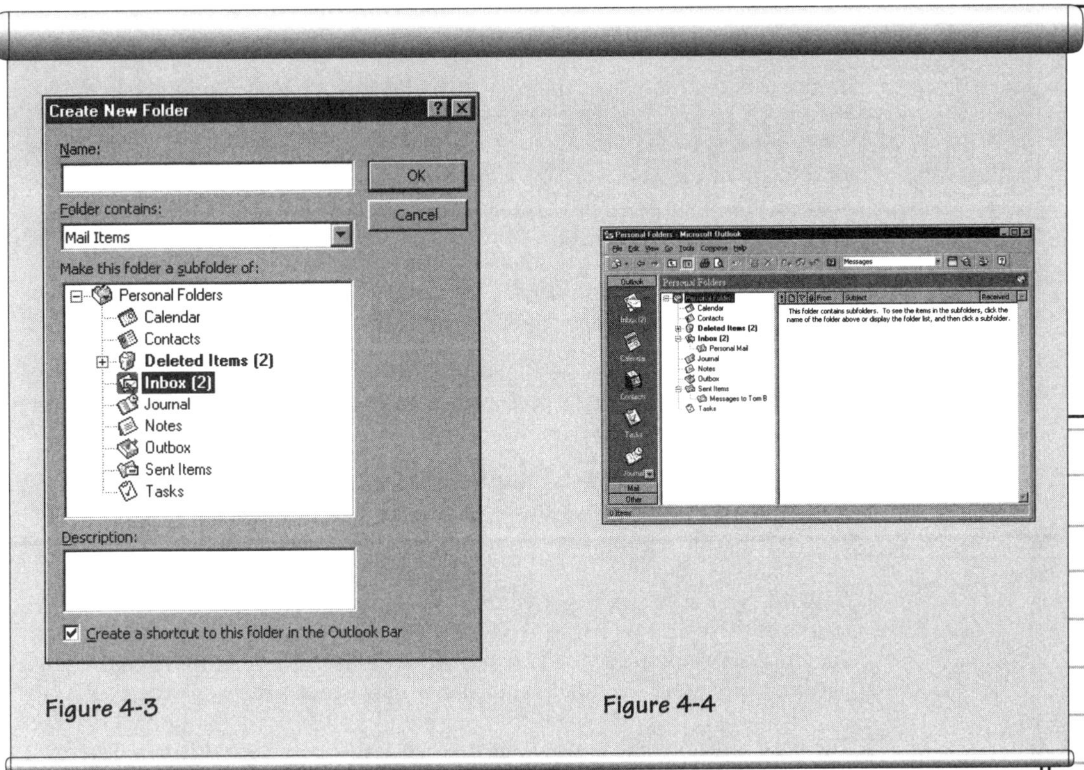

Figure 4-3

Figure 4-4

Figure 4-3: The Create New Folder dialog box walks you through the task of creating a new personal folder.

Figure 4-4: The two folders you created are on the Folder list. Notice the indentation level and the dotted lines between the new subfolders and their parent folders.

from any part of Outlook. This is particularly useful if you are working in an Outlook window and you are not using the Folder list.

8 **Click OK to add this new folder to your Folder list.**

The dialog box goes away and you can see your new folder in the Folder list.

To create another folder to hold the messages you've sent to your boss, follow these steps:

1 **Click the Sent Items folder in the Folder list.**

2 **Choose File⇨Folder⇨Create Subfolder, or right-click the Inbox folder and choose Create Subfolder.**

3 **Type** Messages to *boss* **(substitute the real name of your boss for the word *boss*) in the Name field.**

4 **Press Alt+D to move to the Description field (or click anywhere in the Description field). Type** E-mail sent to *name* **(substituting the actual name you want to use for the word *name*).**

Once again, we skipped over the **Folder contains** field (Mail Items is the correct item type) and the entry box named Make this folder a subfolder of because the Sent Items folder was already selected.

5 **Select Create a shortcut to this folder in the Outlook bar.**

6 **Click OK to add this new folder to your Folder list.**

Now the Folder list displays another new folder (see Figure 4-4).

☑ Progress Check

If you can do the following, you've mastered this lesson:

- ❑ Create a folder and a subfolder.
- ❑ Use computer jargon for parent-child relationships.
- ❑ Use the word hierarchical correctly.

Notice that the Inbox and the Sent Items folder each have a minus sign (–) to the left of the folder name and your new folders are indented to the right (you might have to widen the folder pane to see them). If you click the minus sign next to either the Inbox or Sent Items folder, the minus sign becomes a plus sign (+) and your new folder no longer displays in the Folder list. The plus sign next to a folder is an indication that there are subfolders below it, but they are not currently showing themselves. The plus sign and minus sign are a toggle switches, turning subfolder display on and off. If you create a lot of new folders, the Folder list grows quite large and you'll find that it's helpful to turn subfolder display off for the folders you're not currently using.

Lesson 4-3 Using Folders to Store E-Mail

Now that you've begun to get yourself and your e-mail organized, let's see the results of these efforts. Your Inbox currently has at least two e-mail messages that you've already read (the two you sent yourself during our lessons). There may be many more — in fact, your Inbox may be extremely crowded by now.

keep Inbox as empty as possible

The most efficient way to use your Inbox is to keep it empty for new e-mail. Cluttering it with lots of e-mail you've already read (and probably replied to) makes it harder to use the Inbox because you have to keep scrolling through the list to find the messages you need. Moving old messages into folders, and organizing those messages by topic at the same time, is the perfect way to operate Outlook.

Tip: Messages that aren't important enough to save in a folder should be deleted.

Moving messages from the Inbox into folders

Most of the time, you'll move messages from your Inbox into a folder that you created for a specific purpose or topic. For this exercise, we'll move a personal e-mail message into your new Personal Mail folder, by taking these steps:

1. **Click the Inbox on the Folder list (or on the Outlook bar) to display the contents.**
2. **Click the message you sent yourself titled My formatting lesson.**

   The message listing is highlighted.

   You can also select more than one message and move all of them to a folder at once. Select the first message and then hold down the Ctrl key while you click the additional messages you want to move.

on the test

3. **Click the Move to Folder button on the toolbar and then choose Move to Folder.**

   You can also choose Edit⇨Move to Folder from the menu bar, or right-click the message listing and choose Move to Folder from the menu.

Move to Folder button

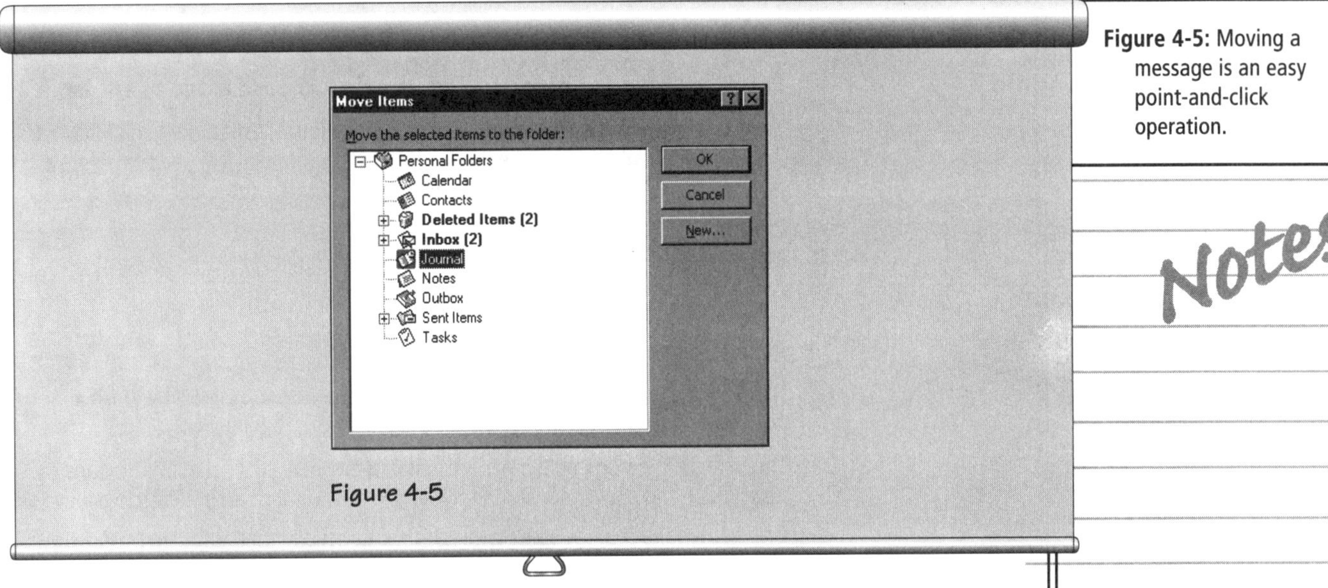

Figure 4-5: Moving a message is an easy point-and-click operation.

Notes:

The Move Items dialog box appears (see Figure 4-5).

4. **Click the plus sign on the left of the Inbox folder.**

   This expands the view of the Inbox folder to display the child folders (subfolders). Of course, as you already know, one of these is the Personal Mail subfolder.

5. **Click the Personal Mail folder to select it.**

   This tells Outlook to move the selected message to this folder.

6. **Click OK**

The dialog box closes and you return to the Inbox. The message about the formatting lesson no longer appears in the Inbox — it's no longer on the message list. Just to reassure yourself that we haven't steered you wrong and sent your message into la la land, click the Personal Mail folder in the Folder list. The message is listed in the right panel. See, it worked!

Moving messages between folders

After you've created some additional folders for topics or projects, you can use the same technique to move messages from one folder to another. In fact, you don't even have to create the folder ahead of time — you can do everything at once. For this exercise, we'll move that message we just placed into your Personal Mail folder into another, new folder. Follow these steps to learn this trick:

You can move messages from one folder to another newly created folder in one fell swoop

1. **Click the Personal Mail folder to display its contents in the right pane.**
2. **In the right pane, click My formatting lesson to select it.**

Notes:

3. **Click the Move to Folder button and then choose Move to Folder.**

   The Move Items dialog box appears and the Personal Mail folder is highlighted. Because we want to move the message out of that folder, we need to select a different folder as the target folder. However, no other subfolder is available that suits our purpose.

4. **Click New.**

   The Create New Folder dialog box appears.

5. **In the Name field, enter** Software Tips.

6. **In the box titled Make this folder a subfolder of, click the Inbox folder.**

   This selects the Inbox as the parent folder of the new subfolder. That means the new folder and the Personal Mail folder are now on the same hierarchical level.

   We skipped the **Folder contains** field for specifying item type again, because we are still working with mail items.

   This time we'll skip the Description field, too, because it isn't required and we don't have to use it if we don't choose to.

7. **Click the Create a shortcut option to deselect it (remove the check mark).**

   This new folder won't be used as frequently as some other, more important folders, so there's no point in cluttering up the Outlook bar.

8. **Click OK to finish creating the new folder.**

   The Move Items dialog box reappears and the new folder is in it, and in fact the new folder is highlighted (see Figure 4-6).

9. **Click OK to move the message into the Software Tips folder.**

   When the Move Items dialog box disappears, the Personal Mail window reappears. The message is gone. Click the Software Tips folder in the Folder list. There it is!

☑ **Progress Check**

If you can do the following, you've mastered this lesson:

- ❑ Move an item from the Inbox to a subfolder.
- ❑ Move an item from one subfolder to another subfolder.
- ❑ Create a new folder from the Move Items dialog box.

Moving messages quickly

After you create all the additional folders you need, moving items between folders gets a lot easier. That's because each time you add a folder to the Folder list, the folder's name is added to the list on the Move to Folder button. Try this quick trick for moving your message back into the Personal Mail folder:

1. **Go the the Software Tips folder.**

2. **Select the message you just placed there (the one called My formatting lesson).**

3. **Click the Move to Folder button.**

   The drop-down list displays all the folders (see Figure 4-7).

4. **Click Personal Mail.**

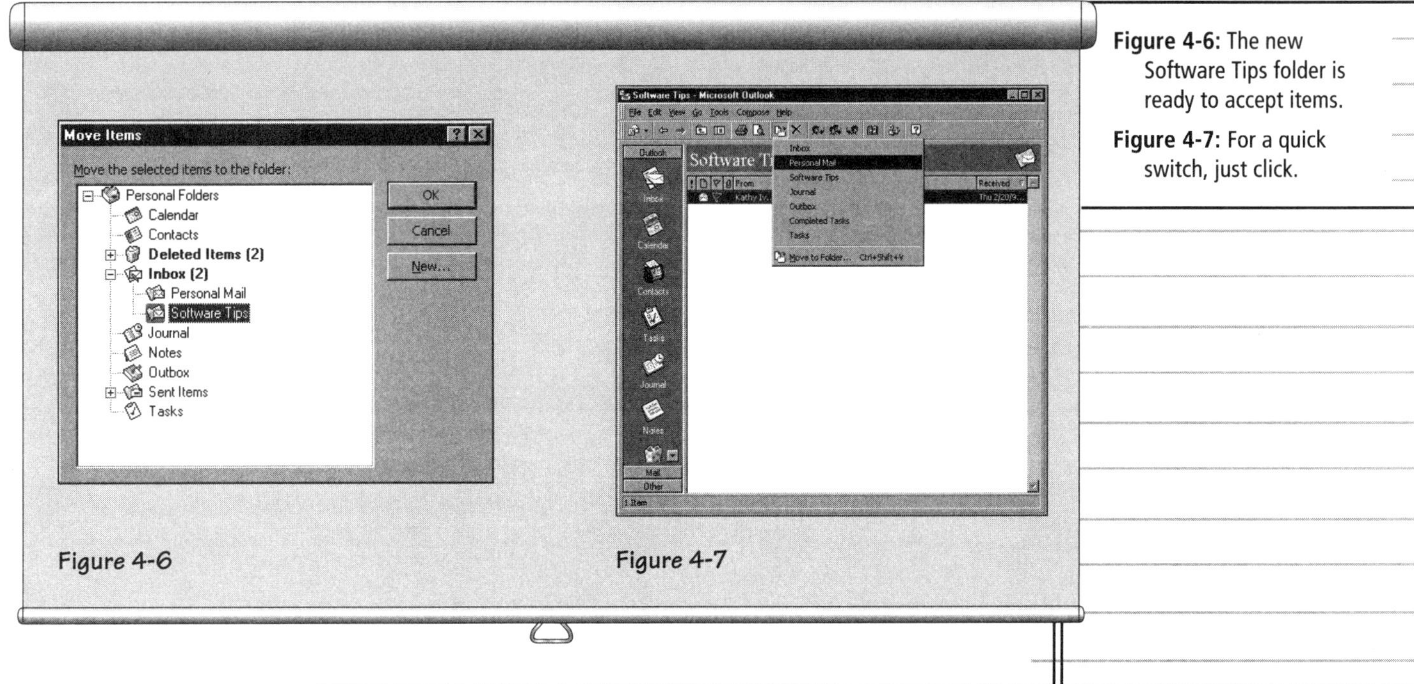

Figure 4-6: The new Software Tips folder is ready to accept items.

Figure 4-7: For a quick switch, just click.

Sorting E-Mail

Lesson 4-4

In Unit 3 we learned to arrange the message listings in the Inbox by clicking the column headings. That's a quick way to sort your messages by a specific column, and to change that sort from ascending to descending order.

When your Inbox or the folders you create to hold messages get crowded, however, that arrangement may not be enough; so Outlook provides more-powerful sorting features that you can use to find and arrange messages.

To learn about some of the ways to sort a list of messages, follow these steps:

1. **Go to the Inbox.**

   We're assuming you haven't created lots of folders yet, so most of your received e-mail is still in your Inbox.

2. **Turn off the Folder list by clicking the Folder list icon.**

   Because we're going to be working with the listings, it's easier to view everything if you devote the whole right pane to the listings.

3. **To sort by Sender, Subject, and Received Date, choose View⇨Sort from the menu bar to display the Sort dialog box (see Figure 4-8).**

   This is useful if you want to see all the messages from a particular sender (the name in the From field of the message), with all the messages from each sender grouped by subject, and you want to see them arranged by date.

Figure 4-8: This is the place to design the order in which you want to display your messages.

Figure 4-9: Head for a specific sender and examine that section of the listing for details.

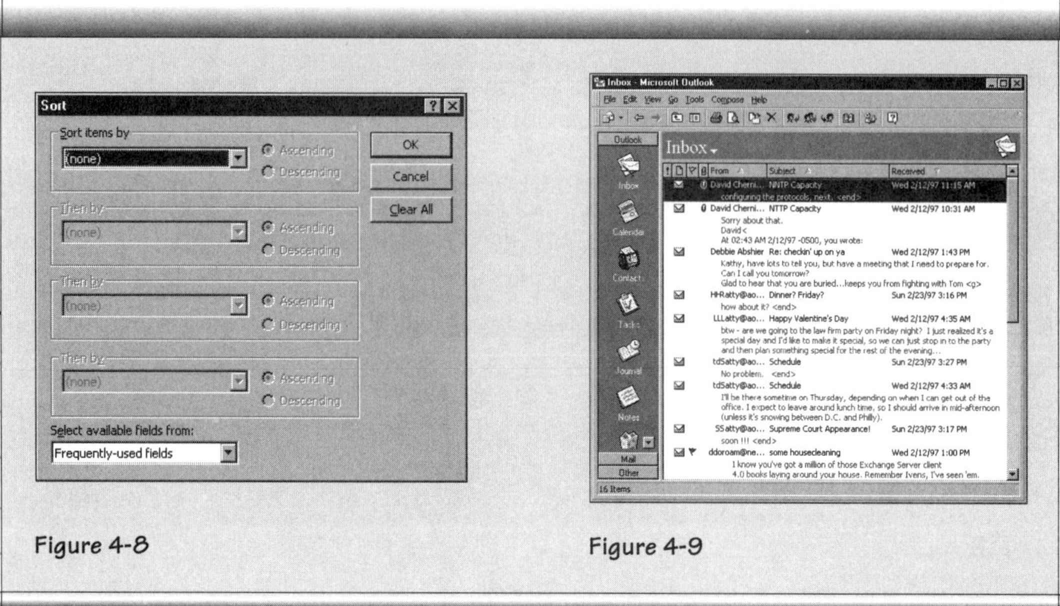

Figure 4-8

Figure 4-9

4 **In the Sort items by selection box, click the arrow to the right of the box and choose From from the drop-down list. Click the Ascending radio button.**

(By the way, radio buttons let you choose one option from two or more options.)

For quicker action, when the drop-down list appears, just type the first letter of the field you're seeking. You'll move to that alphabetic section of the drop-down list immediately. However, it's only the first letter that works. After you type *f* (for from), if you then type *r* you'll move to the R section of this list.

5 **Click the Then by selection box and choose Subject. Click the Ascending radio button.**

6 **Click the Then by selection box and choose Received. Click the Descending radio button.**

You want to see the latest messages from this sender at the top of the list.

7 **Click OK.**

When your messages appear, they're sorted in groups according to the specifications you set and in the order you set (see Figure 4-9).

8 **To gain even more detailed information, choose View⇨AutoPreview.**

9 **To change the message display so that it is unsorted, choose View⇨Current View. Then choose one of the standard views (usually Messages).**

10 **Click Discard the current view... when the Office Assistant asks if you want to redefine Message to match your sorting scheme or you want to discard the current sorting scheme and go back to the standard Messages view.**

☑ Progress Check

If you can do the following, you've mastered this lesson:

- ❑ Configure options in the Sort dialog box.
- ❑ Move from a sorted view to a standard view.

You were introduced to the Office Assistant in Lesson 1-1.

You can repeat this procedure with any fields in the Sort dialog box. The sorting scheme you choose depends on what information you need.

Viewing Messages that Match Criteria

Lesson 4-5

You can tell Outlook which messages you want to see and set the criteria you want to use to view the messages. This is incredibly powerful and helpful, and the more messages you accumulate, the more you'll want to use this feature. It's a way to tell Outlook "Okay, listen up, here are the rules of how to show me my messages." In computer jargon, the term *filter* describes the rules you give Outlook to display your messages.

filter = tells Outlook exactly which messages you want to see

To set up the filters that tell Outlook which messages to show you, follow these steps:

1. **Go to the Inbox.**
2. **Choose View⇨Filter from the menu bar to display the Filter dialog box (see Figure 4-10).**
3. **In the Search for the word(s) field, enter a word or phrase that you know is in every message you want to see.**

   Of course, we can't tell you which words to search for because we can't see the contents of your messages. Therefore, we'll assume (pretend) you need to find all the messages about a project named Green Widgets; you could enter **Green**, **Widgets**, or **Green Widgets**.
4. **In the In field, tell Outlook where to look for the word or phrase you entered.**

   From the drop-down list that appears when you click the arrow next to the field, choose subject field only, or subject field and message body. Choosing more fields slows down the search, and it's almost always true that an important word or phrase is somewhere in those two fields.
5. **Click From to see the names in your Address Book and choose the names you want to use for this search.**

   Usually it's not a good idea to specify anything for this field (unless part of the criteria you want to set is that you only want to examine the messages from specific people).
6. **Click Sent To, which displays your Address Book. Then choose the specific name(s) that must appear in a message's To field in order to match your rule.**

   Unless you're looking specifically for messages to a certain person that contain the word(s) you're searching for in the message text, you shouldn't specify anything for this field.

Figure 4-10: Set criteria to filter out the messages you don't need to find.

Figure 4-11: The filter for this listing was the word Schedule in the Subject field.

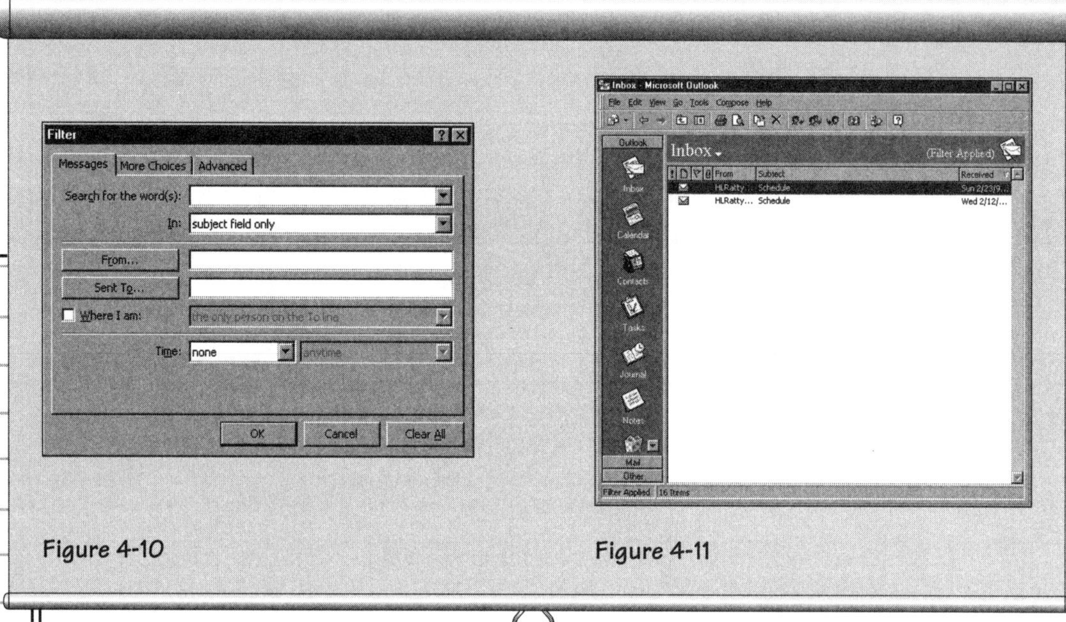

Figure 4-10

Figure 4-11

7 **Select the Where I am check box and then click the arrow to the right of the field and choose the option you want.**

This is another criteria option that is rarely needed. If you do want to use it, the choices are: the only person on the To line; on the To line with other people; and on the Cc line with other people.

8 **If you need to, specify a time filter for the messages.**

You can choose the received time, the sent time, or several other selections involving time, but usually this information isn't important when you're searching for messages.

9 **Click the More Choices tab on the dialog box to move to the More Choices Page.**

10 **Fill in the criteria that fits the filters you need in order to find all the messages you want to see.**

We won't go into the details of these fields (or the fields on the Advanced tab of the dialog box), because they're self-explanatory. Besides, most of the time you won't need them because the standard searching techniques find what you need.

11 **Click OK when you have filled in the fields of interest.**

The message list displays only those items that match your criteria. The rest of the messages have been filtered out. Above the listing, the name of the folder is shown, along with the notation that a filter has been applied (see Figure 4-11).

12 **To turn off the filter, choose View⇨Current View. Then choose one of the standard views (usually Messages).**

13 **Click Discard the current view... when the Office Assistant asks if you want to redefine Message to match your sorting scheme or you want to discard the current sorting scheme and go back to the standard Messages view.**

☑ Progress Check

If you can do the following, you've mastered this lesson:

- ❑ Configure options in Filter dialog box.
- ❑ Move from a filtered view to a standard view.

Grouping Messages

Lesson 4-6

Grouping resembles sorting, but grouping creates a display format that can be much easier to work with, especially if you have a great many messages. Grouping bunches up groups of messages (according to the criteria you set) and then closes each bunch, leaving signs that say, in effect, "Here's the group sorted by this criteria" and "Here's the group sorted by that criteria." You can open each group to examine the individual messages in the bunch without overwhelming yourself.

To group messages, follow these steps:

1. **Move to the Inbox or the folder that contains the messages you want to group.**

on the test

2. **Choose View⇨Group By Box from the menu bar.**

   A sign pops up above the listing box that says "Drag a column header here to group by that column."

3. **To group messages by subject, place your pointer on the Subject column heading and drag the column heading up to the sign.**

   The column heading replaces the sign above the listing box and your messages are grouped in boxes. Each box has a label that proclaims the subject of the messages in the group (see Figure 4-12).

4. **To see the messages in any group, click the plus sign on the group listing.**

   The plus sign changes to a minus sign and the group expands to display the messages (see Figure 4-13). You can expand more than one group if you wish.

5. **Click the minus sign to close the group again.**

   The minus sign changes to a plus sign.

6. **To expand all the groups (or collapse all open groups), choose View⇨Expand/Collapse Groups and then choose Expand All (or Collapse All).**

7. **To group messages within an existing group, drag another column header to the space above the listing box.**

   For instance, you may want to subgroup the current groups (which are grouped by subject) by sender (the From field). Figure 4-14 shows the results for this example.

8. **To change the sort order, move the primary sort column heading to the left of any other column heading.**

   You can use as many column headings as you need when you build groups. The sort order is from left to right, and you can shuffle column headings around to get exactly the sort order you need.

9. **To remove a grouping category, drag the column header back to the column bar.**

Notes:

Figure 4-12: Groups, instead of messages, are shown in the listing box.

Figure 4-13: Expand a group to see the messages.

Figure 4-14: Apparently two different people sent messages about this subject. Expand either or both to see the messages.

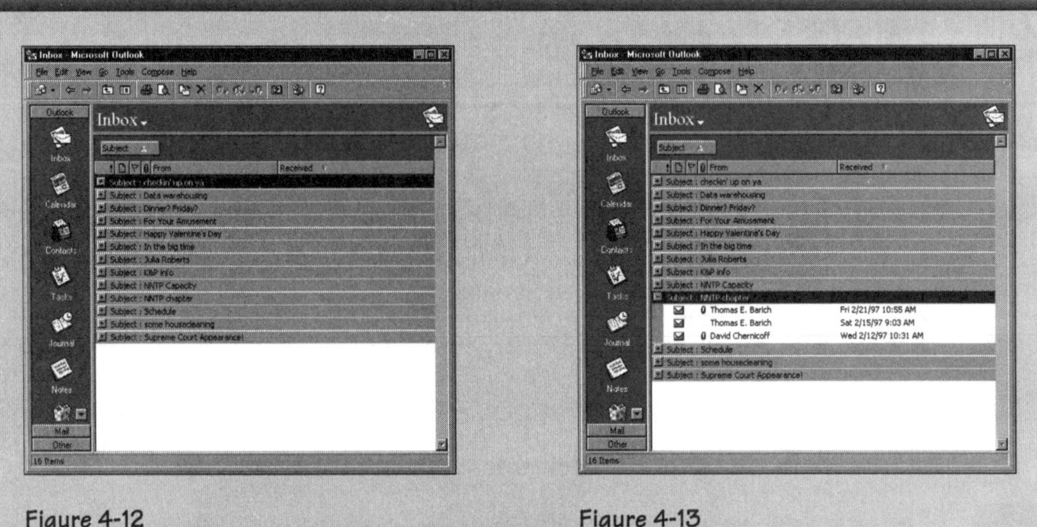

Figure 4-12

Figure 4-13

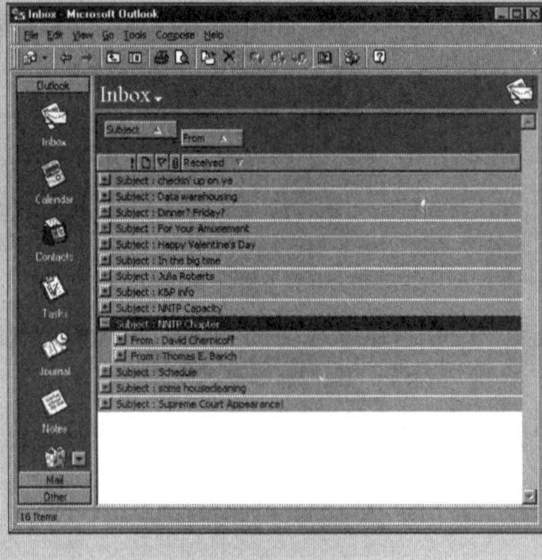

Figure 4-14

☑ Progress Check

If you can do the following, you've mastered this lesson:

- ❑ Group messages in boxes.
- ❑ Modify the sorting scheme by adding more column headings for groups.
- ❑ Change the sorting scheme by moving column headings.

In this example, if you drag the Subject column header back to its place on the column bar, the listing box changes to groups representing the senders. When you move column headers back to the column heading bar, little red arrows appear to remind you where the column belongs.

10 **To remove a grouping, drag all the column headers back to their original place and then choose View⇨Group by Box.**

The space above the column heading bar closes up and your regular listing display returns.

As convenient as grouping can be, overdoing it by adding too many column headings to the sorting scheme can kill its advantages. It's frustrating to click a plus sign, see additional gray group lines, click all those plus signs, see more gray group lines . . . you get the idea. Remember to design these features so that they speed up your work and make you more efficient.

Notes:

Recess

You learned a lot about some fairly complicated subjects. Take a break. Get a soda and grab a package of peanut butter crackers from the vending machine (or splurge and pick Oreos). On your way back to your desk, stop and heckle the Outlook users who are struggling because they don't have this book. Then it's time to take the dreaded quiz. Don't clutch.

Unit 4 Quiz

For each of these questions, circle the letter of the correct answer. We may or may not have played around and put more than one correct answer into the possible answers. We're not telling. You can just figure it out for yourself.

1. **How do you display the Folder list?**

   A. With a colorful mat in a wood frame.

   B. Open the document named Folder List in Microsoft Word.

   C. Click the Folder list button on the toolbar.

   D. Click the large X button on the toolbar.

   E. Call the art department and ask for the display specialist.

2. **What do you do if you can't see the full names of folders in the folder pane?**

   A. Demand a larger monitor.

   B. Adjust the horizontal button on the monitor.

   C. Use a magnifying glass.

   D. Use your mouse to widen the folder pane.

   E. Ask the system administrator to shorten all folder names.

3. **How do you move a message from the Inbox to a folder?**

   A. Open the message and change the text in the subject field.

   B. Select the message and click the Move to Folder button on the toolbar.

C. Delete the message and then click the Oh no! I didn't mean it! button on the toolbar.

D. Leave e-mail for the mailroom to send someone up to handle some moving chores.

E. Ask the sender to send it again.

4. In the correct computer terminology, describe a child folder.

A. A folder that is a subfolder of another folder (the parent folder).

B. A folder that says "Ohh Motherrrrrr!" when you click it.

C. A folder that never responds when you click it, but just stares at you as if you were from Mars.

D. A folder that doesn't arrange its contents neatly, so the messages spill out over the computer (the folder never seems to notice or care).

E. A folder that invites other child folders into the parent folder, and they inhale all the food in the refrigerator in 30 seconds.

5. What does Group By Box mean?

A. You have to print every message in the system and put them into boxes.

B. All messages are printed, then shredded, then the shredded stuff is put into boxes, then the boxes are delivered to Wall Street offices for the next parade.

C. All messages with the word *box* in the subject line are automatically grouped together.

D. All messages are grouped by date and a box icon appears.

E. All messages are grouped and little gray boxes representing the group names are shown in the window.

Unit 4 Exercise

1. Create a folder named after your favorite relative.
2. Move all messages that have a subject line that includes the words "immediate action required" into the new folder.
3. Take a few vacation days.
4. When you return, remember how much fun you had not responding to those messages while you were on vacation.

Part I Review

Unit 1 Summary

- **Starting Outlook:** Double-click the Outlook icon on the desktop.
- **Navigating the Outlook window:** Click the icons in the Outlook bar to move among the Outlook features (Mail, Contacts, Tasks, and so on).
- **Navigating the Mail window:** Click the Inbox icon on the Outlook bar to view your received mail. Click the Folder List button to view the mail folders.

Unit 2 Summary

- **Creating an entry in your Address Book:** Click the Address Book button on the toolbar or choose File➪New Entry. Select an address type and then click OK. Enter the Display Name, E-mail Address, and E-Mail Type. Click OK.
- **Editing and deleting addresses:** Open the Address Book and then double-click the entry you want to change or delete. Make changes and click OK to edit the entry, or press Del to remove the entry.
- **Creating a distribution list:** Open the Address Book. Choose File➪New Entry and then choose Personal Distribution List. Choose names from the address book and then click OK.
- **Composing messages:** Click the New Message Button. Enter the recipient's name, enter names of recipients of copies, and then enter text in the Subject field. Type the text of the message. Click Send to send the message.
- **Formatting message text:** Select the text you want to format and then click the appropriate formatting buttons on the toolbar.
- **Creating an AutoSignature:** Choose Tools➪AutoSignature. Enter the text for your AutoSignature. Click OK.
- **Attaching files to messages:** Compose the message. Click the Insert File button on the toolbar and then select the file you want to attach. Click OK.
- **Setting message options:** Compose the message. Click the Options tab on the Message window. Choose a priority option and a sensitivity option.

Unit 3 Summary

- **Arranging the list of messages:** Go to the Inbox. Click the column heading for the sorting scheme you need. Click again to reverse the order.
- **Reading messages:** Double-click to open a message. Press Alt+F4 to close the message.
- **Opening attachments:** Double-click the attachment icon to open its associated software. Print the attachment from the software window. Close the software to return to the Inbox.
- **Responding to messages:** Open the message. Click the Reply button to send a response to the sender. Click the Forward button to send the message to another recipient. Click the Reply to All button to send a response to all the recipients who received copies.
- **Printing messages:** Select the message and then click the Print button on the toolbar. To preview the print job, open the message. Choose File➪ Print Preview to preview the printing. Click the Page Setup button to make adjustments. Then click Print.

Part I Review

Unit 4 Summary

- **Using the Folder list:** Click the Folder list button on the toolbar. Adjust the width of the folder pane by dragging the vertical bar.
- **Creating a folder:** Choose File⇨Folder⇨Create Subfolder. Enter a Name and Description for the folder. Click the folder you want to use as the parent folder. Click OK.
- **Moving messages into different folders:** Select the message. Click the Move to Folder button on the toolbar. Select the folder where you want to move the message. Click OK.
- **Sorting messages:** Choose View⇨Sort and then choose the fields for sorting the messages. Click OK.
- **Filtering messages:** Choose View⇨Filter. Select the criteria you want to. Click OK.
- **Grouping messages:** Choose View⇨Group By Box. Drag the column heading you want to use as the basis for the group to the top of the listings window.

Part I Test

This test is a metaphor for life. If you do well, you will become rich, famous, and incredibly good-looking. You may even be noticed by a talent scout and cast for your first full-length feature film.

Okay, maybe not. Just take this test to see how much you learned in Part I of this book. To keep you alert, we ask you several kinds of questions. You can find the answers to the test questions in Appendix A.

True False

T F 1. Before you are old enough to retire, *Rocky 88* will be released.

T F 2. An address book entry can be a group instead of an individual.

T F 3. A red exclamation point next to a message listing means high priority.

T F 4. Press Alt+F4 to close a message window.

T F 5. Sorting messages always means putting them in date order.

T F 6. You can only create a new folder if you are the vice president of your company (or higher).

T F 7. Clicking the Forward button on a message window sends the message to somebody who was not on the recipient list.

T F 8. John Wayne had a falsetto voice and all his movies were dubbed with Lauren Bacall's voice to make him sound macho.

Part I Test

T F 9. A drop-down list offers choices for a particular field you have to fill in.

T F 10. You can open an attachment to a message by double-clicking it.

Multiple Choice

Circle the correct answer (or answers if we decided to offer more than one correct answer) for each question.

11. What are the three viewing choices for the Outlook bar?

A. Mailbox, Lunch Menu, Paycheck Stub.

B. Outlook, Mail, Other.

C. His, Hers, Ours.

D. Letters, Pink Slips, Merit Raise Forms.

E. Tasks, W-2 Forms, "We've Moved" Forms.

12. When do you use a Personal Distribution List?

A. To send the same message to a preselected group of recipients all at once.

B. To send a copy of a message to yourself automatically.

C. To remove a group of recipients from your address book because they never reply to your messages.

D. To deliver flowers on Valentine's Day.

E. When you want to send secret codes in your messages.

13. What do you find in the Outbox?

A. A list of people who are "on the outs" with the Personnel Manager.

B. Outdoor plumbing fixtures.

C. Messages waiting to be delivered.

D. All the company memos you received today.

E. A six pack for the company party.

14. How do you move a message?

A. Tell it a sad story.

B. Wait until the light turns green.

C. By pushing it along with your foot.

D. By selecting it and then selecting a different folder from the Folder List.

E. By selecting it and then clicking the "Move to Bob's Desk" button on the toolbar.

15. What does dragging with the mouse mean?

A. Holding down the mouse button and moving the mouse along text to highlight the text.

B. Dangling the mouse cable down the front of your desk.

C. It's the name of a yo-yo stunt.

D. Feeling very tired when you use the mouse.

E. Using Alt+key alternatives every time you should click a button.

Matching

16. Match the buttons with the correct commands.

A.	1. Font Color
B.	2. Delete Message
C.	3. Move to Folder
D.	4. New Message
E.	5. Address Book

17. Match the shows with the characters.

A. *Gilligan's Island*	1. Kookie
B. *Hawaii Five O*	2. The Lads
C. *Magnum P.I.*	3. Grover
D. *The Muppets*	4. Zoe
E. *Cybill*	5. Mrs. Howell

Part I Lab Assignment

Lab assignments ask you to apply the knowledge you acquired in Part I. Later, you find similar lab assignments after the other parts of this book.

We don't tell you how to accomplish the tasks in this lab assignment. If we told you how to do the tasks, we'd have to call this a lesson instead of a lab assignment.

For this lab assignment, you compose and send an e-mail message that is so over-formatted that it looks like a ransom note. It's best to send this message to a friend with a sense of humor. If none of your funny friends have e-mail addresses, you'll have to send it to yourself.

Step 1: Composing a message

Open a Message window and address the message to your friend (or yourself). Make the subject Ransom Note. Make sure the message has a high priority and is confidential. Compose a message about any subject you wish. Talk about your summer vacation, your job, your significant other, your car — whatever you like to talk about.

Step 2: Formatting the message

Make each paragraph in the message a different font. Make the first word of each paragraph a larger font size. Italicize every instance of the word *my* and bold every instance of the word *the*.

Step 3: Sending the message

Send the message and then move it from the Sent Items folder into your Personal Mail folder. Print the message and hang the print out on the wall.

Part II
Staying on Schedule

In this part . . .

Outlook offers incredible scheduling features that will keep you on track no matter how much you have to do. In this part of the book, you learn how to manage your appointments and track your tasks using Outlook.

Actually, you may not want to get too familiar with the scheduling features in this book; after your boss and friends find out that you know how to use Outlook to manage your time and work, you won't get away with being late again.

Unit 5

Making Appointments

Objectives for This Unit

- ✓ Entering appointments
- ✓ Using reminders
- ✓ Setting up meetings
- ✓ Viewing appointments

Prerequisites

- Opening Outlook (Lesson 1-1)
- Understanding the Outlook toolbar (Lesson 1-2)

Although most users will take advantage of Outlook's extensive e-mail features, many will stop there and ignore its wealth of information-management tools. The fact that you are reading this indicates that you are not one of those users. You've made a good choice.

To start organizing your information, take a look at the Calendar folder. The Calendar features enable you to:

- Schedule and manage appointments with ease
- Create annual events
- Set reminders to notify you of important dates
- Organize meeting participants and resources

Before going any further, take a look at Figure 5-1 to familiarize yourself with the Calendar window. The Banner displays events. You record appointments in the Daily Calendar. The Date Navigator provides a minicalendar that has a few tricks up its sleeve. Last but not least is the TaskPad, which, in reality, is the task list from your Task folder.

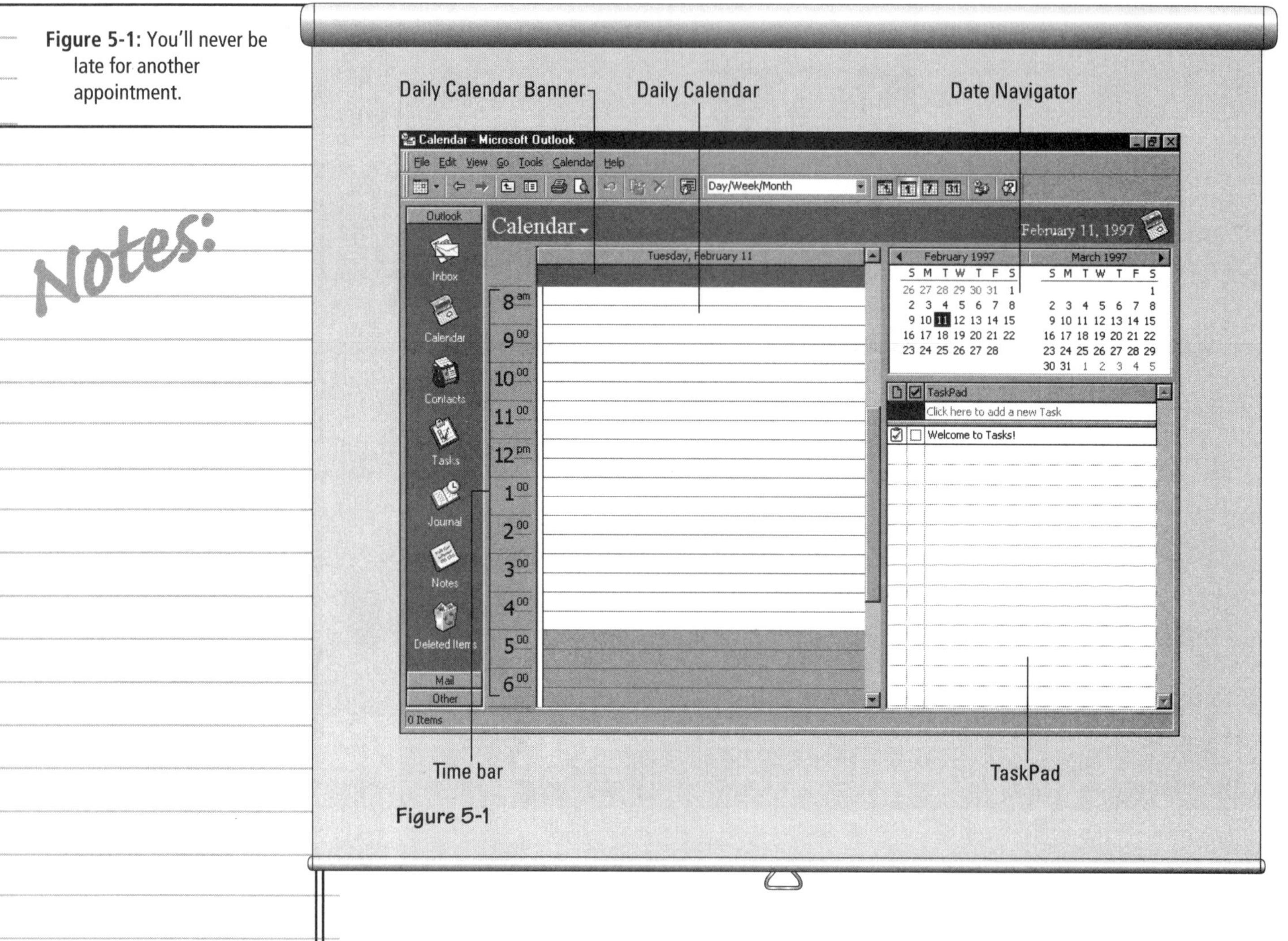

Figure 5-1: You'll never be late for another appointment.

Lesson 5-1 Scheduling Appointments

Although it has many uses, the Calendar's primary functions are scheduling and tracking appointments. Designed to meet the needs of a wide range of users, Outlook offers several ways to accomplish these tasks. You can enter an appointment directly into the Daily Calendar, use a contact name to create an appointment, convert an e-mail to an appointment, or create an appointment by dragging a task onto a specific date in the Date Navigator. In this lesson, we walk you through scheduling an appointment with the Daily Calendar.

Using the Daily Calendar and setting reminders

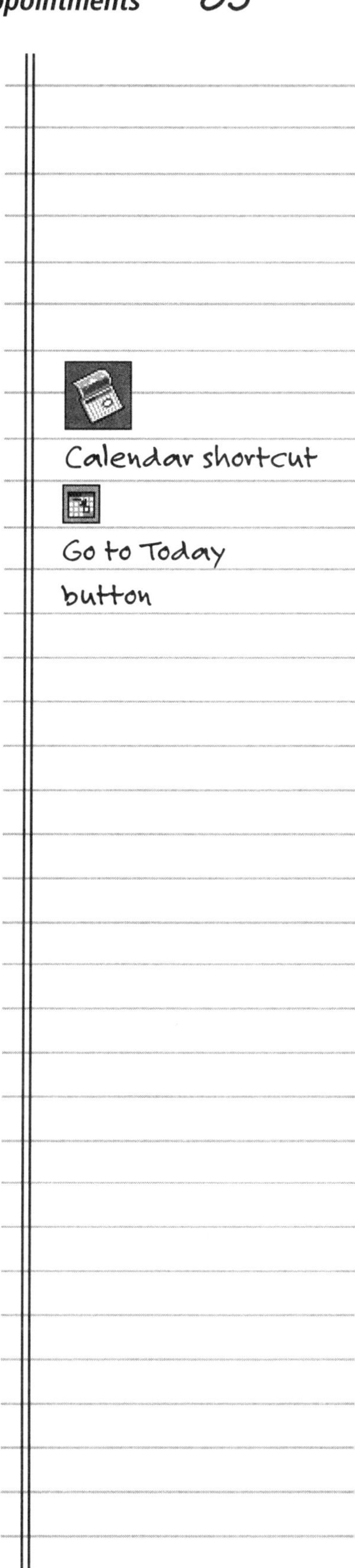

Because the Daily Calendar lets you schedule your day, change dates for your appointments, and record tasks on the fly, you'll probably spend the majority of your scheduling time in this view.

Follow these steps to set up an appointment to talk to your boss about a raise, get your blood pressure checked, or rotate your tires:

1. **Click the Calendar shortcut in the Outlook bar to open the Calendar folder.**

2. **Click the Go to Today button in the Calendar toolbar.**

   Your window should look like Figure 5-1, except for the date. The date in the Daily Calendar column header should be today's date.

   In this lesson, we want you to schedule a sample appointment for one month from today at 2:00 PM.

3. **Choose Go⇨Go to Date to open the Go to Date dialog box.**

4. **In the Date field type** one month from today**.**

   Notice that Outlook understands plain English, at least when it comes to date fields. To go to next Thursday you simply type **next Thursday**, and so on. The date field also provides a drop-down calendar so that you can select a date, if that's more convenient.

5. **Click OK to return to the Daily Calendar.**

6. **Move your mouse pointer to 2:00 on the time bar and double-click.**

   The new Appointment form appears.

7. **Type** Newt Gingrich - Contract negotiation **in the Subject text box and then tab to the Location text box.**

8. **Type** My office **in the Location text box and tab to the Start time hour field.**

   The Location field offers a drop-down list that you access by clicking the down arrow at the right end of the field. The list displays the names of all countries whose holidays you install. The default is the United States (ask your administrator about installing other holidays). Notice, however, that typing **My office** into the Location field automatically adds it to the drop-down list. All subsequent appointment forms provide My office as a selection in the Location drop-down list. By the way, the appointment is actually for 3 PM, not 2 PM, so you need to change it.

Figure 5-2: Creating an appointment is as easy as filling in the blanks.

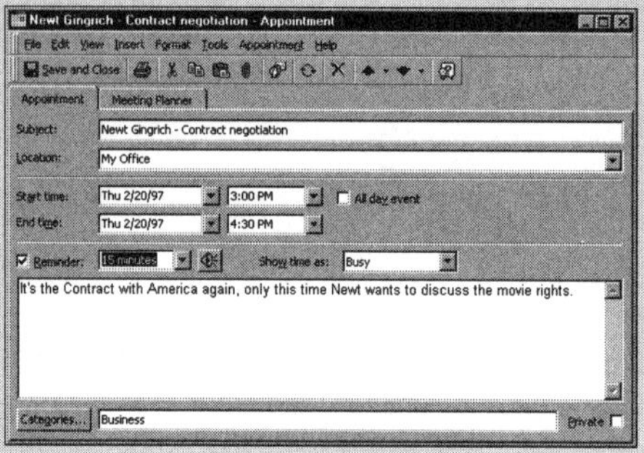

Figure 5-2

Notes:

9 **Click the down arrow and select 3:00 PM from the drop-down list.**

As soon as you click 3:00 PM the End time hour changes from 2:30 PM to 3:30 PM. Outlook automatically sets appointment lengths to 30 minutes. You change the default setting by right-clicking the time bar and selecting from the choices at the bottom of the pop-up menu. Because this meeting involves contract negotiations, it may take longer than 30 minutes; therefore you must allot more time.

10 **Tab twice to the End time hour field, click the down arrow, and select 4:30 PM.**

Because this meeting will not take the entire day, leave the All day event box unchecked.

reminders only work when Outlook is running

on the test

Even the best of us forget about appointments every once in a while, which is why Outlook offers a Reminder option to keep you on your toes.

Reminders are only active while Outlook is running. Don't expect to be tapped on the shoulder by an Outlook reminder after you exit Outlook. Any reminders that occur while Outlook is not running appear as overdue reminders the next time you open Outlook.

11 **Tab to the Reminder option and click to place a check mark in the box.**

12 **Click the down arrow to the right of the reminder time field, and change the setting to 30 minutes.**

Setting the Reminder option to 30 minutes causes a reminder to be displayed 30 minutes prior to the appointment. To insure that you don't miss the reminder when it pops up, Outlook plays a short chiming sound to alert you that the reminder is up.

13 **Click the reminder sound icon to change the sound associated with this reminder.**

14 **From the Reminder Sound dialog box click browse and select a .wav file from the CD files folder.**

Make sure the When reminder comes due, play this sound option is checked.

15 **Click OK to return to the Untitled - Appointment form.**

16 **Designate a status of your time during the appointment by choosing an option in the Show time as drop-down list.**

This option blocks out the time allotted for the meeting in the Daily Calendar in a different color depending on which of the following you choose:

- **Free:** Indicates that the time slot is still available. If your boss wants to take you out for lunch at this time, you're ready.
- **Tentative:** Indicates that the time slot may be tied up, but may become available. This is also known as the waffling option.
- **Out of Office:** The time slot is absolutely tied up because you will not be physically available, even in the event of an emergency.

17 **Tab to the large notes window below and type** It's the Contract with America again, only this time Newt wants to discuss the movie rights.

Use the notes window to include notes, lists of items, things to prepare, or anything else that may be related to the appointment.

18 **Click the Categories button to open the Categories dialog box.**

Categories in Outlook provide an easy way to classify and organize appointments, meetings, messages, and more.

19 **From the Available categories select Business and then click OK to return to the appointment.**

The last option on the appointment form, Private, only applies if you are on a network and allow others access to your Calendar folder. Leave it blank for now. Your appointment form should now look like the one in Figure 5-2.

20 **Click the Save and Close button on the toolbar to save the appointment and close the appointment form.**

The Daily Calendar displays the appointment in a box that blocks out the time from 3:00 PM to 4:30 PM. Also note the blue bar on the left of the box, indicating that you will be busy during that time.

Congratulations! You've scheduled your first appointment. Now, if you can only handle the meeting with Newt with such agility.

Reminder icon

Categories...

Categories button

Save and Close

Save and Close button

☑ Progress Check

If you can do the following, you've mastered this lesson:

- ❑ Open the Calendar folder.
- ❑ Select a date using the Go to Date feature.
- ❑ Open an appointment form.
- ❑ Change the time for an appointment.
- ❑ Set a reminder for an appointment.

Lesson 5-2

Refining Your Reminders

Notes:

15 minutes = default time for reminders

Scheduling appointments and meetings is meaningless unless you remember to attend them. If you have a hectic workday like most of us, an appointment can sneak up on you before you know it. Walking into a meeting late and unprepared is about as much fun as going to a Save the Animals rally in a fur coat. To avoid the unpleasant consequences of either, set a reminder to insure that you'll be ready, on time, and properly attired for your next meeting. You learned how to set a reminder while creating an appointment in Lesson 5-1. Now it's time to pick up the finer points of reminder mastery.

Setting the default reminder time

The Outlook Calendar automatically sets the reminder time at 15 minutes unless you change it in each appointment your create. Some people find that 15 minutes does not provide sufficient warning to adequately prepare for an appointment or meeting. Rather than change the reminder time each time you create a new appointment, you can change the default setting.

To give yourself more time to remember your appointments, follow these steps to reset the default to 30 minutes:

1. **Choose Tools⇨Options from the menu bar to open the Outlook Options dialog box.**

   You can open the Options dialog box from any folder.

2. **Click the Calendar tab to access options relating to the Calendar.**

   The Calendar tab offers numerous options that might be appropriate for you to change, but you should check with your administrator before making any modifications to most of these options. However, the reminder time is entirely a matter of personal choice and can be altered without affecting the rest of the network.

3. **Open the drop-down list in the Reminder field (Appointment defaults).**

   You can set the reminder time for as little as 0 (the reminder activates at exactly when the appointment is scheduled) or as much as two days, with quite a few choices in between.

4. **Select 30 minutes.**

5. **Click OK to return to Outlook.**

The next time you create an appointment, the Reminder field will automatically be set to 30 minutes.

Turning one reminder off

Occasionally you schedule a meeting that you couldn't forget even if you tried. Take the meeting with Newt, for example. You'll probably be burning the midnight oil for days in advance getting ready for that one. Because he's coming to your office, you don't have to worry about being late. The bottom line — there's no need for a reminder. As a matter of fact, a reminder might be more of distraction than a help while you're working. What do you do? Turn the reminder off. How? Glad you asked.

The first thing to do is find the appointment in question. Outlook provides a handy little tool that allows you to find just about anything that you've created or entered into Outlook. It's called Find Items. After you find the appointment, you can make any change to it that you want to make, including turning off the reminder.

1. **Click the Find Items button in the toolbar to open the Find dialog box (see Figure 5-3).**

   Because you're in the Calendar folder, the Look for field already contains Appointments and Meetings and the In field displays the word Calendar.

2. **Tab to the Search for the words(s) fields and type** Newt.
3. **Click the down arrow in the In field to open the drop-down list.**

   Searching for Newt in the subject field alone is probably sufficient to find the meeting with Mr. Gingrich, but to be on the safe side, conduct the search in all the text fields.

4. **Select frequently-used text fields from the In drop-down list.**
5. **Click Find Now to begin the search.**

   The meeting with Newt appears at the bottom of the dialog box, with all relevant information listed, as seen in Figure 5-4.

6. **Highlight the appointment and press Ctrl+O to open the appointment form you filled out for Newt.**
7. **Click the Reminder field to remove the check mark.**
8. **Click the Save and Close button to return to the Calendar.**

Find Items button

Save and Close

Save and Close button

Turning reminders off and on

Every once in a while you experience the kind of day that makes you realize you need a vacation. You know the kind of day — you're understaffed, overworked, and everything has to be done yesterday (so far a normal work-day) *and* your assistant informs you that the figures for your presentation to the board this afternoon are erroneous. That means you have three hours to revise the masterpiece that took three weeks to create. Cancel all appointments, turn off the phone, lock your door, and kill all reminders.

Figure 5-3: Find Items tracks down missing appointments, meetings, messages, and more.

Figure 5-4: Find Items provides the who, what, where, and when for missing appointments.

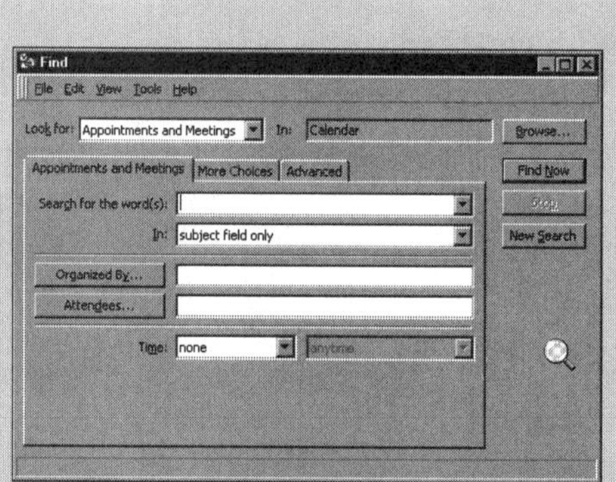

Figure 5-3

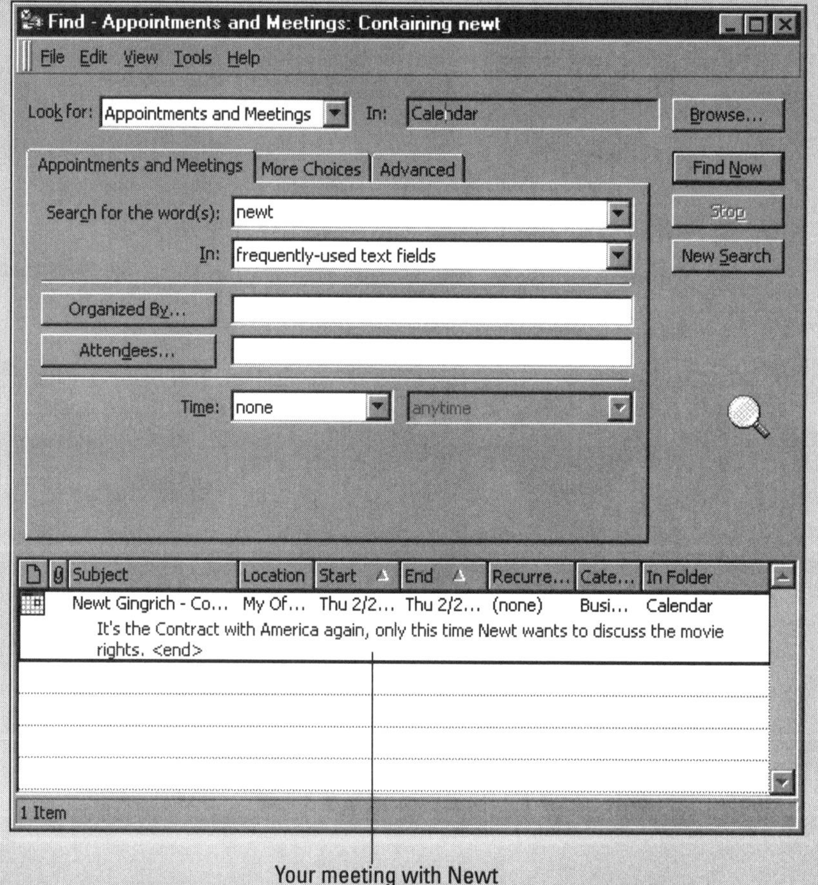

Figure 5-4

1. **Choose Tools⇨Options to open the Options dialog box.**
2. **Click the Reminders tab to see the reminder options.**
3. **Click the Display the reminder field to clear the check mark.**

   Turning off the Display the reminder field option deactivates existing reminders, but does not delete them. Turning this option back on reactivates any reminders that did not expire during the time the option was turned off.
4. **Click OK to return to the Calendar.**

   Hold it — your luck is changing. It turns out that your figures are correct after all. Whew! After you fire your assistant for nearly giving you heart failure, reschedule your appointments, turn on the phone, open your door, and reactivate your reminders by choosing Tools⇨Options, clicking the Reminders tab of the Options dialog box, and clicking the Display the reminder field to place a check mark in the box and enable the option.
5. **Click OK to return to the Calendar.**

to eliminate reminder sound only, leave Display the reminder enabled and disable Play reminder sound

Responding to reminders

When a reminder pops up, you have three options for dealing with it. No, throwing your computer is not one of the options, no matter how tempting that may be. You can, however, choose one of the following:

- **Dismiss:** Shuts down the reminder permanently.
- **Postpone:** Closes the reminder, which then reappears after an interval you specify.
- **Open Item:** Opens the appointment, meeting, or other Outlook item to which the reminder is attached. (Other Outlook items include e-mail messages, contacts, tasks, and journal entries.) If the subject line of your reminder is not clear, you can refresh your memory by opening the item and reviewing it.

To get some practice responding to reminders, we want you to first create an appointment with an instant reminder (so that you have something to respond to) and then do the following:

Go to Today button

1. **From the toolbar, click the Go to Today button.**
2. **Move your mouse pointer to the time bar on the Daily Calendar.**
3. **Double-click the time block nearest to the actual time of day it is right now.**

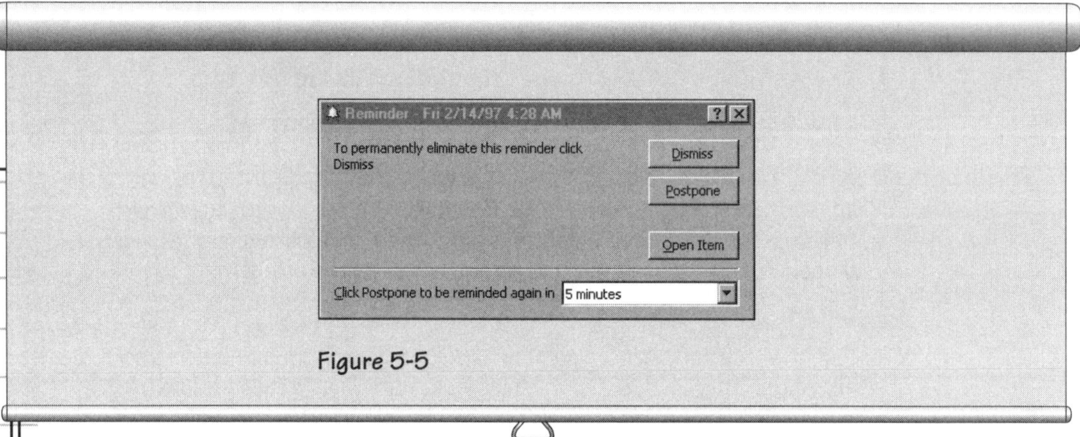

Figure 5-5: Outlook reminders use sight and sound to get your attention.

4. **In the subject field, type** To permanently eliminate this reminder click Dismiss**.**

5. **Open the reminder time drop-down list and select 0 minutes.**

   Make sure the Reminder field is enabled (see "Turning all reminders off" earlier in this lesson).

6. **Move your mouse pointer to the bottom of the screen and bring up your task bar.**

   The Windows 95 task bar which resides at the bottom of the screen, includes a readout of the time. The task bar may be hidden, in which case moving your mouse pointer over the area at the bottom of the screen activates it.

7. **Check the time on the clock at the end of the right side of the task bar.**

8. **Return to the appointment form, move to the Start time hour field, and type in the exact time that's showing on your task bar clock.**

9. **Click the Save and Close button in the toolbar to close the appointment form and activate the reminder (see Figure 5-5).**

   The reminder pops up and chimes to alert you of its presence. Except for the date and time, your reminder should match the one in Figure 5-5.

   heads up

   If the reminder does not appear immediately, check to see if the task bar clock advanced while you were setting the reminder. If so, reset the appointment form Start time hour to match the task bar clock.

10. **When the reminder pops up, click the Postpone button to close the reminder for another five minutes.**

Save and Close

Save and Close button

Now that you've mastered appointment reminders, don't forget that the reminder you created will pop up again in five minutes. Perhaps you should create a reminder to ensure that you remember this (just kidding).

☑ Progress Check

If you can do the following, you've mastered this lesson:

- ❑ Change the default reminder time.
- ❑ Deactivate a single reminder.
- ❑ Turn reminders off globally.
- ❑ Reset a reminder.

Entering Recurring Appointments

Lesson 5-3

Some appointments, such as the Monday morning call to the home office or the monthly team meeting, occur on a regular basis, and usually at the same time and place. These appointments are ideal candidates for recurring appointments.

To create a recurring appointment for the 9:00 AM Monday morning home office call, follow these steps:

1. **Choose Go⇨Go to Date from the menu bar to open the Go to Date dialog box.**
2. **In the Date text box type** next Monday**.**
3. **Move your mouse pointer to 9:00 in the Time bar and left-click to highlight the 9:00 time block.**
4. **Choose Calendar⇨New Recurring Appointment.**

   Immediately, a blank appointment form opens, followed by the Appointment Recurrence dialog box (see Figure 5-6). If you completed the previous steps as indicated, the default settings are accurate. However, because this phone call generally takes more than 30 minutes, you might want to change the duration of the appointment to one hour.
5. **Click the down arrow to the right of the Duration field.**
6. **Select 1 hour and click OK to close the dialog box and move to the new appointment form.**
7. **In the Subject text box type** Home office weekly report **and tab to the Location field.**
8. **Type** Phone **in the Location text box.**

   The reminder time, reminder sound, and Show time as settings are fine, so tab to the Categories field.
9. **Click the Categories button, select Business, and Click OK.**
10. **Click the Save and Close button on the Standard toolbar to return to the Daily Calendar.**

Every Monday morning, come rain or come shine, Outlook will tap you on the shoulder at 8 AM and tell you to get ready for your 9 AM phone call.

Notes:

recurring appointment = appointment at same time and place on regular basis

Categories...

Categories button

Editing recurring appointments

Life is change. Don't panic, you're still in Outlook 101, not Philosophy 101. However, that simple statement applies to everything, including Outlook. Fortunately, Outlook allows you to change as your circumstances change.

Figure 5-6: Recurring appointments are a snap with Outlook.

Notes:

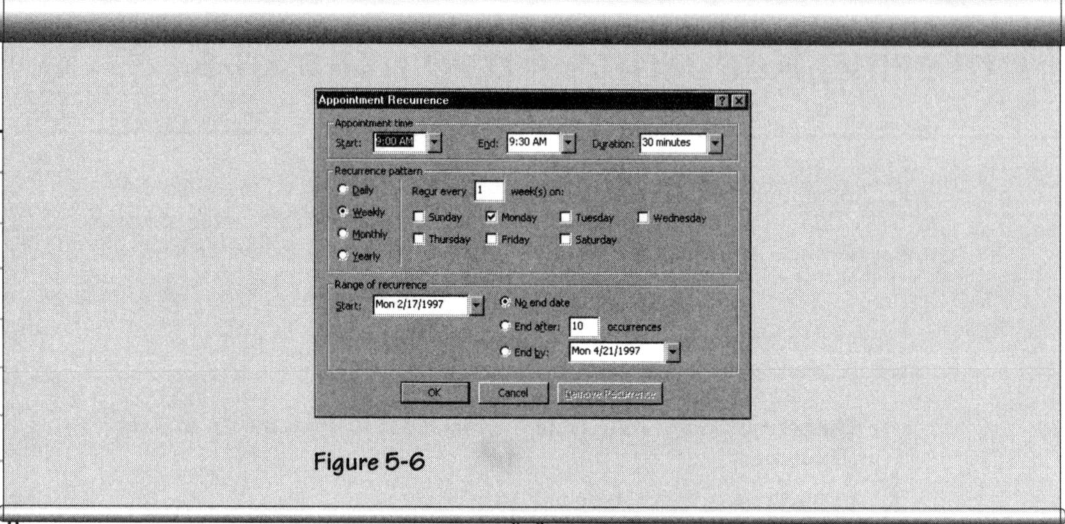

Figure 5-6

As in life, some changes are temporary, and others are permanent. To accommodate your needs, Outlook lets you make temporary changes that affect only a single instance of a recurring appointment, or permanent changes that apply to all future instances of a recurring appointment.

Changing a single occurrence

When the dentist threatens to call your mother unless you come in for an appointment, or you're unable to weasel out of car-pooling the kids to school, you may have to adjust a recurring appointment to accommodate the minor crises that crop up. However, after this appointment, you're not going back to the dentist even if he threatens to call your parole officer. And if worst comes to worst, you can always slash your own tires. Consequently, you only need to change next Monday's occurrence of the home office weekly report. You expect to return from the appointment before 11 AM, so change the start time from 9 AM to 11 AM for this occurrence only.

To...
Go to Date shortcut key = Ctrl+G

1. **Choose Go⇨Go to Date from the menu bar to open the Go to Date dialog box.**
2. **In the Date field type** next Monday.

   If you scheduled your dentist appointment for two weeks from Monday, you could either type the actual date or **two weeks from next Monday**.
3. **Click OK to return to the Daily Calendar.**
4. **Position your mouse pointer over the Home Office weekly report (Phone) appointment in the Daily Calendar.**

   Notice the two icons to the left of the appointment listing. The first, a ringing bell, is the reminder icon, indicating that an active reminder is set for this appointment. The second, a pair of circling arrows, is the recurrence icon, indicating that this is a recurring appointment.

5. **Double-click the Home Office weekly report (Phone) listing to access the Open Recurring Item dialog box.**

6. **Select Open this occurrence and click OK.**

   Any changes you make now only affect the appointment scheduled for this specific date.

7. **Click the down arrow in the Start time hour field to open the drop-down list.**

8. **Select 11:00 AM and click the Save and Close button to return to the Daily Calendar.**

Save and Close

Save and Close button

As long as you let the home office know about the change, you're all set for next Monday's appointment.

Changing the entire series of recurrences

Sometimes the need arises to change all instances of a recurring appointment due to a change or addition to the information you input originally. For example, the home office may call to say that from now on, the weekly call will be on Tuesday, not Monday. No problem.

1. **Double-click the Home Office weekly report in the Daily Calendar.**

2. **In the Open Recurring Item dialog box, select Open the series and click OK to open the appointment form.**

   Notice that this form, unlike the single occurrence form, does not contain Start and End times or an All day event option. To make any changes that affect the series scheduling you must open the Appointment Recurrence dialog box.

3. **Click the Recurrence button in the appointment toolbar to open the Appointment Recurrence dialog box.**

Recurrence button

4. **In the Recurrence pattern option group, click Monday to deselect it and click Tuesday to select it.**

   The only weekday with a check mark now is Tuesday.

5. **Click OK.**

   The dialog box shown in Figure 5-7 materializes to warn you that any single-occurrence changes previously implemented will be lost once you make this global change. This means that next Monday's appointment that you switched from 9 AM to 11 AM will be deleted and a new appointment will be scheduled for next Tuesday at 9 AM. Because you have no conflicting appointments, this is not a problem.

6. **Click OK to return to the appointment form.**

Figure 5-7: Global changes demolish exceptions to the recurring appointment.

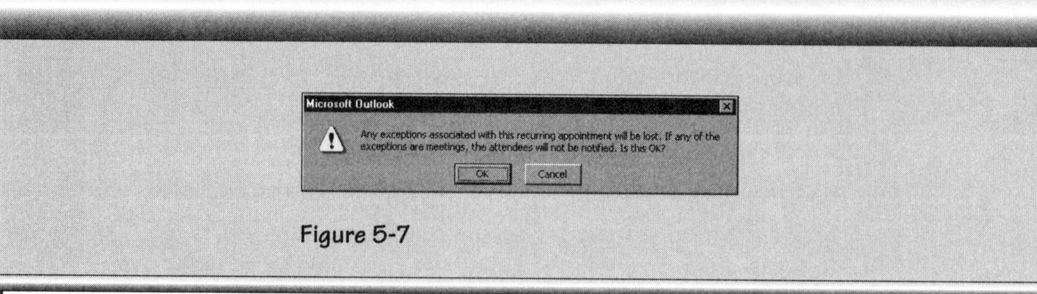

Figure 5-7

7 Click the Save and Close button to save your changes and close the appointment.

Good Job. With a handful of mouse moves you converted all future Monday morning calls to Tuesday morning.

Recess

You've accomplished quite a bit in the last three lessons. This may be a good time to get up, stretch, run a marathon, clean the house, wash the car, or do whatever it is you do on your break. Then come back and dig into the next Lesson, which talks about keeping your events on track.

☑ Progress Check

If you can do the following, you've mastered this lesson:

- ❑ Open a recurring appointment form.
- ❑ Change a single occurrence of a recurring appointment.
- ❑ Change all future occurrences of a recurring appointment.

Lesson 5-4 Creating an Event

What do birthdays, sales conventions, two-day trips to Las Vegas, and anniversaries have in common? If your answer included anything remotely off-color, go directly to Step 4 in the excercise at the end of this unit. The *correct* answer, if anyone is still here, is that they are all activities that last 24 hours or more, and are therefore considered events rather than appointments. The only other feature that distinguishes them from appointments is that they appear in the banner rather than in the body of the Daily Calendar. In this lesson, you create an event for a two-day management seminar offered two weeks from next Thursday.

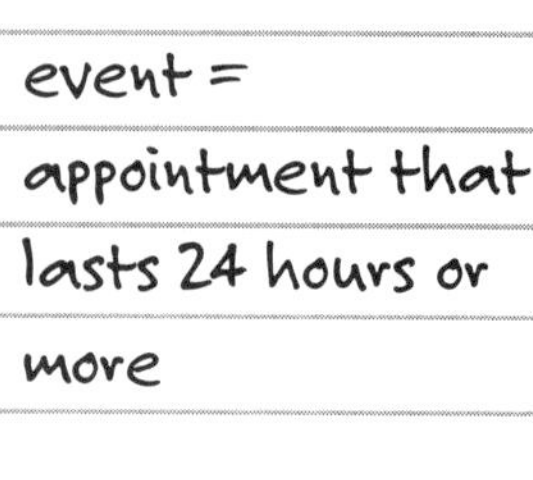

1. **Press Ctrl+G to open the Go to Date dialog box.**
2. **In the Date field type** 2 weeks from thur **and click OK.**

   Notice that you don't have to type the complete name of the day. Outlook date fields recognize standard abbreviations for some date-related items. Use the following abbreviations when you're just too tired to type the whole word:

   mon = Monday

   tues = Tuesday

   wed = Wednesday

   thur = Thursday

   fri = Friday

   sat = Saturday

   sun = Sunday

   wk = week

   mo = month

3. **Choose Calendar⇨New Event from the menu bar to open the new event form.**

   The event form matches the appointment form except for the lack of hourly Start and End times and some default settings.

4. **Type** Management seminar **in the Subject field and tab to the Location field.**
5. **In the Location field type** San Francisco.
6. **Tab to the End time field and type** 2 days.
7. **Click the Reminder field to enable reminders.**
8. **From the reminder time drop-down list select 11 hours.**

   Because an event is a 24-hour (or longer) activity, the start time is considered to be 12:00 AM of the first day. Therefore a reminder set for 30 minutes appears at 11:30 PM the night before the event. Not very useful in most cases.

9. **Tab to the Show time as field, click the down arrow, and select Out of Office from the drop-down list.**
10. **Click the Categories button and select Business.**
11. **Click the Save and Close button to return to the Calendar.**

Notes:

Categories...

Categories button

Save and Close

Save and Close button

Progress Check

If you can do the following, you've mastered this lesson:

- ❑ Explain the difference between an appointment and an event.
- ❑ Open a new event form.
- ❑ Use a shortcut key to open the Go to Date dialog box.

Lesson 5-5 Setting Up a Meeting

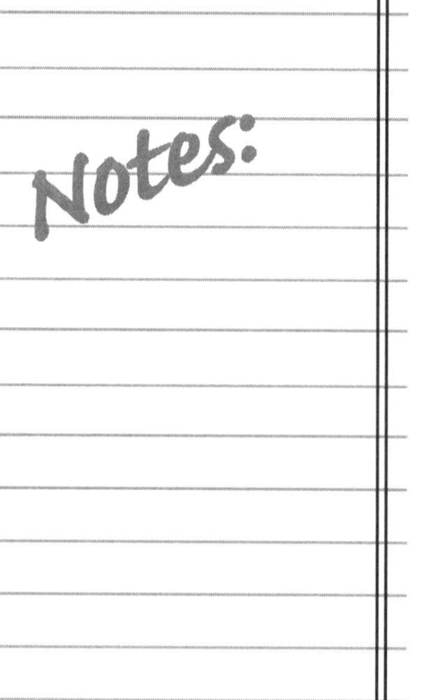

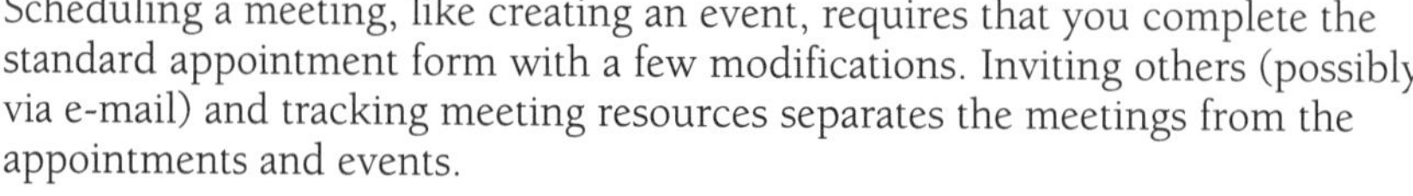

Scheduling a meeting, like creating an event, requires that you complete the standard appointment form with a few modifications. Inviting others (possibly via e-mail) and tracking meeting resources separates the meetings from the appointments and events.

Setting up a meeting necessitates that you have e-mail addresses in your Address Book. Because you created entries for Bill Clinton, Al Gore, and Newt Gingrich earlier, you might as well invite them to a meeting at your office one week from Wednesday.

To assemble this amazing cast (and the people you need for any of your meetings) using e-mail, follow these steps:

1. **Press Ctrl+G to open the Go to Date dialog box.**
2. **In the Date field type** 1 week from wed.
3. **Choose Calendar⇨New Meeting Request from the menu bar to open a new meeting form.**

   Be sure that the All day event option does not have a check mark in it. If it does, the form you see will be an invited event form rather than a meeting form. To remove the check mark click the box to the left of the All day event option.

   As you can see in Figure 5-8 the meeting form includes a To field for e-mail addresses of people you want to invite to the meeting. The addition of the e-mail feature necessitates a revised toolbar to provide e-mail options such as Send, Address Book, and Check Names.

To...

To button

4. **Click the To button to open the Select Attendees and Resources dialog box.**

   At last opportunity knocks. That is, the opportunity to use the Personal Distribution List you created in Unit 2, TopDogs.
5. **Click TopDogs in the address list on the left.**
6. **Click the Optional button to the right of the address list to add TopDogs to the recipient list and at the same time indicate that attendance is optional.**
7. **Click OK to return to the meeting form.**
8. **In the Subject field type** It's the economy! **and then tab to the Location field.**
9. **Type** Oval Office **in the Location field and tab to the End time hours field.**

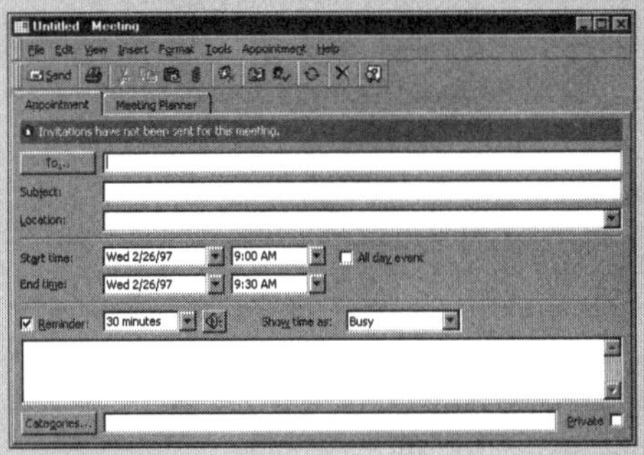

Figure 5-8

Figure 5-8: The meeting form information banner indicates the status of invitations.

10. **Click the down arrow and select 11:00 AM from the drop-down list.**
11. **Click the Categories button and select VIP from the Available categories list.**
12. **Click Send to close the meeting form and send invitations to the members of the TopDogs Personal Distribution List.**

    In case you're wondering, we ignored the Meeting Planner because the majority of its functions are available only with Exchange Server installed. If you're on a network with Exchange Server, ask your administrator about the additional scheduling features available.

Reach around and pat yourself on the back. In five short lessons you've mastered all there is to know about making appointments (well, almost everything).

☑ Progress Check

If you can do the following, you've mastered this lesson:

- ❑ Open a new meeting request.
- ❑ Enter dates using plain English.
- ❑ Use a Personal Distribution List to send e-mail/meeting requests.

Viewing Appointments — Lesson 5-6

on the test

The real value of computers is not their ability to devour the information you put in them, but rather their ability to display that information in a meaningful format. Now that you've created some appointments and events, it's time to take a look at them in ways unimaginable before the advent of computers.

The Calendar window arrives on your desktop with six different views installed. You can use the following views to see just the information about your schedule that you want to see:

- **Day/Week/Month:** The opening view of the Calendar window includes the Daily Calendar, the Date Navigator, and the TaskPad.
- **Active Appointments:** A table (list) view of upcoming appointments, events, and meetings.

- **Events:** A table view of upcoming events (24 hours or longer), including all holidays.
- **Annual Events:** A table view of events that recur yearly.
- **Recurring Appointments:** A table view of all recurring appointments and events.
- **By Category:** A table view of all active appointments, events, and meetings, automatically sorted by category.

Using the Day/Week/Month view

on the test

The most flexible of all the views, the Day/Week/Month view lives up to its name and lets you see all your appointments in daily, weekly, and monthly calendars. Here's where the Date Navigator jumps into the picture with a few neat tricks of its own. To take a look at the three basic views, Day, Week, and Month, starting with the Day view, follow these steps:

1. **Click the Calendar icon in the Outlook Bar to open the Calendar folder.**

2. **Choose View⇨Current View⇨Day/Week/Month from the menu bar.**

   The opening view is the daily (Day) view, which shows the Daily Calendar work hours, the Date Navigator, and the TaskPad. You can also get to Day view by clicking the Day button in the toolbar.

   Day button

3. **Choose View⇨Week from the menu bar or click the Week button in the toolbar to open the Week view.**

   The Week view substitutes a weekly calendar for the Daily Calendar. The rest of the view remains unchanged. Each weekly view begins with Monday and ends with Sunday.

   Week button

4. **To open the Month view, choose View⇨Month from the menu bar or click the Month button in the toolbar to open the Month view.**

   Month button

   The Month view mimics its paper counterpart by blocking off each day and listing the appointments for that day within the box. You can view more than the current month by using the scroll bar to the right of the calendar. Note that when you grab the scroll box a small pop-up window appears with the date. As you move, the date changes, indicating your position on the calendar.

5. **Return to the Day view by choosing View⇨Day from the menu bar.**

   Now, for your viewing (no pun intended) pleasure, may we present the Date Navigator.

6. **Click the first Sunday of this month in the Date Navigator.**

   The Daily Calendar immediately jumps to the date you clicked (be sure to get the first Sunday of this month and not the last Sunday of last month).

7. **In the Date Navigator, position your mouse pointer just to the left of any of the dates in the first column and click once.**

   Not only did you highlight a week's worth of dates on the Date Navigator, you also transformed the Daily Calendar into the Weekly Calendar. Note that regardless of the first day in your week, the Weekly Calendar always starts with

Monday. Be sure not to click the dates themselves or you will only highlight the date. Ready for more?

8. **Move your mouse pointer to the Date Navigator and click anywhere on the weekday header (S M T W T F S) of the calendar.**

   This time you captured the entire month. Not only is it quick, but also it gives you access to the Date Navigator and the TaskPad while you view the Monthly Calendar. Now, suppose you want to see two or three days at a time. Not a problem.

9. **In the Date Navigator click the first Sunday of the month, hold down the mouse button, and drag to the following Tuesday.**

   The Daily Calendar appears, sporting three mini-Daily Calendars. One for each day selected. Pretty slick, eh? Now for the *piece de resistance.*

10. **Move to the Date Navigator and click the first Sunday of the month.**

11. **Hold down the Ctrl key, click the second Sunday of the month, and (still holding down the Ctrl key) click the last Friday of the month.**

    You now have a Daily Calendar that displays each of the 3 nonsequential days. You can include a maximum of 14 days in this view.

Other Calendar views

The Calendar offers a wealth of viewing options. In addition to the split-personality Day/Week/Month view, the Calendar embraces five other viewing options. All the rest of the views are of the table view variety. Table views present information in an orderly fashion by listing each activity and its relevant information row by row. The lessons in Unit 6 deal with using and tailoring views to accommodate your needs. This lesson is just a quick stroll through the different views available in the calendar. You start with the Active Appointments view.

1. **Choose View⇨Current View⇨Active Appointments from the menu bar.**

   The Active Appointments view dominates the Calendar. Notice that all current and future appointments, meetings, events, and holidays appear on the Active Appointments view.

heads up

   The effective use of views depends on your ability to switch between them effortlessly. If you experiment (random clicking) while in any of the table views, you're presented with the Save View Settings dialog box. Unless you've made intentional changes you wish to save, select Discard the current view settings and click OK.

2. **Choose View⇨Current View⇨Events from the menu bar.**

   Like the Active Appointments view, the Events view lists only scheduled events. Because holidays fall into that group you see all the current and future holidays you have installed as well as any events (24 hours or longer) you have recorded.

Progress Check

If you can do the following, you've mastered this lesson:

- ❑ Open a daily view of your appointments.
- ❑ Create a weekly view of your schedule.
- ❑ Preview a month's worth of appointments at one time.
- ❑ Open the By Category view.

3 Choose View⇨Current View⇨Annual Events from the menu bar.

The Annual Events view is identical to the Events view except that only yearly events make this list.

4 From the menu bar choose View⇨Current View⇨Recurring Appointments.

This view provides an easy way to review, edit, and print recurring appointment information alone.

5 Choose View⇨Current View⇨By Category from the menu bar.

Of all the predefined table views, the By Category list offers the best organized view of your appointments, as long as you employ categories when scheduling appointments.

6 Choose View⇨Current View⇨Day/Week/Month to return to the Daily Calendar.

The key to productivity is effective time management. You now possess the basic skills to create a good scheduling system, without which time management becomes little more than a pipe dream.

Unit 5 Quiz

1. How do you record an appointment?

A. Bring a notarized copy to City Hall.

B. Hire a stenographer.

C. Use a new appointment form in the Calendar window.

D. Take a Polaroid and stick it in the appointment album.

E. Recording appointments is for wimps!

2. How do you keep from forgetting an appointment?

A. Paste sticky notes all over your monitor.

B. Set a reminder.

C. Check your calendar every five minutes.

D. Don't schedule any appointments.

E. I can't remember.

3. What's the difference between an appointment and an event?

A. About a buck fifty.

B. You can only make appointments on even days of the week.

C. An event requires a permit from the Mayor's office.

D. Appointments last for less than 24 hours, events, 24 hours or more.

E. One of the above answers.

4. What's the Date Navigator?

A. Slang for a time machine.

B. The small calendar in the Calendar view that shows the current month.

C. How should I know?

D. An airline crew member who keeps track of the international dateline.

E. A new singles forum on the Internet.

5. How do you keep track of your schedule?

A. Hire a private eye.

B. For my money, it's a Ouija board every time.

C. Don't let it out of your sight.

D. Use the Day/Week/Month and other Calendar views.

E. Is this a trick question?

Notes:

Unit 5 Exercise

1. Create events for family members' birthdays.
2. Set two-day reminders for each of the events you create in Step 1.
3. Use the Date Navigator to view next month's schedule.
4. Watch reruns of *Barney* for the next 90 days or until you get your mind out of the gutter, whichever comes first (see Lesson 5-4, introductory paragraph).
5. Create a Daily Calendar view that includes every other day of next week.

Unit 6

Managing Appointments

Objectives for This Unit

- ✓ Editing appointments
- ✓ Using drag and drop with appointments
- ✓ Archiving appointments
- ✓ Printing your calendar

Prerequisites

- Opening the Calendar folder (Lesson 5-1)
- Creating an appointment (Lesson 5-1)
- Using the Date Navigator (Lesson 5-1)
- Using Calendar views (Lesson 5-6)

- TaxRefrm.doc

A half dozen Clydesdales grazing in the pasture is a pretty sight. Round up those same six horses and hitch them to a wagon, and you've got a powerhouse of locomotion. The Outlook Calendar offers the same potential. Properly harnessed, your Outlook appointments form the core of a powerful time-management machine. Unit 6 provides the tools and skills you need to harness all the power of Outlook's scheduling features.

Modifying Appointments — Lesson 6-1

Nothing lasts forever, not even a well planned schedule. Eventually you'll find yourself making changes to some of the appointments you create. Editing appointments involves following the same steps used to create them and making some changes along the way. You can practice on the appointment with Newt Gingrich that you created in Unit 5. First make sure you are in the Calendar folder, and then work through this lesson to see how to change an appointment when your schedule changes.

Changing the date

Follow these steps to reschedule your appointment with Newt.

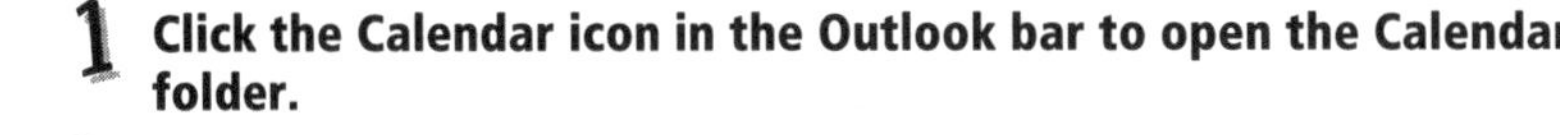

1. **Click the Calendar icon in the Outlook bar to open the Calendar folder.**

on the test

2. **From the menu bar, choose Tools⇨Find Items to open the Find dialog box.**

   You can also press Ctrl+Shift+F to open the Find dialog box shown in Figure 6-1. Of course, before you can edit an appointment, you first have to find and open it, and the Find dialog box helps you do just that.

3. **In the Search for the word(s) text box type** newt.
4. **Click the Find Now button.**

   The appointment with Newt appears in the display window at the bottom of the Find dialog box.

5. **Press Ctrl+O to open the appointment form.**

   Newt called and said he can't make it on the original date and would like to postpone the meeting for another month. You cordially offer to reschedule for a month from the previous date.

6. **Click the down arrow to the right of the Start time date field to open the drop-down calendar.**

   The appointment date is highlighted.

7. **Click the right arrow located in the calendar header to advance the calendar one month.**

   While you could use plain English to change the date command, it's simpler to do it from the drop-down calendar this time.

8. **Click the appropriate date for the meeting next month.**

   The calendar closes and returns you to the appointment form.

9. **Click the Save and Close button to save your changes and close the message form.**
10. **Use the shortcut key Alt+F4 to close the Find dialog box and return to the Daily Calendar.**

Adding an attachment

Because the meeting with Mr. Gingrich is about the Contract with America, why not include a copy of the document? It just so happens there's one on the CD that comes with this book.

1. **Use the shortcut key Ctrl+Shift+F to open the Find dialog box.**
2. **In the Search for the word(s) text box type** newt.
3. **Click the Find Now button.**

   The appointment with Newt appears in the display window at the bottom of the Find dialog box.

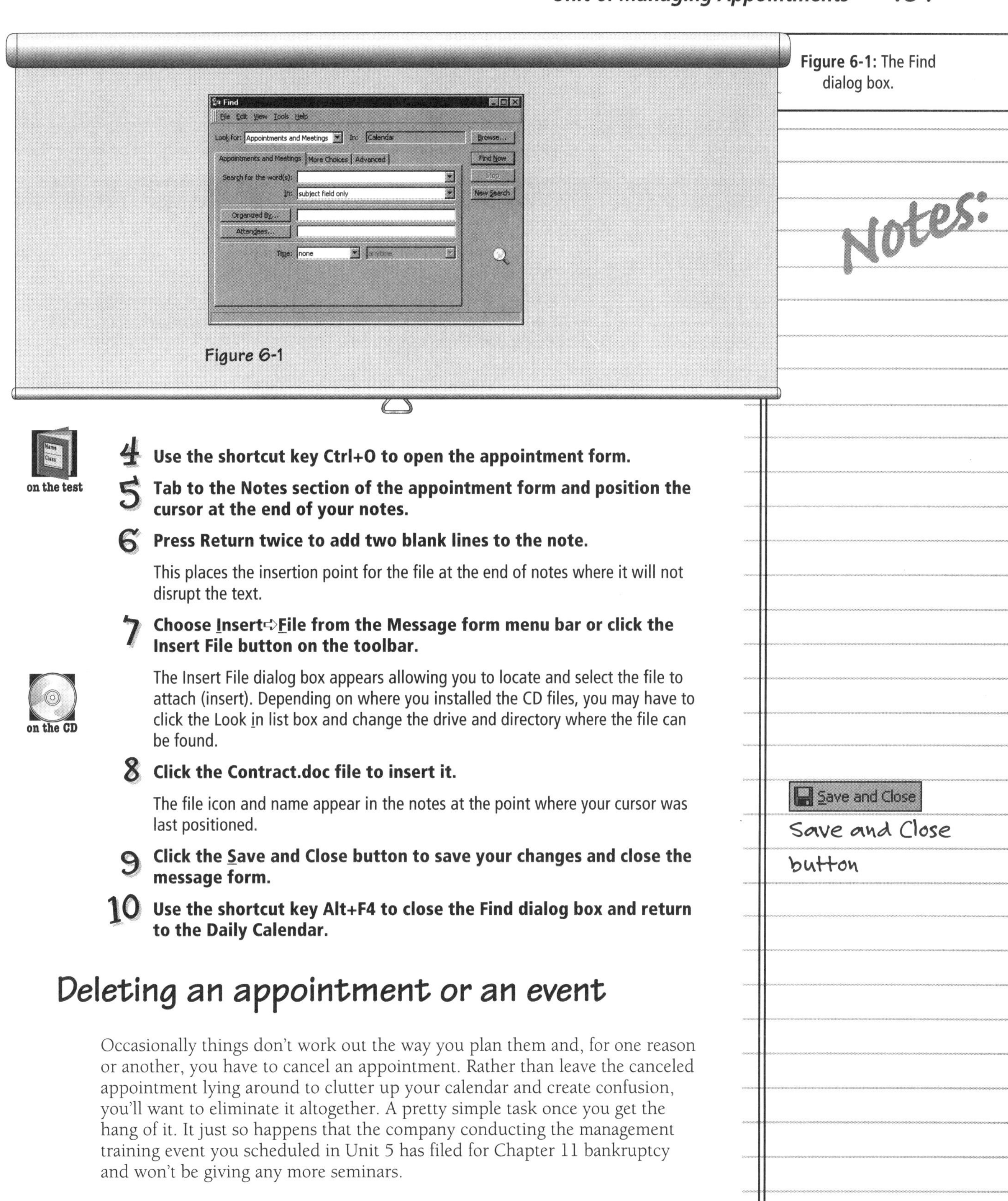

Figure 6-1

Figure 6-1: The Find dialog box.

on the test

4. **Use the shortcut key Ctrl+O to open the appointment form.**
5. **Tab to the Notes section of the appointment form and position the cursor at the end of your notes.**
6. **Press Return twice to add two blank lines to the note.**

   This places the insertion point for the file at the end of notes where it will not disrupt the text.
7. **Choose Insert⇨File from the Message form menu bar or click the Insert File button on the toolbar.**

   The Insert File dialog box appears allowing you to locate and select the file to attach (insert). Depending on where you installed the CD files, you may have to click the Look in list box and change the drive and directory where the file can be found.

on the CD

8. **Click the Contract.doc file to insert it.**

   The file icon and name appear in the notes at the point where your cursor was last positioned.
9. **Click the Save and Close button to save your changes and close the message form.**
10. **Use the shortcut key Alt+F4 to close the Find dialog box and return to the Daily Calendar.**

Deleting an appointment or an event

Occasionally things don't work out the way you plan them and, for one reason or another, you have to cancel an appointment. Rather than leave the canceled appointment lying around to clutter up your calendar and create confusion, you'll want to eliminate it altogether. A pretty simple task once you get the hang of it. It just so happens that the company conducting the management training event you scheduled in Unit 5 has filed for Chapter 11 bankruptcy and won't be giving any more seminars.

Progress Check

If you can do the following, you've mastered this lesson:

- ❑ Use the Find feature to locate a scheduled appointment.
- ❑ Add an attachment to an appointment.
- ❑ Delete an appointment.
- ❑ Retrieve a deleted appointment.

1. **Press Ctrl+Shift+F to open the Find dialog box.**
2. **In the Search for the word(s) text box, type** management.
3. **Click the Find Now button.**

   The Management seminar event appears in the display window at the bottom of the Find dialog box.
4. **Click the event to highlight it.**
5. **Press Ctrl+D to delete the event.**

   Without a warning, the event vanishes from the display window and your calendar. On the off chance that you occasionally act impulsively, Outlook takes the precaution of transferring the event to the Deleted Items folder for temporary storage.
6. **Press Ctrl+F4 to close the Find dialog box and return to the Daily Calendar.**

Retrieving deleted appointments

It turns out that the information you received about the management seminar cancellation was inaccurate. When you call to see about getting your deposit back, you discover that the company did not file for Chapter 11. It's true that one of the officers was indicted for racketeering, but that in no way affects the seminar schedule. Because it means two days away from the office, you decide that you might as well attend anyway. Now you have to dig the deleted event out of your electronic wastebasket and put it back on your calendar.

1. **Click the Deleted Items shortcut in the Outlook bar to open the Deleted Items folder.**
2. **Click Management seminar event to highlight it.**
3. **Press Ctrl+Shift+V to open the Move Items dialog box.**
4. **Click the Calendar folder in the Move Items dialog box.**
5. **Click OK to close the Move Items dialog box and return the deleted event to the Calendar.**
6. **Click the Calendar shortcut in the Outlook bar to return to the Calendar.**

Recess

With editing, deleting, and retrieving appointments under your belt, you're due for a little R and R, so take a break. Go to the donut shop and treat yourself to a well-deserved cup of coffee and a donut. To alleviate some of the guilt of eating that donut, you might want to jog there and back.

Editing Appointments with Drag and Drop

Lesson 6-2

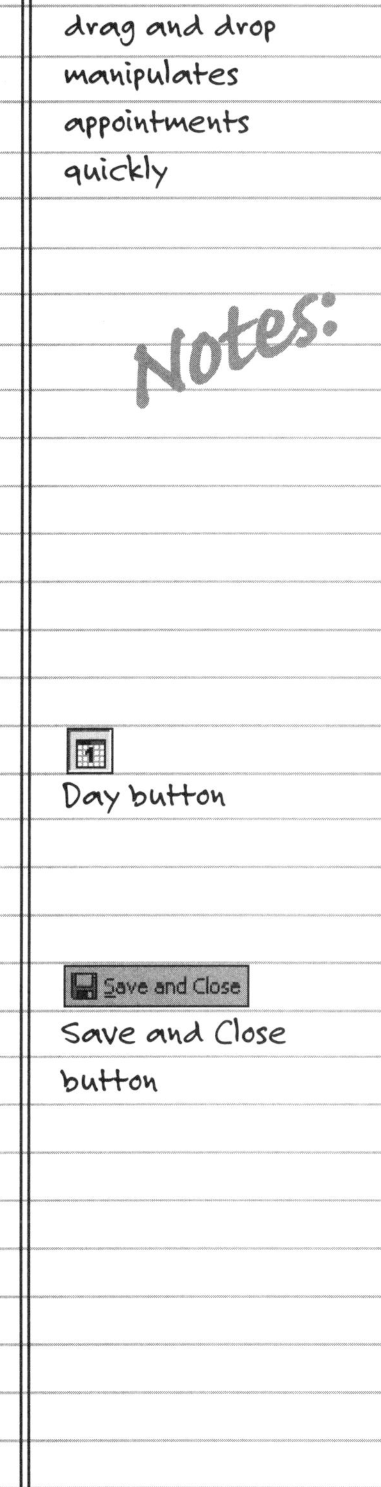

While it is possible to edit appointments in a variety of ways, drag and drop beats them all, hands down, for ease-of-use and speed.

Using drag and drop with appointments you can:

- Change appointment start and end dates
- Change appointment start and end times
- Create other Outlook items from an appointment
- Delete an appointment

If you can't do it with drag and drop, it's probably not worth doing anyway.

Changing the date, time, and length of an appointment

In Lesson 6-1 you learned to change an appointment date by opening the appointment and editing the date field. It works, but so do you. Now try a simpler way. First, create a quick test appointment to use and then follow these steps:

1. **Choose Go⇨Go to Today from the menu bar to start on today's date.**
2. **Press Alt+1 or click the Day button on the Calendar toolbar to bring up the Daily Calendar view.**
3. **Press Ctrl+N to open a new appointment form.**
4. **Type** Test **in the Subject field.**
5. **Move the cursor to the Notes section and type** This is the Notes section.
6. **Click the Save and Close button on the appointment form toolbar.**

   The Test appointment appears on your Daily Calendar in the 8am time slot (it may be different if your calendar working options have been changed from the default settings).

7. **Move your mouse pointer to the left of the side of the Test appointment in the Daily Calendar until the mouse pointer turns into a pair of double-ended arrows in the shape of a cross, as seen in Figure 6-2.**
8. **Click and hold down the left mouse button.**
9. **Drag the appointment to the Date Navigator and drop it on tomorrow's date.**

The Daily Calendar changes to tomorrow's date and the Test appointment appears in the same hour slot on tomorrow's date. It doesn't get much easier than this. Changing the Start time is just as easy.

You can simultaneously move or change multiple appointments by holding the Shift key down, selecting the appointments, and performing the action (move date, change hours, expand duration). Do not let go of the Shift key until you complete the action.

10. **Move the mouse pointer to the left side of the Test appointment until the pointer turns into a cross.**

11. **Click the left mouse button, hold it down, and drag the appointment down and drop it in the 1pm time slot.**

    If you open the appointment form you can see that the start and end times have changed. One last thing you can do here is change the length of the appointment.

12. **Move the mouse pointer over the bottom edge of the appointment until it turns into a double arrow, as seen in Figure 6-3.**

13. **Click the left mouse button, hold it down, drag the bottom of the appointment box down, and drop it on 2:00.**

Using drag and drop, you'll rearrange your schedule in less time than it takes your boss to say no when you ask for 16 weeks of paid vacation. As a matter of fact, it will save you enough time so you can start working on your resume.

Creating other Outlook items from an appointment

Data entry is not exactly a glamorous job. There are plenty of other things you'd rather be doing — hanging out at the coffee machine, listening to your favorite CD, or working on next year's budget.

Finding shortcuts to finish tedious jobs in half the time is what computers are all about. Suppose you create an appointment that includes a list of items you'll need during the appointment. Wouldn't it be great if you could send an e-mail message to your assistant, and ask him to pull the list of items together, without having to reenter everything from the appointment into the e-mail message? Well, it just so happens you can. Outlook allows you to create an e-mail message that contains all the information in an appointment form, simply by dragging and dropping the appointment form onto the Inbox icon in the Outlook bar.

Drag and drop also lets you carry information from an appointment over to an Outlook task, journal entry, contact, or note using the same technique we show you in this section. You learn more about tasks, journal entries, contacts, and notes later in this book. For now, just get a little practice with using appointment information in e-mail.

1. **In the Date Navigator, click tomorrow's date.**

2. **Move the mouse pointer to the left side of the Test appointment until it turns into a cross.**

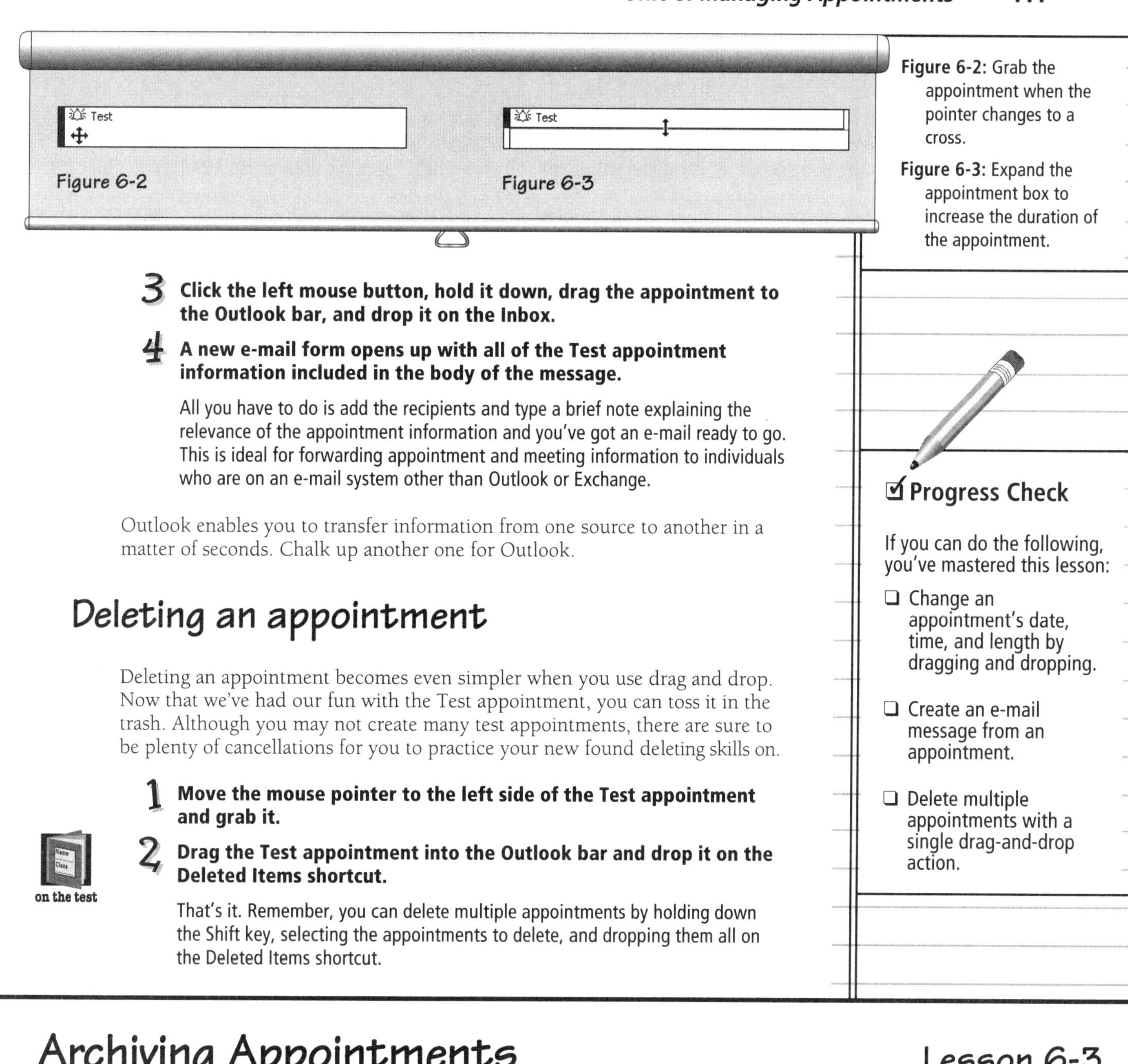

Figure 6-2

Figure 6-3

Figure 6-2: Grab the appointment when the pointer changes to a cross.

Figure 6-3: Expand the appointment box to increase the duration of the appointment.

3. **Click the left mouse button, hold it down, drag the appointment to the Outlook bar, and drop it on the Inbox.**
4. **A new e-mail form opens up with all of the Test appointment information included in the body of the message.**

   All you have to do is add the recipients and type a brief note explaining the relevance of the appointment information and you've got an e-mail ready to go. This is ideal for forwarding appointment and meeting information to individuals who are on an e-mail system other than Outlook or Exchange.

Outlook enables you to transfer information from one source to another in a matter of seconds. Chalk up another one for Outlook.

Deleting an appointment

Deleting an appointment becomes even simpler when you use drag and drop. Now that we've had our fun with the Test appointment, you can toss it in the trash. Although you may not create many test appointments, there are sure to be plenty of cancellations for you to practice your new found deleting skills on.

1. **Move the mouse pointer to the left side of the Test appointment and grab it.**
2. **Drag the Test appointment into the Outlook bar and drop it on the Deleted Items shortcut.**

   That's it. Remember, you can delete multiple appointments by holding down the Shift key, selecting the appointments to delete, and dropping them all on the Deleted Items shortcut.

☑ Progress Check

If you can do the following, you've mastered this lesson:

- ❑ Change an appointment's date, time, and length by dragging and dropping.
- ❑ Create an e-mail message from an appointment.
- ❑ Delete multiple appointments with a single drag-and-drop action.

Archiving Appointments

Lesson 6-3

Most of us maintain a love-hate relationship with our computers. It's ironic that more often than not, the features we love are also the features we hate. Think about the paperless office. Computers were supposed to eliminate the need for printed copy, but because they do such a great job of information storage and retrieval, they make it temptingly easy to create hard copy, and they provide more material to print. The result — more paper than ever, floating around in every office.

archive old information to get it out of the way and save space

The same thing applies to electronic data that we create and store. It's so easy to amass and store megabytes of information that it sometimes become more of a hindrance than a help. That's where *archiving* steps in and lends a hand. Archiving simply means preserving important, but outdated, data in a file separate from the one you use regularly. Copies of your old appointments with Newt and any notes you took could come in handy if you get called before a Senate subcommittee. In addition, archiving lets you free up space and increase the ease and speed with which you access and use the more current information.

archive appointments, e-mail, notes, tasks, contacts, and journal entries

Archiving is not just for appointments. You can use it to save copies of other Outlook items, including e-mail messages, notes, tasks, contacts, and journal entries.

There may come a point when, after a period of substantial activity, the Calendar folder becomes unwieldy and requires archiving. To archive the Calendar folder follow these steps:

1. **Choose File⇨Archive from the Calendar menu bar to open the Archive dialog box as seen in Figure 6-4.**
2. **Select Archive this folder and all subfolders.**
3. **Select the Calendar folder from the folder list.**
4. **In the Archive items older than field, type** 6 months ago.

   You can also type in a date or choose one from the drop-down calendar.
5. **Click OK to carry out the manual archive.**

   Your Calender is archived as soon as you click OK. There's no turning back.

Retrieving archived items

pull up archived information when you need it again

Now that you've got all those valuable bits and pieces of important data stashed in your archive file, how do you get to them when you need to review the information? Actually, it's fairly easy, but it does require a little setup. You have to tell Outlook where the archive file is and what kind of file it is, and how Outlook should interact with it.

Follow these steps so that Outlook can open the archive file and let you look in and use the information as you please:

set up archive file as information service

1. **Choose Tools⇨Services from the menu bar to open the Services dialog box.**

   The Services dialog box contains the various information services installed in Outlook. Information services are groups of settings that enable the sending, receiving and storage of messages and other items, including address books and personal folders. For Outlook to use the archive file, it must first be setup as an information service.
2. **Click Add to open the Add Service to Profile and add the archive file to the list of information services.**

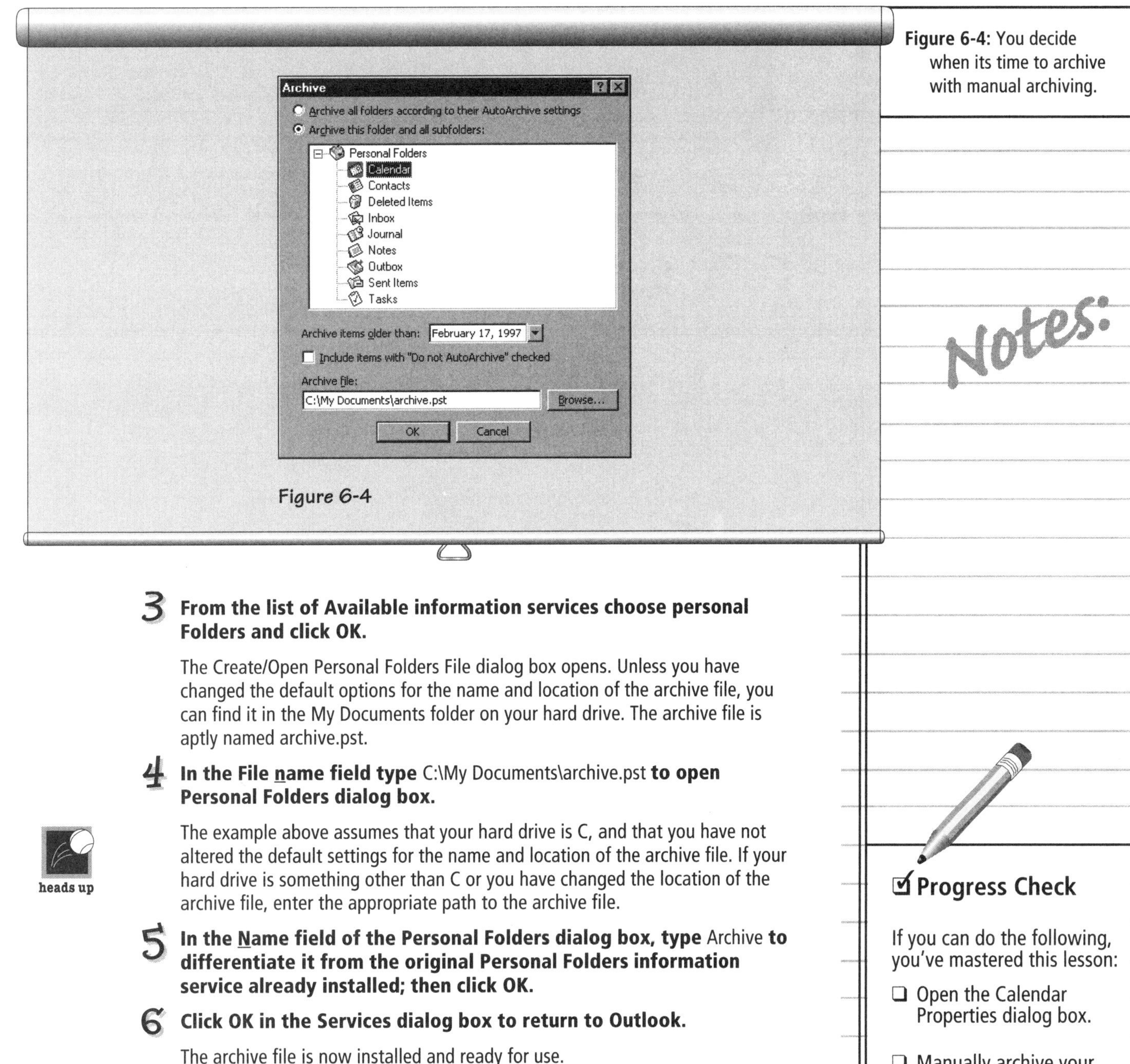

Figure 6-4: You decide when its time to archive with manual archiving.

Notes:

3 From the list of Available information services choose personal Folders and click OK.

The Create/Open Personal Folders File dialog box opens. Unless you have changed the default options for the name and location of the archive file, you can find it in the My Documents folder on your hard drive. The archive file is aptly named archive.pst.

4 In the File name field type C:\My Documents\archive.pst **to open Personal Folders dialog box.**

heads up

The example above assumes that your hard drive is C, and that you have not altered the default settings for the name and location of the archive file. If your hard drive is something other than C or you have changed the location of the archive file, enter the appropriate path to the archive file.

5 In the Name field of the Personal Folders dialog box, type Archive **to differentiate it from the original Personal Folders information service already installed; then click OK.**

6 Click OK in the Services dialog box to return to Outlook.

The archive file is now installed and ready for use.

7 Click the Folder List button in the Calendar toolbar to open the Folder list.

You now see a new folder called Archive. This contains all the folders and items that you have archived up to this point.

8 Click the plus sign to the left of Archive to expand the subfolders.

The subfolders are duplicates of your original personal folders — Calendar, Contacts, and so on — except that they contain only archived items. When you click one of the Archive subfolders, it opens the subfolder. You can then view,

☑ Progress Check

If you can do the following, you've mastered this lesson:

- ❑ Open the Calendar Properties dialog box.
- ❑ Manually archive your appointments.
- ❑ Get to and use your appointments after you archive them.

copy, move, delete and do anything to the archived items within the Archive subfolder that you can do with unarchived items in any of your original Personal Folders.

Now that wasn't so bad, was it? In one lesson you've learned how to preserve your important information and how to restore it when you need it.

Lesson 6-4 Printing the Calendar

printing lets you take your Calendar anywhere

Whether you are on the road a lot or just like to have a hard copy of your schedule to take to meetings, you will undoubtedly want to print some portion of your calendar at one time or another. Outlook provides a wide array of printing options.

Follow these steps to print out a calendar for a little light reading at the dentist's office. It's one of the few times you'll wish you were back at work.

on the test

1. **Press Ctrl+P or choose File⇨Print to open the Print dialog box.**
2. **Select the correct printer from the Name drop-down list.**

   Outlook uses the default printer from your Windows 95 setup, so you shouldn't have to change this setting unless you have more than one printer and wish to use one other than the default.
3. **Scroll down the Print style list and click Tri-fold Style.**

   As you can see, you have four choices of print styles, Daily, Weekly, Monthly and Tri-fold. Daily, Weekly, and Monthly are self-explanatory. Tri-fold creates a printed calendar that resembles an 8 1/2 by 11-inch brochure folded into thirds, with your choice of what information appears on each of the thirds (see Figure 6-5). If you have an appointment highlighted you also receive a fifth choice, Memo Style.
4. **Click the Page Setup button to open the Page Setup dialog box.**

   Page Setup...

   Page Setup button

   The default setup for the Tri-fold style is the Daily Calendar in the left section, the TaskPad in the center, and the Weekly Calendar in the right section.
5. **Click the Print Preview button to see what the Tri-fold style looks like with the default settings.**

   Print Preview

   Print Preview button

   Because we are only dealing with appointments and not tasks so far, remove the TaskPad and make the printout all calendars. (Don't worry — you learn more about tasks later in the book.)
6. **Click the Page Setup button in the menu bar to return to the Page Setup dialog box.**
7. **Click the down arrow on the right side of the Middle section field to open the drop-down list, and select Weekly Calendar.**
8. **From the Right section drop-down list select Monthly Calendar.**

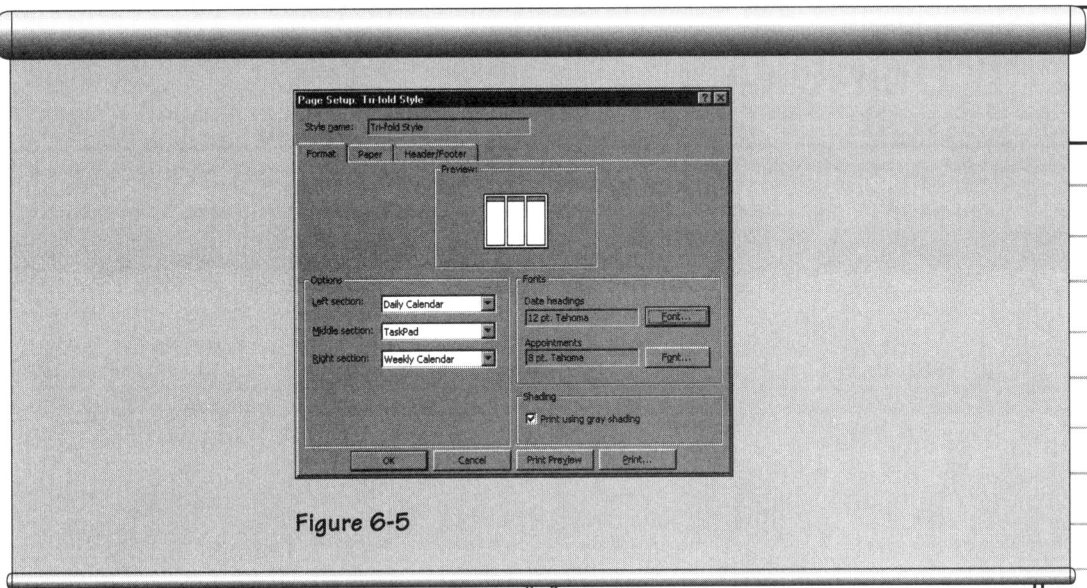

Figure 6-5: The Tri-fold print style offers the most bang for your buck.

Notes:

9 **Click the Print Preview button.**

Note that the TaskPad is gone, the Weekly Calendar has moved to the middle section, and the Monthly Calendar has been added to the right section.

10 **Click the Print button to return to the opening Print dialog box.**

heads up

Be advised that any changes you make to the Page Setup of any style automatically become the new default for that style, unless you click the Cancel button. If you make changes and click any button other than Cancel, Outlook does not ask you if you want to save the changes, it merely saves them.

Print button

Another quirk of the print feature is that once you go to Print Preview and return to Page Setup, the Cancel button no longer returns you to the original Print dialog box, but rather dumps you out of Print and back into the Calendar window.

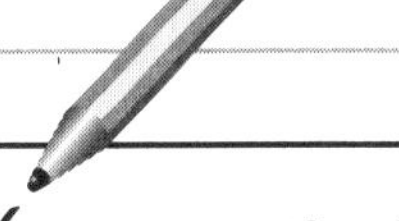

11 **Tab twice to the Print range Start field and type** today.

12 **Tab to the End field and type** 1 week.

Because you specified a one-week time frame, any appointments that fall within that date range will appear on at least two (Weekly and Monthly), and possibly all three of the calendars printed on the Tri-fold.

13 **Click OK to print the calendar.**

If you use a Franklin or Day-Timer planner you'll be pleased to know that you can print your calendar in that format, and even on the forms that can be used with those planners.

Congratulations, you've survived another unit. By this point it should be clear to you that getting organized with Outlook is well within your reach. You've mastered the two major components, e-mail and appointments. After you finish the Quiz and the Exercise, you'll be ready to tackle the rest without even breaking a sweat.

☑ Progress Check

If you can do the following, you've mastered this lesson:

- ❑ Open the Print dialog box.
- ❑ Change the Page Setup for the Tri-fold style.
- ❑ Preview your job before printing.
- ❑ Print the Calendar.

Unit 6 Quiz

Notes:

1. **How do you find an existing appointment if you forget the start date?**

   A. Get on your hands and knees and look under the desk.

   B. Put up a reward.

   C. Ask your assistant (hey, that's cheating!).

   D. Outlook's Find Items feature.

   E. Call the Psychic Hotline.

2. **How do you retrieve a deleted appointment?**

   A. With a string and some chewing gum.

   B. I'm not putting my hand in there!

   C. Whistle repeatedly while clapping your hand against your thigh.

   D. Open the Deleted Items folder, highlight the deleted item, and move it back to the Calendar folder by pressing Ctrl+Shift+V.

   E. If you don't mind picking through the bag, a high-powered vacuum cleaner ought to do the trick.

3. **What is drag and drop?**

   A. A little bar down on Tenth Street.

   B. What you do at the end of a long day.

   C. A quick and easy way to change appointment start dates and times.

   D. Okay, I give up.

   E. A game you play with people you don't like.

4. **Why do you archive appointments?**

   A. For posterity.

   B. I don't know what else to do with them.

   C. To keep a backup copy in case it's ever needed.

   D. Because you enjoy it.

   E. Because your neighbor does it.

5. **How do you open the Print dialog box?**

   A. Try a crowbar.

   B. It's too pretty to open.

   C. Press Ctrl+P.

   D. Remove the screws first and then lift the top off.

   E. Tell your spouse not to open it under any circumstances.

Unit 6 Exercise

1. Retrieve the Test appointment that you deleted in Lesson 6-2.
2. Add location information and notes to the Test appointment.
3. Move the newly revived Test appointment to next Tuesday using drag and drop.
4. Print a Tri-fold copy of your calendar and include the TaskPad in the middle section.

Unit 7

Tracking Tasks

Objectives for This Unit

- ✓ Understanding tasks
- ✓ Entering tasks
- ✓ Creating recurring tasks
- ✓ Linking tasks for the same project
- ✓ Handling completed tasks

Prerequisites

- Opening Outlook (Lesson 1-1)
- Using the Outlook bar (Lesson 1-1)
- Changing the view in the Calendar window (Lesson 5-6)

In Outlook, a *task* means exactly what it meant when your mother made you perform tasks around the house — an errand, a chore, or any other kind of duty that's fallen on your shoulders. Today, when you have a task to perform it's probably something related to work, and with any luck it's possible to delegate some of the details involved in the task.

task = stuff you have to do

Outlook has a whole set of functions designed to help you track your tasks. In fact, you can use Outlook to track tasks that aren't even business-related. If you have a personal task to perform (maybe something you have to do for your mother; old habits die hard), Outlook still makes everything easy to keep track of.

Some tasks are more complicated than others. For example, being responsible for coordinating a major event is more complicated than writing a one-page report. In this unit we'll discuss tasks that are simple one-step procedures and also learn how to deal with major tasks, which involves tracking all the individual tasks involved in a large project and connecting them.

track simple and complicated tasks with Outlook

Lesson 7-1

Recording a Task

Notes:

Outlook provides two ways to record a task: using the Task window in the Tasks folder and using the Calendar window in the Calendar folder.

For this exercise, you enter two tasks into Outlook. The first task (which you were told about via e-mail) is to make copies of all the correspondence with the Unicorn Uniform company and send it to the lawyer for your own company. The other task facing you is the need to go through all your personal bank statements for the past five years and find every canceled check that was written when you added that family room (you're selling the house and your accountant says you have to prove the new cost basis for the house to avoid taxes on the profits).

Entering a task in the Task window

When you receive an assignment, usually you just have to create a record of it, mostly to remind yourself that the assignment has to be completed.

Of course, it also doesn't hurt to have a long list of completed assignments just to prove to yourself (or others) how much work you do outside the day-to-day chores that are part of your job description.

To enter a task into the Tasks window, follow these steps:

1. **Open Outlook and click the Outlook button on the Outlook bar.**

   This displays the icons for the Outlook functions (in case the Outlook bar is displaying the icons for the Mail functions).

Tasks icon

2. **Click the Tasks icon to move to the Tasks folder.**

   The Tasks window appears (see Figure 7-1) . Notice that the top listing in the task list part of the window isn't a task, it's a note that says "Click here to add a new Task."

3. **Click the top line of the list section of the window, which clears the text and presents a blank line. Type** Unicorn correspondence.

4. **Press Enter.**

   The task appears magically on the TaskPad.

Entering a task in the Calendar window

If you're working in the Calendar window and enter an appointment that requires a task (or receive a telephone call that assigns you a task), you don't have to move to the Tasks folder to enter it. You can enter the task directly into the TaskPad on the Calendar window.

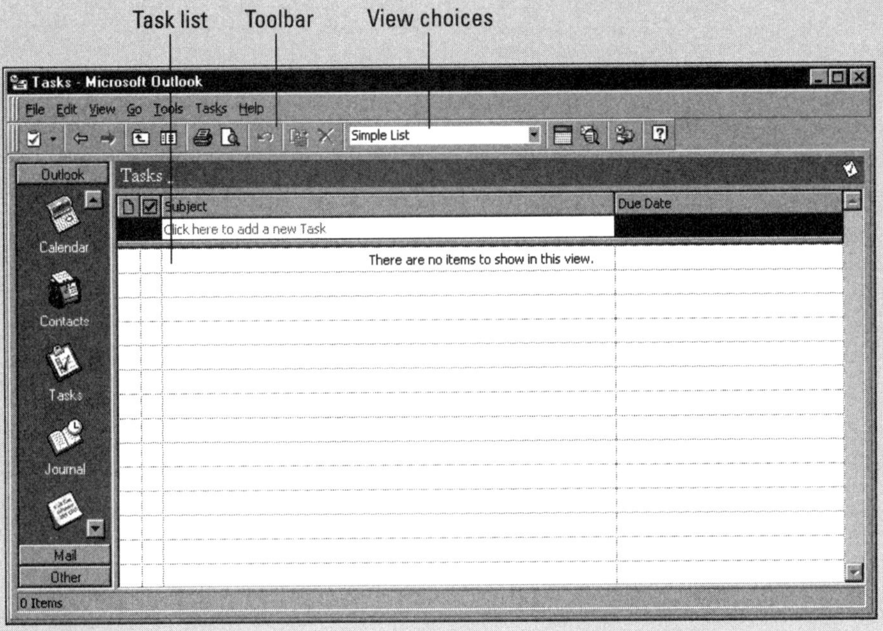

Task list Toolbar View choices

Figure 7-1

Figure 7-1: The Tasks window opens, displaying a list of tasks.

Because you're not currently working in the Calendar at the moment, you'll have to go there to follow along with this exercise. So click the Calendar icon in the Outlook bar to move to the Calendar folder (if you were working in the Calendar you wouldn't have to do this, of course). Now you're ready to enter the canceled checks task.

Calendar icon

To enter a task from the Calendar window, follow these steps:

1. **If you're using the Month view in the Calendar window, switch to either the Week or Day view. (The TaskPad doesn't appear in the Month view of the Calendar window.)**
2. **Click the top line on the TaskPad where it says "Click here to add a new Task".**
3. **Enter the task by typing** Canceled checks.
4. **Press Enter to record the task.**

   The task appears on the TaskPad (see Figure 7-2).

When you return to the Tasks window, the new task appears on the task list. The two Outlook elements (the Tasks window and the TaskPad on the Calendar window) are connected, and information is displayed in both places. This is nagging at its best.

☑ Progress Check

If you can do the following, you've mastered this lesson:

- ❑ Open the Tasks folder.
- ❑ Enter a task while working in the Tasks window.
- ❑ Enter a task while working in the Calendar window.

Figure 7-2: You can add a task to your Tasks folder from the Calendar window.

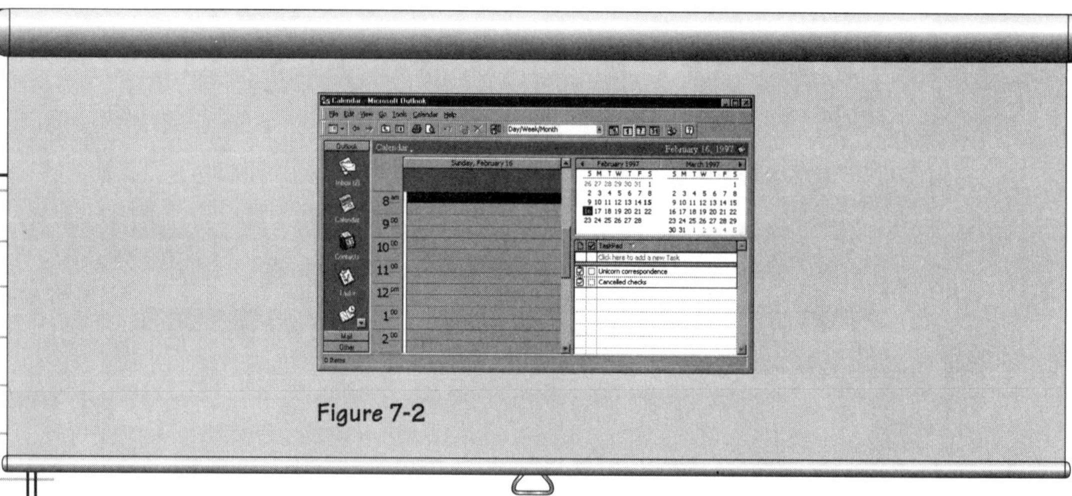

Figure 7-2

Lesson 7-2

Entering Details about a Task

Notes:

Sometimes a task is more than a reminder or an item on a To Do list. There might be a due date or you might have to keep track of how much of the task has been completed by a given date. Outlook provides a way to enter details about a task so that you can keep track of its status.

For this exercise, you'll enter the information for a task you've been assigned that requires completion by a specific date. You have to collect the name, sex, age, and holiday wish list for every child of the employees in the company. Mr. Scrooge, the vice president for human resources, has decided to give gifts to the employees' children this year in addition to the annual bonus (there's a story going round that he had this idea as a result of a dream, but that's just a rumor). In order to make sure that everything goes smoothly, your report is due by November 14. Mr. Scrooge is a fussbudget and we all know that somewhere around October 15, he'll demand to know how much of the information you've managed to collect. Because today is October 1, you'd better get moving, so follow these steps:

New Task button

1. **Make sure you're working in the Tasks window.**
2. **Press Ctrl+N or click the New Task button on the toolbar to open a new Task window.**

   The new Task window appears, and your cursor is waiting in the Subject field (see Figure 7-3).
3. **You have to enter a title for this task in the Subject field, so type** gifts.
4. **Press Tab to move to the next field, Due date.**

   move to field by clicking it instead of using Tab key
5. **Because this task has a due date, click the Due radio button. Then click the arrow to the right of the date field and click November 14 on the calendar. Use the left (back) and right (forward) arrows on the calendar to move to November.**

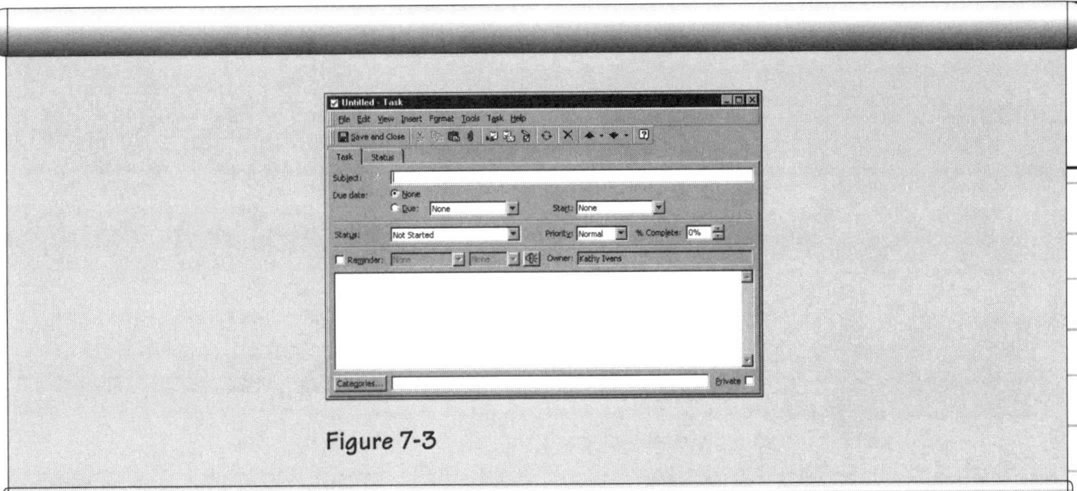

Figure 7-3

Figure 7-3: The new Task window has fields for the important details about a new task.

radio button = choose one of two or more options

6 **Press the Tab key to move to the Start field. Click the arrow to the right of the field to see a calendar with today's date highlighted. Move through the months to get to October and select October 1 as the start date.**

7 **In the Status field, the default choice of Not Started is accurate, so you can skip it and move on.**

You should, however, click the arrow to the right of the field to learn what the choices are.

move to field by pressing Alt+ underlined letter on field name (aka hot key)

8 **The Priority field offers three choices: Low, Normal, and High. The default, Normal, seems appropriate.**

Using a priority option of high or low for tasks is useful because you can sort tasks by priority in the Tasks window. That way, when your task list becomes long, you get an instant clue about what to work on first.

on the test

9 **Skip the % Complete field and move on to the Reminder field. Schedule a reminder by selecting the Reminder check box.**

By default, the reminder is scheduled for 8:00 AM on the due date. I don't know about you, but for me this is much too late to be reminded.

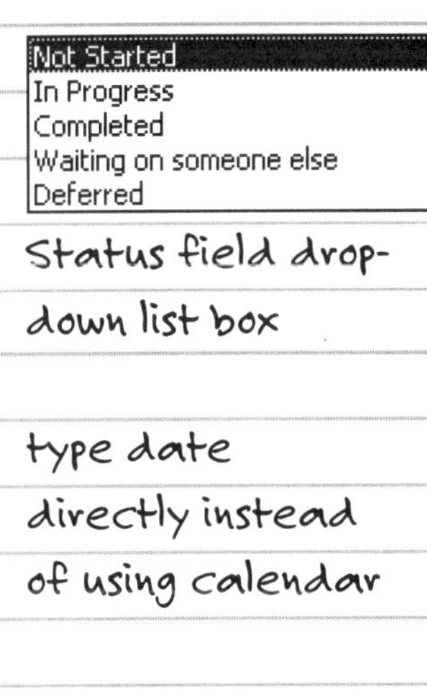

Status field drop-down list box

10 **Click the arrow to the right of the Reminder field and select a new (earlier) date. Use the left arrow to move back to October and then select October 14 (the day before you think you'll need to issue an interim report). You can also type a date directly into the Reminder field instead of using the calendar.**

type date directly instead of using calendar

11 **Click the Reminder button to configure the reminder.**

The reminder itself is a pop-up message that appears on your screen at the appointed date and time. To draw your attention to the message, Outlook also plays a sound. You can make the following choices about the sound:

- Change the sound that plays by clicking the Browse button and selecting a different sound file (any file that has an extension of .wav).

Figure 7-4: Now the Task form has all the details you need to begin working on this task.

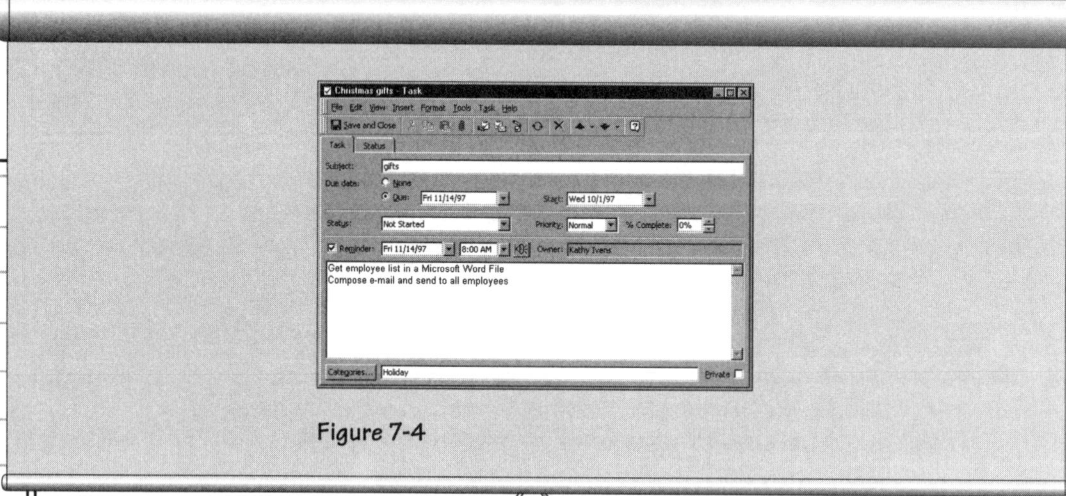

Figure 7-4

Notes:

- Click the check mark box to remove the check mark and deselect the sound altogether.
- Choose Cancel to leave things the way they are.

If you need to brush up on setting and working with reminders, look at Lesson 5-2.

Save and Close button

12 **Press Tab to move to the text section of the Task form, where you can enter notes, comments, or reminders to yourself about this task. Type** Get employee list in a Microsoft Word file**. Press Enter to move to the next line. Type** Compose e-mail and send to all employees**.**

The text section is like a mini word processor. You can use the toolbar at the top of the window to cut, copy, and paste text just as you can in your word processor. You can use the menu bar to format text. You can also click the right mouse button while you are working in this section to choose text-manipulation options, such as copy and paste.

13 **Click the Categories button at the bottom of the window. When the list of categories appears, click Holiday.**

Using categories enables you to sort your tasks by category in the Tasks list window. If you get any additional tasks in the same category, chances are they'll be connected (Mr. Scrooge may assign you the task of shopping for the gifts).

Your task and the details about it are entered, and you're finished with the task (see Figure 7-4).

14 **Click the Save and Close button on the toolbar to complete the entry of this task.**

As you begin working on the individual chores you need to accomplish, you can update the task file. We'll cover the procedures for that later in this unit.

☑ Progress Check

If you can do the following, you've mastered this lesson:

- ❑ Open a Task window.
- ❑ Enter information about due dates and start dates.
- ❑ Set a reminder.
- ❑ Enter comments in a Task window.
- ❑ Choose a category for a task.

Creating a Recurring Task

Lesson 7-3

on the test

The vice president in charge of office morale, Johnny B. Jolly, just sent you e-mail to tell you that he's scheduling a monthly luncheon in his office for department heads on the third Monday of every month, and you're in charge of collecting the monthly list of attendees (at least you don't have to do the cooking or the washing up). Every month the same items will need your attention.

recurring task = something you do over and over

When a task occurs over and over, it's called a *recurring task*. Luckily, Outlook has a feature that makes recurring tasks easy to enter. Did you think you'd have to go through the task list, entering each monthly date one at time? Think again!

To create a recurring task, start in the Tasks window and follow these steps:

1. **Press Ctrl+N to open a new Task form.**
2. **In the Subject field type** Monthly luncheon.
3. **Click the Recurrence button on the toolbar.**

   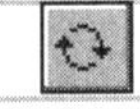
   Recurrence button

   The Task Recurrence dialog box appears (see Figure 7-5); Outlook has preconfigured it based on today's date. Because today's date has no bearing on this task (you'll find it usually works that way), you need to fill in the fields with the correct information.
4. **Select Monthly in the Recurrence pattern portion of the dialog box.**

   Note that when you change the Recurrence interval, the rest of the options in the Recurrence pattern section of the dialog box change to match the interval.

   Because this luncheon isn't scheduled for a particular date in every month, but rather for a particular day (Monday), you need to tell Outlook that.
5. **Click the arrow next to the first field in the option and select Third, then click the arrow in the next field and select Monday. The last field is correct because it assumes that this task will recur every month.**

   If this were a bimonthly event you would change the last field in the row to 2.
6. **Skip the Regenerate new task option.**

   heads up

   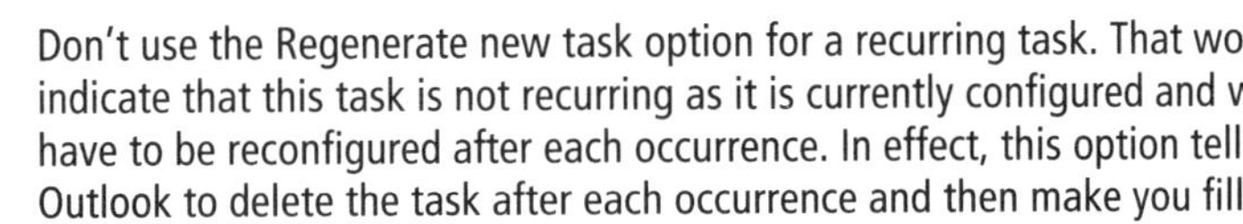

   Don't use the Regenerate new task option for a recurring task. That would indicate that this task is not recurring as it is currently configured and would have to be reconfigured after each occurrence. In effect, this option tells Outlook to delete the task after each occurrence and then make you fill in the configuration all over again. That's a big bunch of trouble.

   don't use the Regenerate new task option
7. **In the Range of recurrence section, enter the first luncheon date for this event.**

   Choose the third Monday of next month for this exercise — we won't give you a specific date to fill in because there's no way to know when you're reading this.

Figure 7-5: Replace the guesswork with the correct information in the Task Recurrence dialog box.

Figure 7-6: Everything is set and this is now a third-Monday-of-the-month event.

Figure 7-7: The task is set up as a recurring task, and the due date automatically matches the information from the recurring task configuration.

Notes:

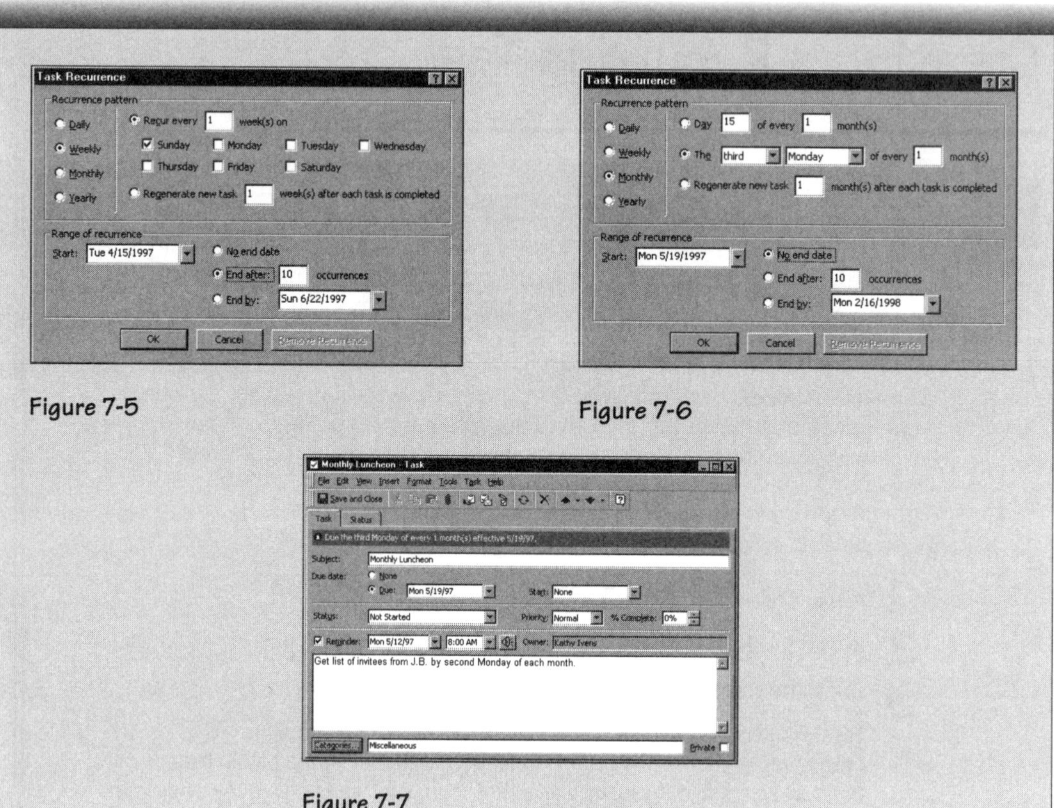

Figure 7-5

Figure 7-6

Figure 7-7

8 Choose No end date because this is not a task with a finite life span.

Even though you can see data in the other two options in the end date section, it's meaningless because the options themselves aren't selected. If this were a recurring event that ceased after a certain number of occurrences, you would select that option and then enter the right information.

You've said everything you want to say about this recurring task, and now it should look similar to Figure 7-6.

9 Choose OK to make the recurrence information part of the task.

The Task Recurrence dialog box closes and the original Task form appears. There's a note indicating its recurrence pattern above the Subject field (see Figure 7-7).

10 Change the Reminder field to one week before the event so you have plenty of notice and can get any preliminary work done. Click the arrow to select that date, or enter the date into the Reminder field directly.

If you wish, configure the sound reminder as you learned to in Lesson 5-2.

11 **In the text box, type** Get list of invitees from J.B. by second Monday of each month.

12 **Click the Categories button to see the list and then select Miscellaneous. Click OK to close the list.**

13 **Click the Save and Close button on the toolbar to put the task into your Outlook Tasks window.**

The recurring task feature in Outlook is a great time saver. Think about all the things you need to do every month, and it won't take long for you to think up plenty of uses for this feature.

☑ Progress Check

If you can do the following, you've mastered this lesson:

- ❑ Open the Recurrence dialog box.
- ❑ Enter details about a recurring task.

Editing Tasks

Lesson 7-4

You may come across two reasons to edit a task. The first, which is obvious, is that something in the data has changed: perhaps the due date has moved or you've thought of an additional chore you want to make note of in the text box. The second reason is to put detailed data into a task you entered onto the task list of the Tasks window or the Calendar window. When you entered those tasks (in Lesson 7-1) you just named them. Sometimes you'll find it's necessary to add a bit more information to a task entered in this manner.

To edit the information about a task, follow these steps:

1 **Be sure you're in the task list of the Tasks window.**

2 **Click the listing for the task named Canceled checks to highlight it and then press Ctrl+O to open it, or place your mouse pointer on the listing and double-click. You can also highlight a task and then choose File⇨Open to open it.**

heads up

When you're pointing at a task listing in preparation for opening it, be careful not to let your mouse pointer land on the check box in the second column. That's the column you use to indicate that a task has been completed (we'll discuss that later in this unit). Anywhere else on the line that holds the listing is safe for double-clicking.

3 **Click the Categories button to display a list of descriptive choices. Select Personal as the category and then click OK to close the categories list.**

4 **Click the box next to the Private field to make this a private task (see Figure 7-7).**

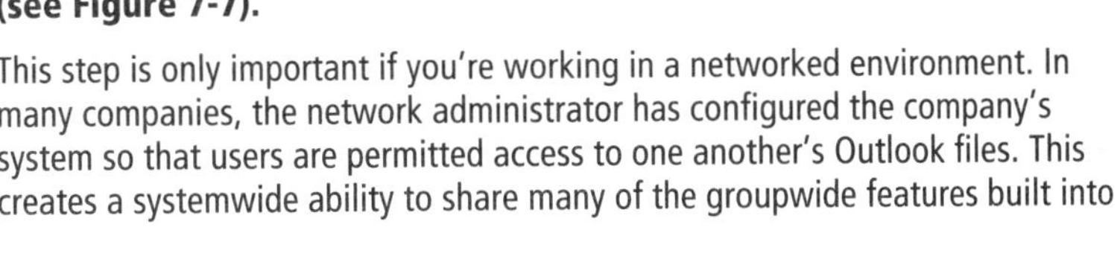

This step is only important if you're working in a networked environment. In many companies, the network administrator has configured the company's system so that users are permitted access to one another's Outlook files. This creates a systemwide ability to share many of the groupwide features built into

Figure 7-8: This task is personal and private; you know it, and now Outlook knows it.

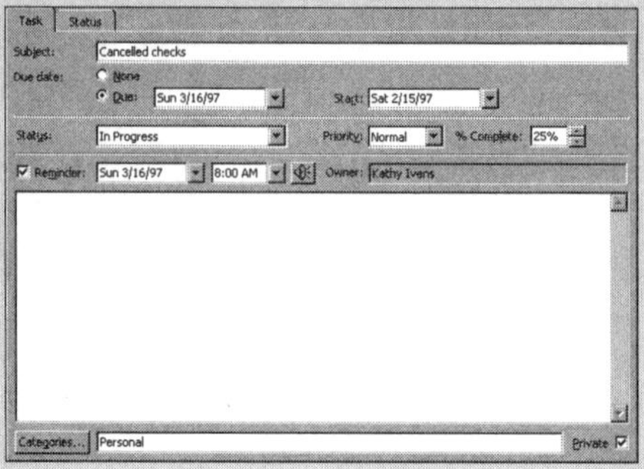

Figure 7-8

Outlook. When the Tasks folder is shared, you can share the work by assigning chores to other users and letting them access the task's information file to update the Task window as they complete their work.

Making a task private means that when someone else connects to your computer from his or her computer, that task is invisible. It appears on the task list when *you* look at it, but not if it's viewed from a connected computer.

5 **Click the Save and Close button on the toolbar.**

The changes you made are saved and are now part of the task's data (see Figure 7-8).

If you change your mind about the edits, press Alt+F4 to close the file without saving the changes. Click No when Outlook asks if you want to save changes.

☑ Progress Check

If you can do the following, you've mastered this lesson:

- ❑ Open an existing task.
- ❑ Add or change data in an existing task.
- ❑ Make a task private.

You can make changes to the task information for any task, whether it has no detailed information (perhaps because you originally created it from the Calendar folder TaskPad, as in this exercise) or it has a great deal of original information, some of which has changed. As you work with tasks, you'll probably find that the most common change you'll have to make is the due date.

Lesson 7-5 Changing Recurring Tasks

If the information about a recurring task changes, you can make those changes easily. Several scenarios could occur, and we'll cover them in this lesson:

- The day or date for the recurring task changes.
- A recurring task that had no end date now has one.
- A recurring task that had an end date now has a different one.
- A recurring task is canceled and becomes a one-time task.
- You need to skip one occurrence of a recurring task.

Changing the recurrence information

Mr. Jolly has sent you e-mail outlining the changes he wants to make to the monthly luncheons. With the list in front of you, implement his changes by following these steps:

1. **Open the Monthly luncheon recurring task.**
2. **Click the Recurrence button on the toolbar to display the Task Recurrence dialog box.**
3. **To change the recurrence pattern, move to the Day field (it currently says Monday) and enter Tuesday, or click the arrow and select Tuesday from the drop-down list.**
4. **To change the frequency from every month to every other month, change the 1 in the "every month" box to a 2.**
5. **Change the Start to the third Tuesday of next month.**
6. **Click OK to save the changes in the recurrence pattern and return to the Task window.**
7. **The information in the Task window reflects the changes you made. Click Save and Close to record the changes.**

Other changes in the recurrence pattern or the start date are just as easy to accomplish. You can change a monthly task to a weekly one, change a monthly task recurrence pattern from a day of the week to a date, or make any other changes that become necessary. You can change the start date, change an existing end date, or add an end date where there wasn't one.

Canceling future recurrences

When you cancel a recurring task, you change it into a one-time task. This is not the same as deleting the task (we discuss deleting tasks later in this unit). Follow these steps to cancel future recurrences of a task:

1. **From the Tasks window, open the recurring task you want to change (Monthly Luncheon).**
2. **Click the Recurrence button on the toolbar to display the Task Recurrence dialog box.**
3. **To change a task from a recurring task to a one-time task, click the Remove Recurrence radio button.**

   The Task Recurrence dialog box closes and you return to the Task window. The task is a one-time task with a due date that matches the first occurrence date of its original recurring status. You have several options, depending on the situation:

   - If the date for this task is still correct, you don't need to do anything.
   - If the date for the task has changed, move to the Due field and change the date (don't forget to change the Reminder information, too).

Notes:

4 **In this case, because you don't really want to destroy the recurring nature of the Monthly Luncheon task, don't change anything.**

In fact, click the Recurrence button again, and when the dialog box opens you'll find that your original recurrence configuration information is still there. Click OK to put it all back now that you've seen the results.

Remember, when you do this on your real tasks, you won't take Step 4.

5 **Click Save and Close to record your changes.**

When you really make the changes, the task appears on your Tasks window's task list as a regular, one-time task. Incidentally, even though you put everything back the way it was for this exercise, you still have to click Save and Close. Once any keystrokes have been entered, there has been a change, and you have to save the change even if there is a second change reversing the original one. That's just the way software works.

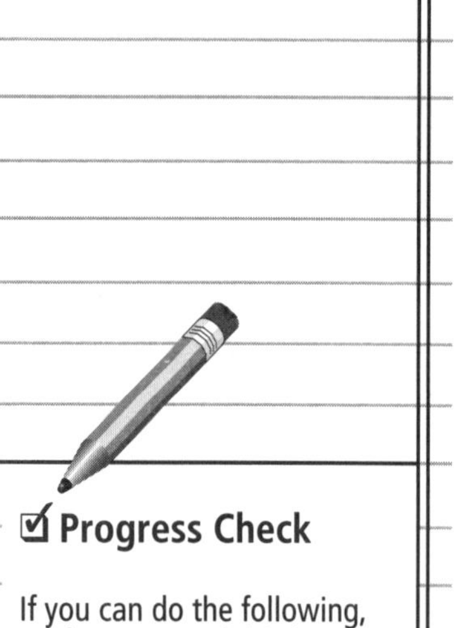

☑ Progress Check

If you can do the following, you've mastered this lesson:

- ❑ Open the Task Recurrence dialog box for a recurring task and make changes to any field.
- ❑ Change a recurring task to a one-time task.
- ❑ Configure a recurring task to skip the next scheduled occurrence.

Skipping an occurrence

If a regularly scheduled occurrence of a task has to be canceled, that's a one-time-only change and after the missing occurrence, things will proceed normally. To tell Outlook to skip the next occurrence of a task, follow these steps:

1 **Open the recurring task Monthly Luncheon.**

2 **Choose Task⇨Skip Occurrence from the toolbar.**

The Task window information changes to a due date reflecting the fact that the next occurrence is no longer expected.

3 **Click Save and Close to record the changes.**

If the recurring task has a specific number of occurrences in its configuration, the skipped occurrence counts as an occurrence. If you have to make up the missed occurrence, open the Task Recurrence dialog box and increase the number of occurrences by one.

Lesson 7-6 Charting the Progress of a Task

As you work on a task and accomplish some of the chores and goals, you have to tell Outlook about your accomplishments. Then you can give a coherent and accurate report about the status of the task.

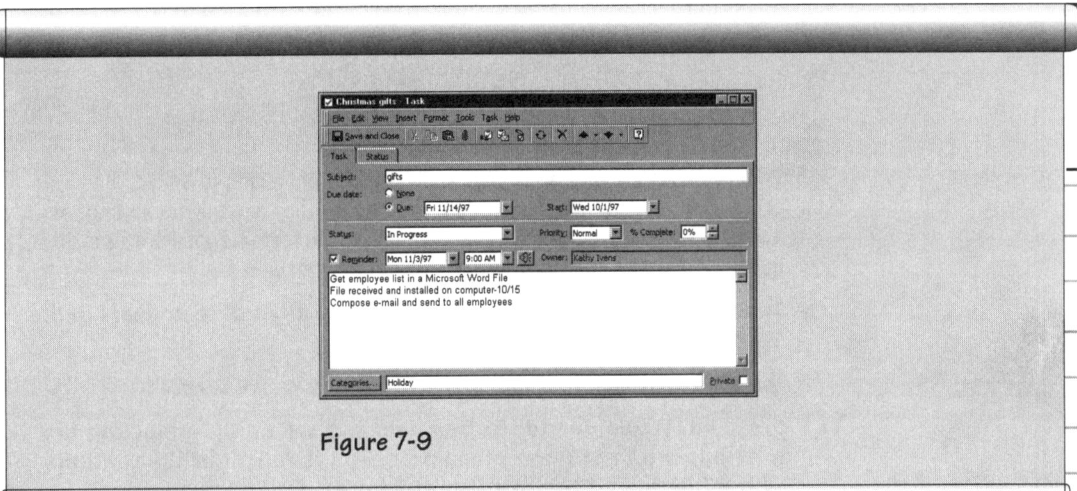

Figure 7-9

Figure 7-9: If anyone asks, you can report your progress by peeking at the Task window.

Updating tasks is really a form of editing a task (you learned about that in Lesson 7-4). However, there are two major differences: You get to use some of the fields that are concerned only with the completion of the task; and it feels better to edit a task in order to note progress than it does to make changes in the configuration. There's nothing like the feeling of accomplishment — and even more important, tracking progress on a very large and complicated task means that you can begin to believe there's a light at the end of the tunnel.

For this exercise, we'll update the status of the holiday gifts recurring task to indicate that you've been working on this task. We'll also update the progress for the Canceled checks task.

To begin updating these tasks, follow these steps:

1. **Open the gifts task.**
2. **Click the arrow to the right of the Status field and select In Progress.**

   Now this task is underway, which is a major form of progress.
3. **Move to the text box and click at the end of the first line to place the insertion point there. Then press Enter to insert a new line.**
4. **Type** File received and installed on computer 10/15**.**

   It's the middle of October and you have the file you'd made a note about when you created the task (the list of employees), so that chore is completed. Good going!
5. **Move to the Reminder field and set a reminder for 11/3/97. Set the time of the reminder for 9:00 AM.**

   Your notes say that your next job is to compose the e-mail you want to send to employees. You should probably do that in a few weeks, so this reminder is for that chore.
6. **Your progress changes for this task are finished (see Figure 7-9). Click Save and Close to record them.**

Not Started
In Progress
Completed
Waiting on someone else
Deferred

choices for the Status field

Notes:

7. **Open the Canceled checks task.**

8. **Press Alt+R to move to Start field.**

   When you use the Alt+*underlined letter* method of moving to a field, any contents in the field are highlighted. That means they're ready for editing. As soon as you enter your first keystroke, the original text disappears. This is a quick way to replace existing text with your new text.

9. **Type** yesterday **and then press Enter. Yesterday's date appears in the Start field.**

   Outlook understands the terms *yesterday, tomorrow, next week.*

10. **Press Alt+D to move to the Due field and select it (deselecting the previous choice of None), then press Tab to highlight the contents of the Due field. Type** next month **and press Enter.**

    When you entered a start date, the Due field automatically changed from None to the start date you just entered. You can't have a start date with no due date. The decision to use a due date of next month is arbitrary in this case, but it seems to be good timing. When there's no explicit due date — sometimes you just have to lie.

11. **Move to the Status field and change the status to In Progress.**

12. **Move to the text box and type** 1992 completed.

13. **Move to the % Complete field and change the value to 25.**

    Because you've completed one of the five years you have to investigate, you're 25 percent of the way there. You can use the arrow next to the value field to display the available choices (25, 50, 75, 100) or enter the value directly into the field. If you're editing a task that is at 20 percent completion, you must enter the value directly into the field because there's no matching choice.

14. **Click the Status tab on the Task window to move to the status page.**

    The Status tab can track a variety of items as the task progresses. You can track mileage and billable expenses and keep track of the contacts and companies you interacted with as you worked on the task. In this case we're going to track the number of hours the task took.

15. **In the Total work field type** 50 hours**, which is the total number of hours you expect to spend finishing this task. Press Tab to move to the Actual work field and type** 12 hours **to indicate the time you've spent on the task so far. Press Enter.**

    As soon as you press Tab or Enter, Outlook changes your hours into days (see Figure 7-10).

16. **Your update is complete, so click Save and Close to make the changes permanent.**

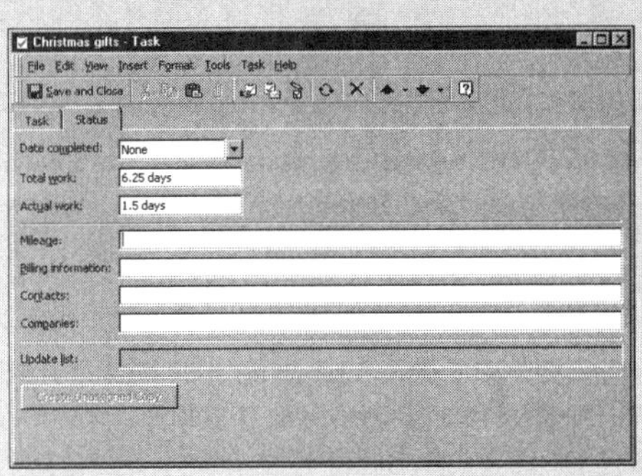

Figure 7-10

Figure 7-10: Use the Status tab of the Task window to track time, money, and contacts.

Wow, not only did you get work done, but you recorded that fact on a computer. That makes it incredibly official, especially for those folks who think that anything that comes from a computer is absolute fact. You have one of those famous, important paper trails. Sometimes you just have to go along with corporate mentality. And, besides that, it's nice to know that you don't have to rely on your memory to give a report of a task's status.

Defining days and weeks

You can establish your own criteria for the way the calculation works when Outlook changes hours into days. To do this, follow these steps:

1. **Choose Tools⇨Options from the menu bar to display the Options dialog box.**
2. **Go to the Tasks/Notes tab of the dialog box.**
3. **In the Task working hours section of the dialog box, make any necessary changes to Hours per day (the default is 8) or Hours per week (the default is 40).**
4. **Click OK to save any changes.**

This changes the default calculation for all the tasks you work on in Outlook.

☑ Progress Check

If you can do the following, you've mastered this lesson:

- ❑ Indicate that the work on a task has been started.
- ❑ Reset reminders.
- ❑ Update the status of a project.
- ❑ Enter the estimated time for completing a task.
- ❑ Enter the time spent on a task in progress.

Recess

You've done so much work in so many different areas of Outlook Tasks that your brain probably hurts. Go get a soda and some chips or pretzels. Put your feet up. Gossip with the person in the next office. When you come back, there's more to learn, but all of it is fun and interesting. Okay, most of it is fun and interesting.

Lesson 7-7 Tracking Tasks as Projects

Some tasks are very large and involve a lot of steps. When you begin working on one of these, you realize very quickly what the limitations are. For instance, if a task involves three or four major components, you could make notes to yourself in the text portion of the Task form about each component — what's finished, what's not started yet, what's partially completed (and when), and so on.

heads up

One caveat of this approach is that if someone asks you for a detailed report on the status of the task, you'll have to spend a lot of time reading those notes and putting the information together as a report.

categories track parts of a multi-part task

There's an easier way to track the progress of multipart tasks (like you didn't know we'd say that). You can create a project by making each component of the project a task and then connecting all those tasks. Don't panic — you don't have to learn about another Outlook feature, and you don't have to learn another set of keystrokes that work in a different Outlook window. There's no special part of Outlook called Projects — you can do everything you have to do by using the skills you already have. Here's a hint: You accomplish this amazing feat with categories, and it's the categories that provide the connection between the tasks.

Pretend that your company is developing a new product. It's a big secret, so it's called Secret Product (your marketing department needs a creativity infusion). You have to track the progress of the Secret Product, involving research, marketing, sales, finance, manufacturing, and personnel. As usual, each department head wants specific reports on how it's going for his or her department. And when you hear the phrase "I want a report," you know that creating a task is the only way to track the information. But eventually, somebody will want a comprehensive, total report, so you have to develop a way to tie all the individual tasks together.

Creating a category

The first step is to create the first task involved in completing this project. Then you'll create a category for that task and you'll use the same category for every task you create for this project. Start by taking these steps:

1. **Starting in the Tasks window, press Ctrl+N to create a new task.**
2. **In the Subject field, type** Research-SP.
3. **Fill out fields as follows: Due date is** 1 year from today**; Start date is** today**; Status is** In Progress.

   Remember you can type in text and Outlook interprets the dates for you.
4. **Click the Categories button.**
5. **When the Categories list appears, click in the "Item(s) belong to these categories:" text box. Then type** Secret Product **(see Figure 7-11).**

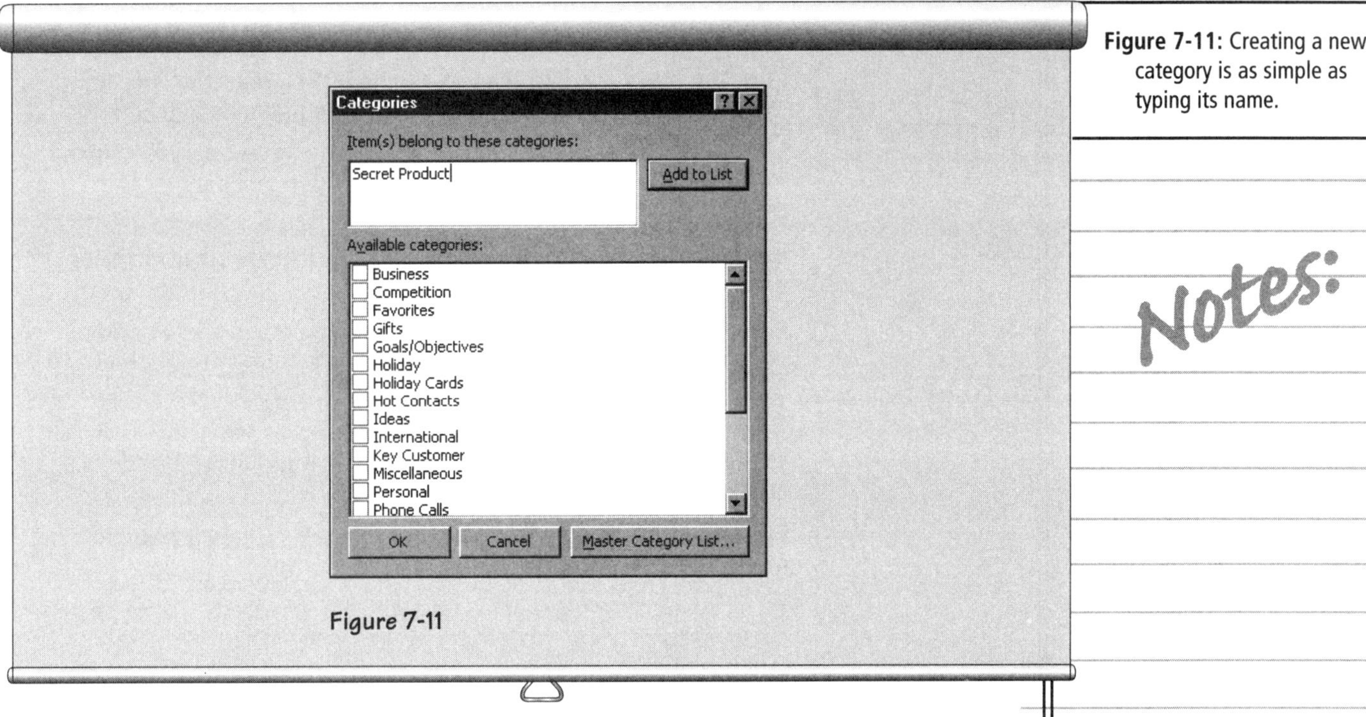

Figure 7-11

Figure 7-11: Creating a new category is as simple as typing its name.

Outlook offers you some ready-made categories in the Available Categories list, but you want to create your own category that's more descriptive of the task at hand.

6. **Click Add to List to place your category on the categories list.**

   The new category is on the list in its proper alphabetical place (you may have to scroll through the list to find it) and there's already a check mark next to it, indicating that the Research task is assigned to it.

7. **Click OK on the categories list.**

   The list closes and you return to the Task window, where the category Secret Product is inserted in the Categories field.

8. **Click Save and Close to finish this task.**

Now the first task for the secret product is in your Outlook system. But, besides research, there are all those other departments involved, and each of them needs task tracking.

Wait, don't start repeating all these steps to create the other tasks you need, there's an easier way.

Copying a task

The quickest way to create all the new tasks you need is to use the task you just finished as a model. You simply copy that task, and then you can create all the tasks you need by changing the tasks' names in the Subject field of the copies you've made. Here are the steps:

Notes:

1 **Click the check mark in the box on the left edge of the listing for the Research-SP task you just created. The listing is highlighted, indicating that it has been selected.**

2 **Press Ctrl+C or choose Edit⇨Copy from the menu bar.**

This places a copy of the item on the Windows Clipboard. The Clipboard is an area of memory that accepts data and holds it so that you can use it somewhere else.

3 **Press Ctrl+V or choose Edit⇨Paste from the menu bar. Another copy of this task is now listed immediately below the original one.**

The item you placed on the Windows Clipboard is pasted into your Tasks window. However, the item is still on the Clipboard, and will remain there until you put something new on the Clipboard (by using the Cut or Copy command on the Edit menu) or until you exit Windows.

4 **Press Ctrl+V again. Another copy of this task is now listed immediately below the first copy.**

You now have three copies of this task; you need three more to complete the tasks for all six departments that are involved in this project.

5 **Press Ctrl+V three more times.**

Isn't this great? It's like magic! You have six copies of a task, with all the data filled in, and it only took a couple of seconds to do it. Uh-oh, wait, they're all called Research. You have to fix that.

6 **Move to the second copy of the Research task in the task listings and double-click to open it.**

When the Task window opens, the insertion point is in the Subject field, which is exactly what you want to change. Notice that all of the dates and other data are exactly the same as the original task's values.

7 **Delete Research and type** Marketing**. The Subject field now says Marketing-SP.**

You can also highlight the word Research by holding down the Shift and Ctrl keys and then pressing the right arrow. Once it is highlighted, as soon as you start typing the new word, the original word is deleted.

8 **Click Save and Close to save your changes.**

9 **Move to the next duplicate of the Research task and repeat the process, changing the Subject field to the next department name, using the departments involved in this project. Continue this until each duplicate has the correct Subject name.**

You're all set to track each task individually, knowing they're linked as a category. You'll use that information to arrange the display of your tasks (we'll cover that later in this unit).

☑ Progress Check

If you can do the following, you've mastered this lesson:

- ❑ Create a category.
- ❑ Copy a task.
- ❑ Paste a task.

Sorting Tasks

Lesson 7-8

By default, Outlook displays your tasks in a list. In fact, Outlook calls this list the Simple List, and that's a pretty good description of it. It simply lists your tasks in the order you add them to the list.

Rearranging the way tasks appear on this list can help you work more efficiently. You can sort tasks by a variety of criteria, such as the Due Date or the Subject.

Sorting with the Current view box

The easiest way to sort your tasks is with the Current view box on the toolbar. Follow these simple steps to sort your task list and see only the information you want to see:

Simple List
Detailed List
Active Tasks
Next Seven Days
Overdue Tasks
By Category
Assignment
By Person Responsible
Completed Tasks
Task Timeline

choices in the Current view box

1. **Click the arrow to the right of the Current view box to see the available choices.**
2. **Choose Detailed List to see each task listed along with details under the headings Status, Due Date, % Complete, and Categories.**
3. **Choose By Category to arrange the tasks by their assigned categories. When you select this view, only the categories appear on the task list (see Figure 7-12). Click the plus sign (+) to the left of the Category name to expand the list to include the tasks in that category (see Figure 7-13).**

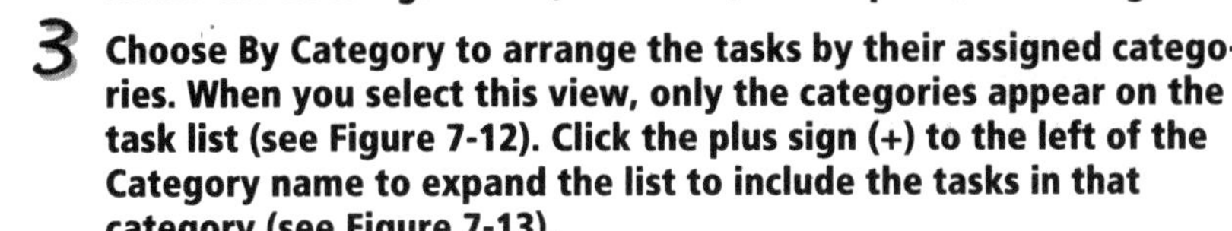
on the test

   This is a good way to get to a specific task when your task list has grown quite long.
4. **Experiment by selecting the other available choices to see the results on your listing.**

heads up

It's a good idea to return to the Simple List after you've seen the results of different views, in order to continue these lessons.

Adding columns

If you wish, you can see another detail about the task (perhaps you want to know if it's in progress, or you want to see the percent complete figure), you can add another column to the window quite easily.

To add a new column, follow these steps:

1. **Choose View⇨Show Fields from the menu bar to bring up the Show Fields dialog box (see Figure 7-14).**

   The Show Fields dialog box has two panels. The left panel lists the available fields that are not currently displayed on the window. The right panel lists the fields that are currently displayed.

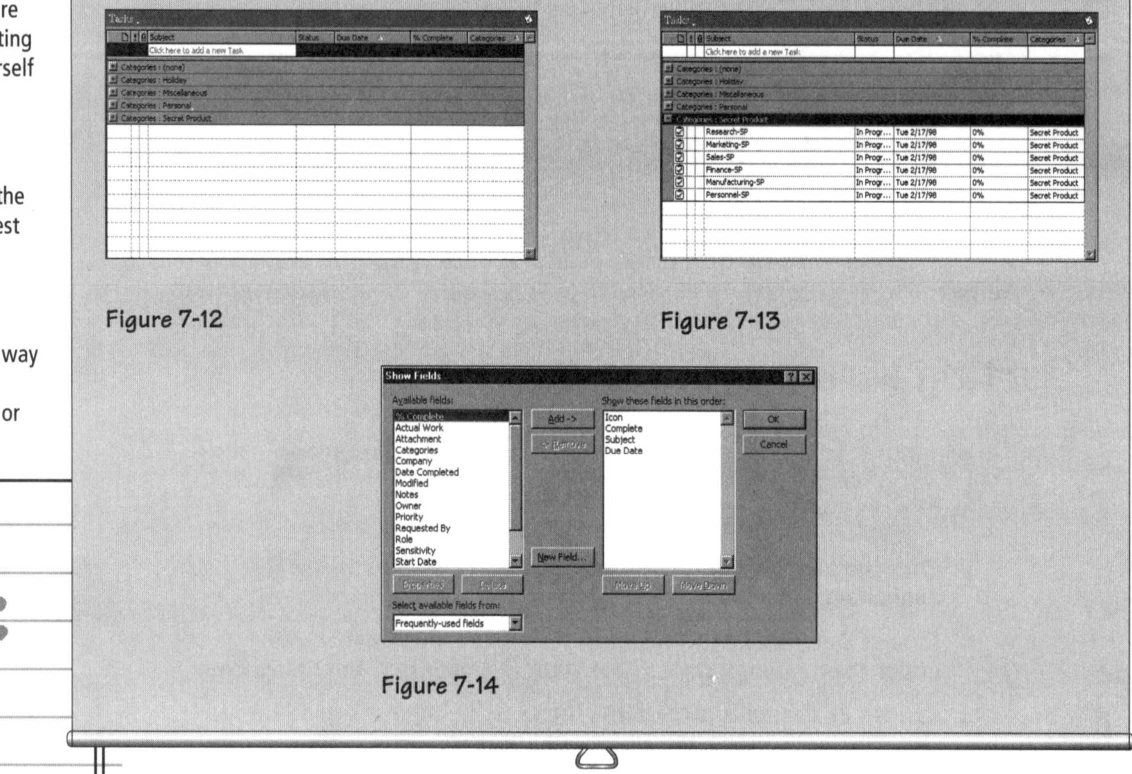

Figure 7-12: The Categories view lists the categories you're currently using, letting you decide for yourself which category of tasks you want to view.

Figure 7-13: Expand the categories of interest to see the tasks assigned.

Figure 7-14: You can custom-design the way your task listing appears by adding or removing columns.

Notes:

2. **In the left pane, click % Complete and then click Add.**

   The % Complete field appears in the right pane, indicating that it is now a column in the Simple List display of tasks.

3. **In the left pane, click Status (you may have to scroll through the list to find it) and then click Add.**

   You now have two new columns for your display.

4. **To rearrange the order, select (highlight) Status and then click Move Up. The Status column now precedes the % Complete column in the display.**

   Select % Complete and then click Move Down to reestablish the original order.

5. **Click OK to complete the process.**

You return to your Tasks window and the new columns appear, with appropriate information for the columns displayed for each task.

Changing the width of a column

There's a small problem when you add columns — the columns are frequently so narrow that it's hard to read the data for each task. Luckily, this is an easy problem to fix. In this exercise, you'll start by narrowing a column in order to make room for a column you want to expand. Follow these steps to change the width of a column:

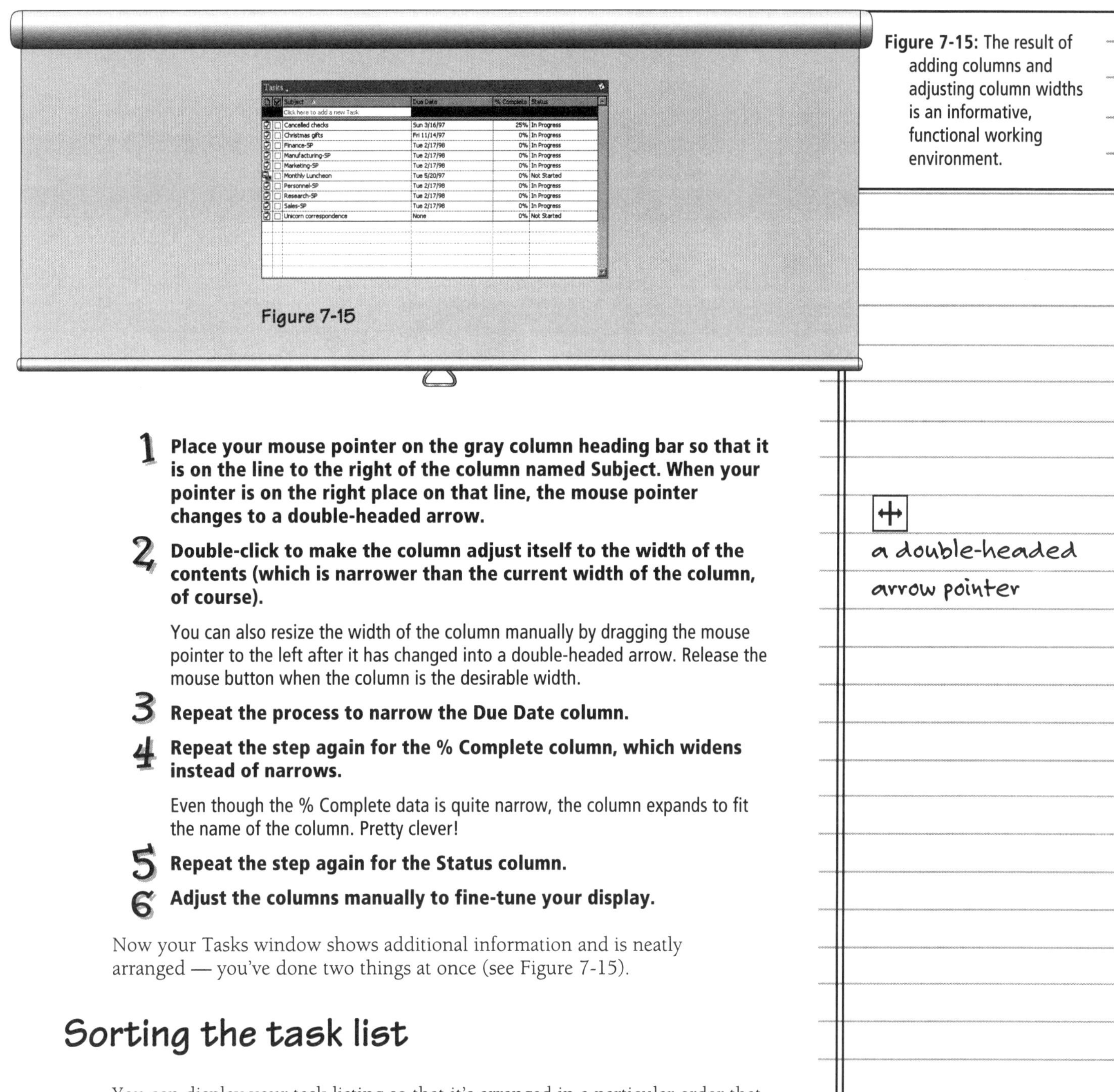

Figure 7-15

Figure 7-15: The result of adding columns and adjusting column widths is an informative, functional working environment.

1. **Place your mouse pointer on the gray column heading bar so that it is on the line to the right of the column named Subject. When your pointer is on the right place on that line, the mouse pointer changes to a double-headed arrow.**

2. **Double-click to make the column adjust itself to the width of the contents (which is narrower than the current width of the column, of course).**

   You can also resize the width of the column manually by dragging the mouse pointer to the left after it has changed into a double-headed arrow. Release the mouse button when the column is the desirable width.

3. **Repeat the process to narrow the Due Date column.**

4. **Repeat the step again for the % Complete column, which widens instead of narrows.**

   Even though the % Complete data is quite narrow, the column expands to fit the name of the column. Pretty clever!

5. **Repeat the step again for the Status column.**

6. **Adjust the columns manually to fine-tune your display.**

Now your Tasks window shows additional information and is neatly arranged — you've done two things at once (see Figure 7-15).

Sorting the task list

You can display your task listing so that it's arranged in a particular order that matches what you need to know about your tasks. For example, you may want to see all your tasks arranged by due date or by percent complete. To rearrange the order to your specifications, follow these steps:

1. **Click the column heading for Due Date. Your list appears listing each task according to the due date of each task.**

   A small triangle appears in the Due Date column heading. If the triangle is pointing down, the tasks are arranged by due date in descending order. If it is pointing up, the tasks are arranged by due date in ascending order.

Figure 7-16: You can sort and subsort your task list by any field.

Figure 7-17: The task list is sorted according to the instructions you gave in the Group By dialog box.

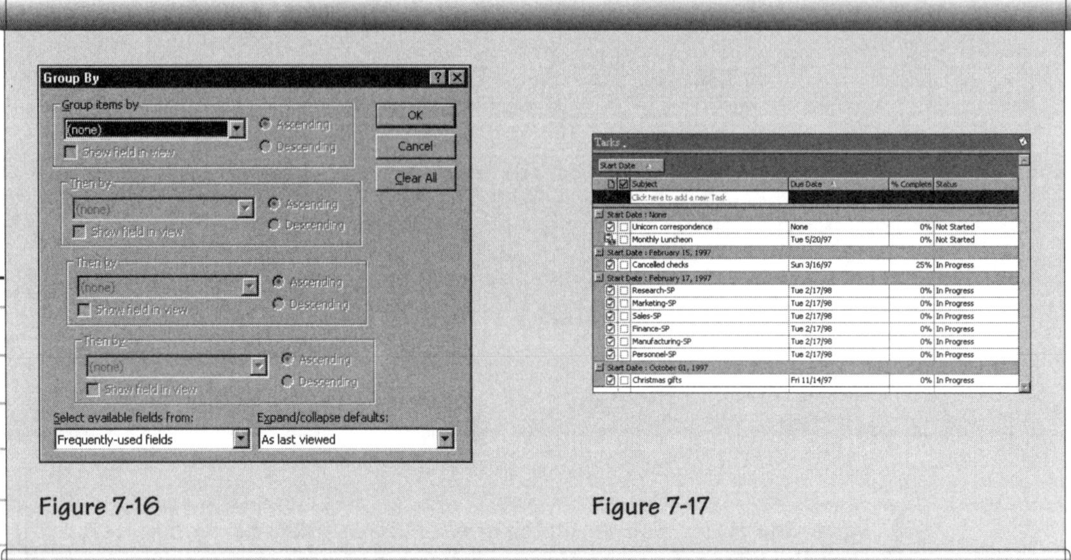

Figure 7-16

Figure 7-17

2. **To reverse the current order, click again on the Due Date column heading.**
3. **Repeat this process with the % Complete column heading to arrange the tasks according to that data.**

This is a quick and easy way to view your tasks according to the criteria you need at the moment.

Even better, and more useful, is the fact that you can arrange the tasks according to the data in a field that isn't even shown on the Tasks window. For example, suppose you want to sort your task list by the start dates for each task, even though Start Date is not a column on the Tasks window. To do this, follow these steps:

1. **Choose View⇨Group By from the menu bar to display the Group By dialog box (see Figure 7-16).**
2. **Click the arrow to the right of the box named Group items by and then select Start Date.**

   Note that you can also opt to show the field's column in the display (but we're choosing not to).
3. **Click Ascending to group your list in ascending order by Start Date.**
4. **At the bottom right of the dialog box, click the arrow next to the Expand/collapse defaults box. Choose All expanded.**

   This choice determines whether you see a display of the sort category (Start Date) with a plus sign (+) next to each Start Date choice or you see the expanded list of tasks under each Start Date choice. If the list were not expanded, you would have to click the plus sign to see the tasks that belong to that Start Date choice. In this case, you want to see all the tasks.

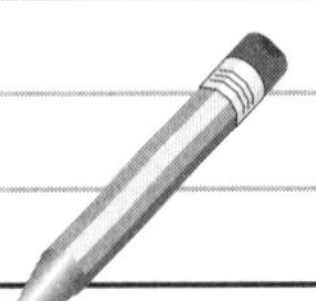

☑ Progress Check

If you can do the following, you've mastered this lesson:

- ❑ Change the current view of your task list.
- ❑ Add a column to your Tasks window.
- ❑ Change the width of columns.
- ❑ Sort the list by the data under each column heading.
- ❑ Sort the list by the data in a field that doesn't have a column on the window.

Click OK.

The task list is sorted exactly the way you wanted to see it (see Figure 7-17). Aren't you clever!

To change the sorting scheme, repeat this process. To eliminate it, just select None from the Group items by box.

Printing Task Reports

Lesson 7-9

Some people thought that the wide-spread use of computers would create the paperless office. Unfortunately, it hasn't happened and it probably never will. *Hard copies* (the computer jargon for printouts of information contained in computers) are still demanded and filing cabinets are still being used. Eventually, you will need to print out a report about your tasks — probably so you can give a copy to those in your office who can't use Outlook as well as you can.

To print a task report, follow these steps:

1. **Open the Canceled checks task.**
2. **Choose File⇨Print Preview to see what the printed report will look like.**
3. **In the Print Preview window, click the Actual Size button on the toolbar (it's the third icon).**

   The Print Preview window displays the report exactly as it will print, as seen in Figure 7-18. This gives you a chance to make changes to the printing format before committing the report to paper. This is especially important if you have to walk down the hall to the printer in order to see what the report looks like.
4. **If you don't like what you see, you can make some page design changes. Click the Page Setup button on the toolbar to bring up the Page Setup dialog box.**

   This dialog box is named Memo Style because that's the style used for task reports.
5. **Click the Font button next to the Fields font box.**
6. **Find the font named Times New Roman and click to select it.**

   When you open the Font drop-down list, the name of the current font is highlighted. If you know the name of the font to select you can type the first letter(s) of the font name to bring it up quickly. In this case, type **t** to bring your pointer immediately to the section of font names that begin with *T*. Type **i** after the t and you'll be right where you want to be.
7. **Click OK to return to the dialog box.**

Notes:

Figure 7-18: The Print Preview is an on-screen printout.

Figure 7-19: A header or footer (or both) makes a report easier to read and more professional looking.

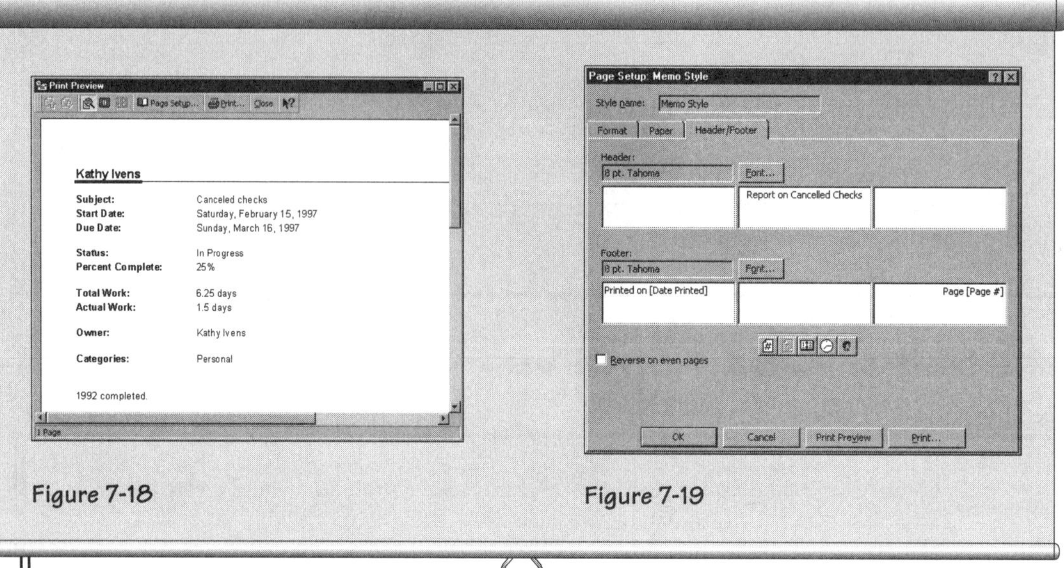

Figure 7-18

Figure 7-19

Header/Footer icons (l to r) = page number, total pages, date printed, time printed, user name

8 **Click the Header/Footer tab to move to that page of the dialog box (see Figure 7-19).**

Headers and footers appear at the top (header) or bottom (footer) of every page of a report. You only have to enter the text once.

You see three boxes for the Header and three boxes for the Footer. Those boxes represent (from left to right) placement on the left side of the page, placement in the center of the page, and placement on the right side of the page.

9 **In the center box of the Header section, type** Report on Canceled Checks**.**

10 **Click the Font button in the header section and select Times New Roman. Select 14 from the Size list box. Then click OK.**

11 **In the left box of the Footer section type** Printed On**. Press the spacebar to leave a space and then click the third button from the left on the toolbar below the footer section.**

This inserts a code that translates to the date you print this report. If you print it again next week, it will carry the new date.

12 **In the right box of the footer section, type** Page**, leave a space, then click the first button (page number) on the toolbar (delete the page number in the center section).**

13 **Click the Print Preview button to return to the Print Preview window.**

You can't see the entire page in Print Preview if you're viewing the window in actual size, but you can see what the fonts look like. To see where the headers and footers fall, click the One Page button on the toolbar (the fourth button).

14 **Click the Print button to send the report to your printer.**

The familiar Windows Print dialog box appears. Click OK (unless you have to select a printer as part of your normal Windows procedures).

☑ Progress Check

If you can do the following, you've mastered this lesson:

- ❑ Open the Print Preview window.
- ❑ Change fonts and font sizes.
- ❑ Create a header.
- ❑ Create a footer.
- ❑ Use icons to insert date, time, page number, and other header/footer information automatically.

This returns you to the Task form for Canceled checks. Click Save and Close.

The reason you save the task again is to save this print format with it. Otherwise, you'd have to repeat all those steps again the next time you wanted to print this report.

Handling Task Housekeeping

Lesson 7-10

Now that you know how easy it is to use the Tasks feature in Outlook, you'll probably use it constantly. Eventually you'll have many tasks on your list, some of which are completed, some of which have been abandoned, and perhaps others which are still in progress but are not your responsibility (you've handed them off to others and you don't care about receiving status reports).

In this exercise, you're going to update completed tasks, delete tasks that are no longer of interest, and create a folder to hold completed tasks (in case anyone wants information about them later, you don't want to delete them just yet). To keep your task list current and productive, follow these steps:

Notes:

1. **Click the Complete box for the Unicorn Correspondence task.**

   This marks the task as completed. A line appears through the data on the listing. It's important to do this every time you complete a task.

2. **Click the task icon (the first column) of the listing for Finance-SP and then press Delete.**

   on the test

   The task is deleted from your list. It has moved to the Deleted Items folder, which you can open from the Outlook bar in case you deleted the task by mistake and want to restore it.

3. **Choose File⇨New⇨Folder from the menu bar to bring up the Create New Folder dialog box (see Figure 7-20).**

   Note that by default, the new folder is placed into the Tasks folder, so it becomes a subfolder for your work in Outlook Tasks.

   Note also that the option to create a shortcut to this new folder in the Outlook bar has been selected. This means that your Outlook bar will have an icon for this folder, providing easy access to it whenever you need it. If your Outlook bar is already crowded (or if you are planning to create lots of folders that will eventually crowd the Outlook bar), you can deselect this option by clicking the check mark.

4. **In the Name box enter** Completed Tasks.

   If you wish, you can also enter a description of this folder in the Description box, but I find that if I name the folder properly I don't need to add a description.

5. **Click OK to finish creating this folder.**

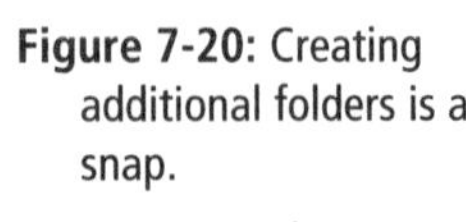

Figure 7-20: Creating additional folders is a snap.

Figure 7-21: The Move Items dialog box is a quick way to put a task into another folder.

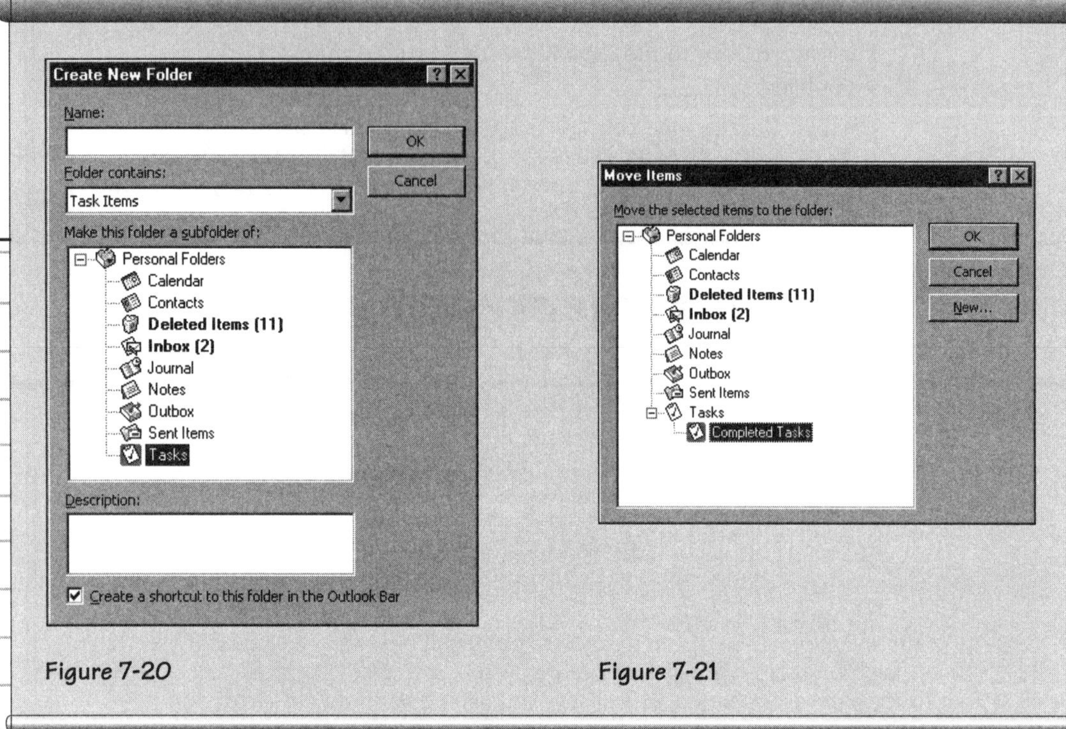

Figure 7-20

Figure 7-21

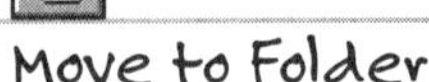

Move to Folder button

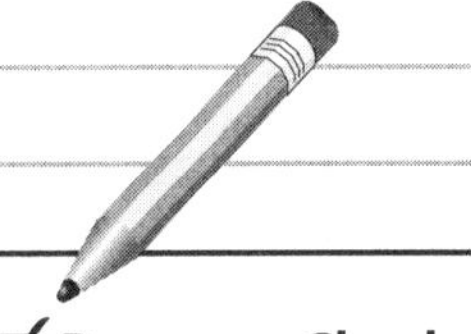

6. **Click the task icon for the Unicorn correspondence task to select it.**
7. **Click the Move to Folder button on the toolbar or press Ctrl+Shift+V and then choose Move to folder. The Move Items dialog box appears.**
8. **Click the plus sign (+) to the left of the Tasks folder to reveal the subfolders (see Figure 7-21).**
9. **Click the Completed Tasks folder. Then click OK.**

   The Unicorn Correspondence task is no longer on your task list. Just to reassure yourself, click the Completed Tasks icon on the Outlook bar. There it is! Now click the Tasks icon on the Outlook bar to come back.

You've done quite a bit of housekeeping, and everything is neat and tidy. Don't forget to take these steps on a regular basis as you continue to work with tasks in Outlook.

☑ Progress Check

If you can do the following, you've mastered this lesson:

- ❑ Mark a task completed.
- ❑ Delete a task.
- ❑ Create a folder.
- ❑ Move a task into another folder.

Recess

Congratulations! POP (sound of champagne cork leaving its bottle)!! You've accomplished an incredible amount of work. This calls for a celebration. We're here having champagne in your honor, but if there isn't any champagne around where you are, grab a soda or a cup of coffee and raise it in a toast to yourself. We're certainly toasting you for a job well done. Mmmm, good bubbly. Oh no, we don't have any caviar. When you come back after recess, there's a quiz. You know this stuff cold — you'll ace it.

Unit 7 Quiz

For the following questions, circle the letter of the correct answer. We're pretty sneaky, so there might be more than one correct answer for some questions. You can find the answers to the questions in Apppendix A.

1. **What is the Outlook bar?**

   A. A country-and-western dive where the men are macho and the women wear gingham.

   B. The area on the left side of the Outlook window that holds icons for folders.

   C. A plumber's tool.

   D. A breed of dogs.

   E. A book by Fyodor Dostoyevsky.

2. **How do you tell Outlook to remind you to work on a task?**

   A. Set a date in the Reminder field.

   B. Tie a string around the mouse.

   C. Put Post-it notes all over the monitor.

   D. Call the Psychic Network.

   E. Vocalize a command into the speakers connected to your computer's sound card.

3. **What is a recurring task?**

   A. Housework.

   B. A task with a due date of last year.

   C. A dream that repeats itself every Saturday night.

   D. A task that's configured to occur regularly.

   E. The latest album from the artist formerly known as Prince.

4. **What does sorting by category mean?**

   A. Sorting the task list so that tasks with the same category are contiguous.

   B. Rearranging the telephone wires in a wall jack so that the colors are in the same order as the rainbow.

   C. Slang for doing the electric slide at a wedding.

   D. Putting all the dishes in your kitchen cabinet into boxes and replacing them with the contents of your kitchen junk drawer.

   E. Writing poetry where nothing rhymes.

Notes:

5. **What happens when you delete a task?**
   A. You can take the rest of the day off.
   B. A popping noise issues from the computer and smoke rises from the monitor.
   C. A secret red phone automatically rings in your boss's office.
   D. The task moves to the Deleted Items folder.
   E. Nothing, because all tasks must go on forever as a form of job security.

Unit 7 Exercise

1. Create a task named Gimme a Raise.
2. Make the due date one month from today.
3. Enter all the text necessary to explain the task.
4. Print a task report and leave it on the appropriate desk by accident.

Part II Review

Unit 5 Summary

- **Opening a new appointment form:** Select a date in the Date Navigator and double-click on the appropriate time slot in the Daily Calendar.
- **Returning to today's date:** Click the Today button in the Calendar window.
- **Resetting the default reminder time:** Use the Options dialog box.
- **Resetting a reminder:** Choose the time interval and click Postpone.
- **Entering Date fields in Outlook:** You can type **one week from today** or **next Saturday** instead of the actual date.
- **Scheduling a recurring appointment:** Choose Calendar⇨New Recurring Appointment and fill out the information in the Appointment Recurrence dialog box.
- **An event:** An activity that lasts for 24 hours or more.
- **Switching between the three Day/Week/ Month views:** Click the Day, Week, and Month buttons on the Calendar toolbar.

Unit 6 Summary

- **Locating an appointment for editing:** Use the Find Items feature.
- **Adding an attachment to an appointment:** Use the Insert File feature from the appointment form menu bar.
- **Deleting an appointment:** Highlight the appointment and press Ctrl+D to send it to the Deleted Items folder.
- **Changing an appointment date quickly:** Drag the appointment to the Date Navigator and drop it on the new date.
- **Opening the Calendar Properties dialog box:** Position your mouse pointer over the Calendar shortcut in the Outlook Bar, right-click, and choose Properties from the pop-up menu.
- **Modifying the selected Print style:** Click the Page Setup button in the Print dialog box. Make any changes that you want to make.

Part II Review

Unit 7 Summary

- **Entering a task:** Enter a task either in the Tasks window or in the TaskPad of the Calendar window.
- **Opening a new task form:** Open the Tasks window and press Ctrl+N.
- **Creating a recurring task:** Open the Task Recurrence dialog box by clicking the Recurrence button on the new task form toolbar.
- **Editing an existing task:** Highlight the task and press Ctrl+O to open it. Make the necessary changes and click the Save and Close button to save your edits and return to the Tasks window.
- **Deleting a single occurrence of a task:** Use the Skip Occurrence feature found by choosing Task⇨Skip Occurrence.
- **Tracking time, money and contacts related to a particular task:** Use the Status tab of the task form.
- **Tracking multiple tasks that belong to a single project:** Create a new category for the project and assign related tasks to the new project category.
- **Adding or removing columns from a Tasks window view:** Use the Show Fields dialog box.
- **Sorting data in your task list:** Click the header of the column to sort by or use the Group By dialog box by choosing View⇨Group By from the Tasks window menu bar.

Part II Test

The following test questions correspond to the material covered in Units 5 through 7 of Part II. You can find the answers to the questions in Appendix A.

True False

T F 1. You can create an appointment by dragging a task onto a specific date in the Date Navigator.

T F 2. Outlook date fields accept plain English input as well as numerical date information.

T F 3. The default reminder time is a fixed number that can't be changed.

T F 4. You can only change a recurring appointment by deleting it and entering a new recurring appointment.

T F 5. The Day/Week/Month view of the Calendar window contains the Daily Calendar, the TaskPad, the Date Navigator and a calculator.

T F 6. Once you delete an appointment it is gone forever.

T F 7. You can use the drag and drop feature to change an appointment date.

T F 8. You can use AutoArchive to save your old appointments to a separate file and remove them from your main file.

T F 9. To enter a new task you must be in the Tasks window.

T F 10. There's an easier way to make duplicates of tasks other than by opening a new task form and reentering all the information.

Multiple Choice

Circle the letter of the statement(s) that best answers the question (some questions may contain more than one correct answer).

11. Which of the following options is *not* available for resetting a reminder?

A. Dismiss, which turns the reminder off permanently.

B. New Time, which resets the reminder to go off at a specified time.

C. Postpone, which delays the reminder for a specified time period.

D. Tomorrow, which sets the reminder to activate the following day at the same time.

E. Open Item, which opens the appointment to which the reminder is attached.

12. Which of the following entries is *not* valid for an Outlook date field?

A. 12/14/99

B. Three months from Saturday.

C. Sometime next week.

D. January 22, 1999

E. The first Monday in May.

13. You can use drag and drop to perform which of the following tasks?

A. Turn off a reminder.

B. Change an appointment date.

C. Change the category to which an appointment is assigned.

D. Create an e-mail message from an appointment.

E. Change views in the Calendar window.

Part II Test

14. **Where is the TaskPad located?**
    A. In the Tasks folder.
    B. In the Phone List view of the Contacts folder.
    C. In the Day/Week/Month view of the Calendar folder.
    D. Argentina.
    E. On the Status tab of the new task form.

15. **The most efficient way to track several tasks related to one project is to:**
    A. Use specialized project tracking software.
    B. Assign all tasks the same due date.
    C. Give each task for the project a High priority status.
    D. Create a new category for the project and assign each task to the new category.
    E. Add a reminder to each task with a note indicating that it belongs to the particular project.

Matching

Draw a line from the item in the left column to the closest match in the right column.

16. **Match the following shortcut keys to the actions they trigger.**

A.	Ctrl+Shift+F	1. Open the Go To Date dialog box.
B.	Ctrl+O	2. Open an existing contact form.
C.	Ctrl+Shift+V	3. Open the Find Items dialog box.
D.	Ctrl+G	4. Copy the highlighted item.
E.	Ctrl+C	5. Open the Move Items dialog box.

17. **Match the following buttons to the functions they represent.**

A.		1. Set the reminder sound.
B.		2. Open the Find Items dialog box.
C.		3. Go to today's date on the calendar.
D.		4. Indicates that the item has a reminder.
E.		5. Designates a recurring appointment.

Part II Lab Assignment

Now comes the moment of truth — putting it all to work. The purpose of this lab assignment is to use the Secret Product project you created in Unit 7 as the basis for creating appointments, meetings, and additional tasks. You will assign each task to a task leader, set up an appointment with each task leader, set up a meeting of all task leaders, and assign some new tasks.

Step 1: Assigning the Secret Project tasks to task leaders

Open Outlook and click the Tasks shortcut to move to the Tasks window. Change the view to the By Category view and expand the Secret Project category. If you and all the task leaders were connected to the same network using Exchange Server, you could use the Assign Task function. For this exercise we will assume that is not the case and therefore, you must assign the tasks manually. Open the Research-SP task and at the top of the notes section of the task form type **Task leader: Bill Clinton** (Rhodes scholars must be good at research, don't you think?). Save the task and return to the Tasks window. Repeat the process for the remaining Secret Project tasks assigning each one to a different individual from your Personal Address Book.

Step 2: Setting up meetings with task leaders

Open the Calendar window and select the date that is two weeks from next Monday for the individual project meetings. Select one hour intervals and create an appointment for each of the team leaders you assigned to the various tasks. After filling out the appointment information, set a reminder for ten minutes before each appointment.

Step 3: Confirming assignments and appointments by e-mail

In the appointment form, choose Appointment➪Invite Attendees to open your Personal Address Book. Select William J. Clinton. In the notes section of the appointment (meeting) form type **Bill, I would like you to take an active role in the upcoming Secret Product project by handling the Research task. I've attached a copy of the task for your review. Let's meet two weeks from this Monday to discuss it further.** Use the Insert Item feature to attach a copy of the Research task. Send it off and you're all set.

Part II Lab Assignment

Step 4: Adding more tasks

Open the Tasks window and create new tasks for packaging and product testing. Assign the tasks and notify the task leaders.

Managing
Your
Contacts
Part
III

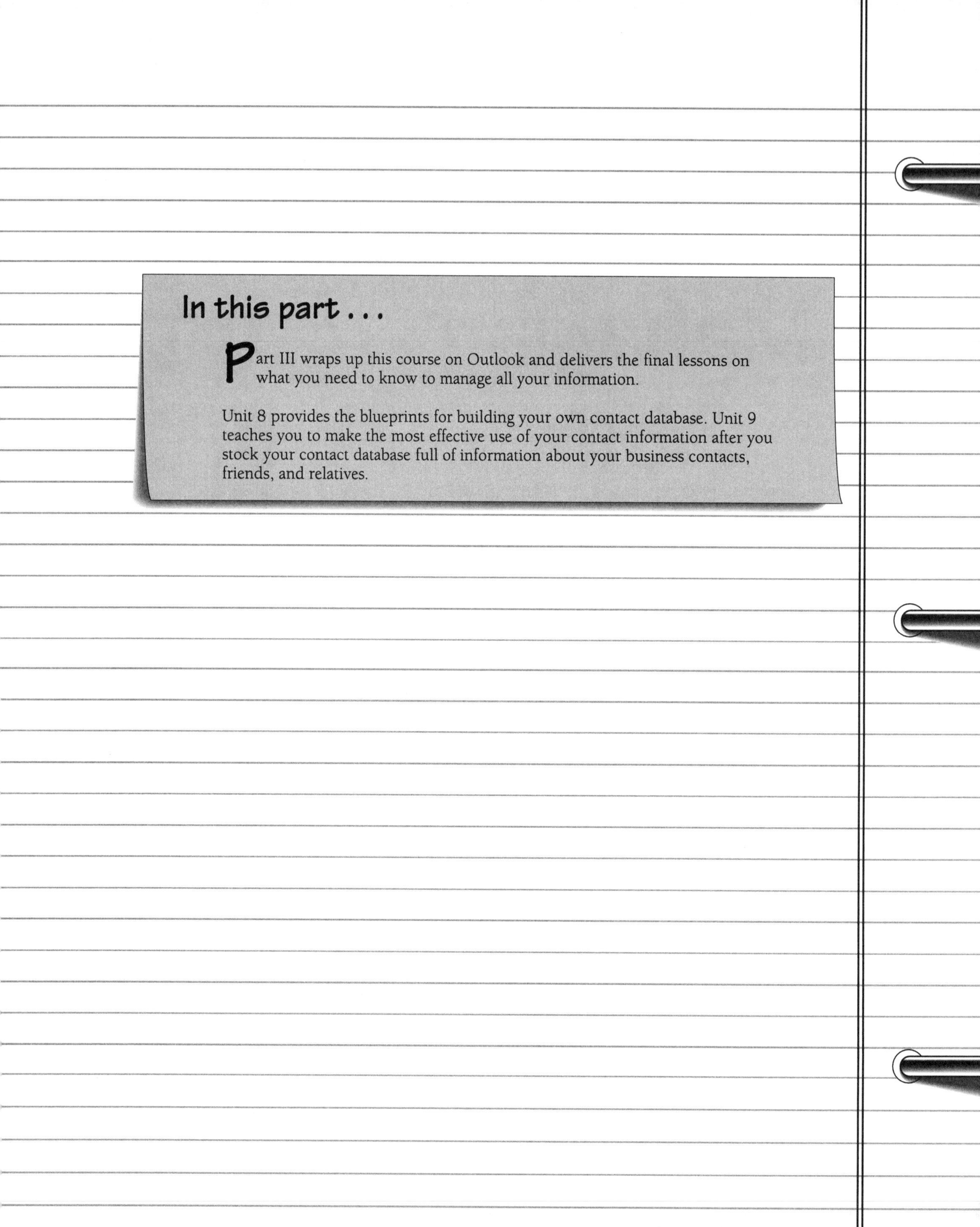

In this part . . .

Part III wraps up this course on Outlook and delivers the final lessons on what you need to know to manage all your information.

Unit 8 provides the blueprints for building your own contact database. Unit 9 teaches you to make the most effective use of your contact information after you stock your contact database full of information about your business contacts, friends, and relatives.

Unit 8

Setting Up the Contacts Database

Prerequisites

- Opening the Contacts folder (Lesson 1-2)
- Opening an e-mail message (Lesson 3-2)

on the CD

- Governor.mdb

Objectives for This Unit

- ✓ Entering a new contact
- ✓ Setting Journal options
- ✓ Importing contacts from the Address Book
- ✓ Importing contacts from another program
- ✓ Formatting the Address Cards view

Organization is the key to time management. Chaos lurks behind every office door and cubicle wall. How much time do you squander searching for an address, phone number, notes about a conversation, or some personal information relating to a business or personal acquaintance? If the answer is none, you need a good contact-management system.

In addition to its other assets, Outlook provides an effective contact-management feature. Gather up your business card collection, as well as all your cocktail napkins, matchbook covers, and sticky notes, and start building a contact database.

Entering Contacts

Lesson 8-1

If you've ever used a Rolodex file or an address book of any sort, you already understand the basics of contact management. The first rule is: No matter

where your contact information comes from, your first job is to put it into a format that you can manipulate to suit your needs. When using Outlook to manage your contacts, the primary tool for entering contact information is the new contact form.

The new contact form enables you to retain as much detail as you want for each contact. Follow these steps to get intimately acquainted with the new contact form:

1. **Click the Contacts shortcut in the Outlook bar to open the Contacts window (Figure 8-1).**

   The Contacts window opens in the Address Cards view, which displays individual cards with basic contact information and a letter bar down the right side from which you navigate the contact database.

2. **Press Ctrl+N to open a new contact form, as seen in Figure 8-2, and click the General tab.**

   The new contact form provides four tabs that contain input fields for a variety of information. You record the type and amount of information that accommodates your needs.

   - **General:** Basic contact information, including the name, address, phone number, and so on.
   - **Details:** Less critical, but often helpful information such as names of the contact's assistant and boss, as well as some personal information about the contact.
   - **Journal:** Journal entry options and a display list of recorded journal entries for the contact.
   - **All Fields:** Outlook fields and their values for this contact.

3. **Type** Attila T. Hun **in the Full Name text box and then tab to the Job title field.**

   When typing the contact name, use the first name, middle initial (or name), last name format.

   heads up

   Outlook requires that you enter a first and last name in the Full Name field. If you enter a partial name, the Check Full Name dialog box appears (Figure 8-3) asking you to enter more detailed name information. Title, Middle Name, and Suffix are optional.

4. **Type** Oppressor **in the Job title text box and tab to the Company field.**

5. **Type** Barbarians "R" Us **in the Company text box and tab to the File as field.**

   on the test

   As soon as you entered the Full Name, Outlook automatically entered the File as information. Note that Outlook files the name in the last name, comma, first name, middle name format so that you can search and sort by last name.

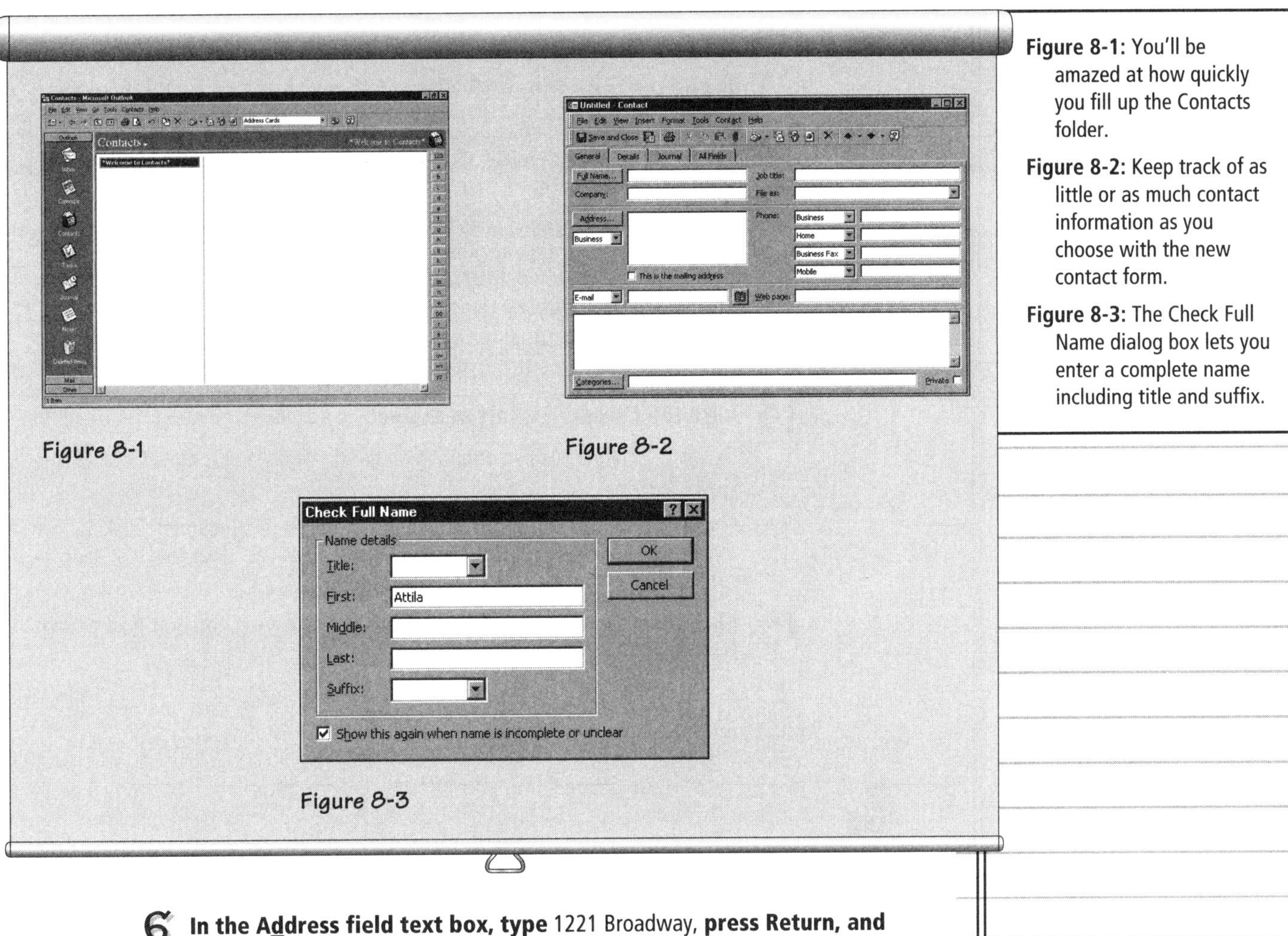

Figure 8-1

Figure 8-2

Figure 8-3

Figure 8-1: You'll be amazed at how quickly you fill up the Contacts folder.

Figure 8-2: Keep track of as little or as much contact information as you choose with the new contact form.

Figure 8-3: The Check Full Name dialog box lets you enter a complete name including title and suffix.

6 **In the Address field text box, type** 1221 Broadway, **press Return, and type** Hoboken, NJ 12345**.**

The drop-down list below the Address button indicates that this is a business address. Note that the mailing address box is checked. Any correspondence you create for this contact uses the Business address as the mailing address. The next task is to enter a home address.

7 **Click the down arrow to the right of Business and choose Home.**

The text box clears, and the cursor jumps back to the Address text box.

8 **Type** 1832 The Steppes**, press Return, and then type** Ulan Bator, Outer Mongolia**.**

9 **In the Business phone field, type** 2015551357**, and then tab to the Home phone text box.**

You can click the down arrows next to the Phone fields to open drop-down lists of other types of phone numbers to enter, such as pager, car phone, and so on. Also note that when you tab from phone field to phone field, Outlook places parentheses around the area code and a dash between the exchange and last four digits of the number you just entered.

10 **Type** 37-8521 **in the Home phone text box and tab to the Business Fax field.**

11 **Type** 201-555-2468 **in the Business Fax text box and then tab to the E-mail field.**

12 **Type** ahun@barbarians.com **in the E-mail text box and then tab to the Web page text box.**

Notice that the E-mail field has a drop-down list that enables you to enter as many as three different e-mail addresses for one contact. This comes in handy when a contact has more than one online account — such as Internet, CompuServe, and America Online.

13 **Type** http://www.barbarians.com **as the address for the Barbarians "R" Us Web page.**

Categories...

Categories button

14 **Click the Categories button and select Key Customer.**

Now you have the basic information on file for Attila, and it should look like Figure 8-4.

From here you can choose to include more detailed information by clicking the other tabs of the new contact form, or you can close this form and add another contact by redoing Steps 1 through 14.

Save and Close

Save and Close button

15 **Click the Save and Close button to save the new contact and return to the Contacts window.**

After you close the contact form, the new contact appears with name, address, phone numbers, and e-mail address visible (see Figure 8-5).

heads up

Most things in life change, and your contact information is no different. People move and change jobs and as a result get addresses, phone numbers, and new e-mail addresses. To edit contact information, simply open the contact form by highlighting it and pressing Ctrl+O, make the necessary changes, and click the Save and Close button.

☑ Progress Check

If you can do the following, you've mastered this lesson:

- ❑ Open a new contact form.
- ❑ Move through the fields of the contact form.
- ❑ Enter information for a contact.

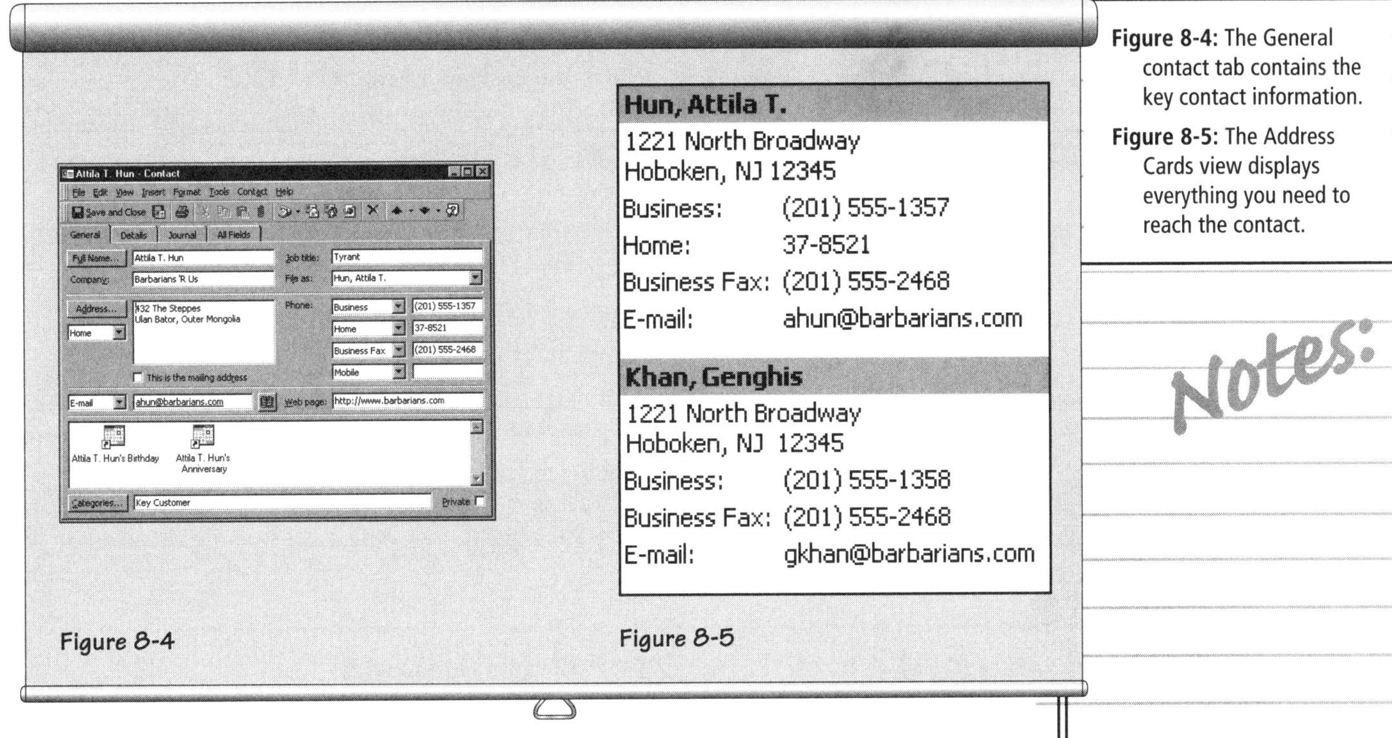

Figure 8-4

Figure 8-5

Figure 8-4: The General contact tab contains the key contact information.

Figure 8-5: The Address Cards view displays everything you need to reach the contact.

Notes:

Entering Repetitive Contact Information

Lesson 8-2

As is often the case, you have more than one contact at Barbarians "R" Us. Now you want to add the next contact, Genghis Khan, but you dread reentering all the same information you just entered for Attila T. Hun. No need to worry. Outlook is one step ahead of you. To simplify your life, Outlook enables you to create a new contact based on a previous contact.

Follow these steps to enter a new contact from the same company:

1. **Click the previous contact (Attila T. Hun in this case) to use as the basis for the new contact.**

on the test

2. **Choose Contacts⇨New Contact from Same Company from the menu bar.**

   A new contact form opens with the Company, Business Address, and Business Phone numbers carried over from Attila's contact form.

3. **Type** Genghis Khan **in the Full Name text box and tab to the Job title field.**

4. **Type in** Oceanic Ruler **and tab to the Business Phone field.**

   Hey, that's what Genghis Khan means!

   Because you never have occasion to contact him at home, you can skip the home address or phone.

☑ Progress Check

If you can do the following, you've mastered this lesson:

- ☐ Save yourself time by basing a new contact on a previously entered contact.
- ☐ Impress your friends and colleagues with the Outlook skills you've mastered.

5. **Type** 201-555-1358 **in the Business Phone text box.**

   Business associates rarely share the same telephone number, so unfortunately, you have to type the phone number.

6. **Place your cursor in the E-mail text box by clicking the text box once.**
7. **Type** gkhan@barbarians.com **and tab to the Web page field.**
8. **Type** http://www.barbarians.com**.**
9. **Click the Categories button and choose Key Customer.**
10. **Click the Save and Close button to add the new contact to the contact database and return to the Contacts window.**

    The new contact is added to the Address Cards view alphabetically, by the File as name. Note that this time the Home phone number does not appear for the new contact. The reason is simple — you didn't add one. Unless you change the default settings, Outlook displays only fields that contain information.

Lesson 8-3 Entering Detailed Contact Information

Sometimes general contact information is sufficient for your records. Other times, however, you require more detailed information — especially when you're dealing with very important contacts, whether personal or business. It's always a good idea to keep track of a certain amount of personal information about good clients. They appreciate your remembering a birthday or the names of their spouse and children. It's the little things that sometimes clinch a business deal. When it comes to personal contacts, you can't afford to forget some things, like anniversaries and special events.

To include more detailed information for Attila, follow these steps:

1. **Highlight Attila T. Hun in the Address Cards view of the Contact window.**

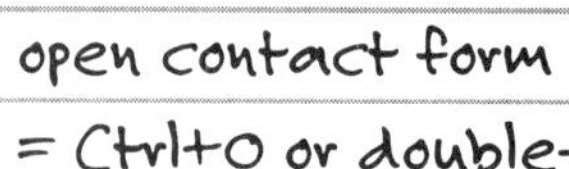

open contact form = Ctrl+O or double-click contact in Address Cards view

on the test

2. **Press Ctrl+O to open the Attila T. Hun contact form.**
3. **Click the Details tab to open the personal details form.**
4. **Type** Field Management **in the Department text box and then press the tab key to go to the Office field.**
5. **Type** Yak Skin Tent **in the Office text box and press tab to go to the Profession field.**
6. **Type** Pillager/Plunderer **in the Profession text box and then tab to the next field.**

heads up

Don't forget to regularly save anything you are working on to insure it is not permanently lost in case of a power failure or system crash. If one of those things happens, all data entered since the last save is lost.

7 **Press Ctrl+S to save the contact form with the newly entered information.**

8 **Type** Bleda **(his brother) in the Assistant's Name text box and tab to the Manager's Name field.**

9 **Type** Genghis Khan **in the Manager's Name text box and tab to the Birthday field.**

10 **Type** 3/1/06 **in the Birthday text box and tab to the Anniversary field.**

As best we can tell, Attila was born in 406 AD.

11 **Type** 2/14/50 **in the Anniversary text box and tab to the Nickname: field.**

This is the date of the last of many marriages. As you might guess from some of his contact information, Attila T. Hun is not an easy guy to live with.

12 **Type** Scourge of God **in the Nickname text box and tab to the Spouse's Name field.**

13 **Type** Honoria **in the Spouse's Name text box.**

14 **Click the Save and Close button to return to the Contacts window.**

Notice that none of the information in the Address Cards view changes. Filling out the Details form results in a couple of changes to the contact information on the General tab. To see them, open up Attila T. Hun's contact form again.

15 **Highlight Attila T. Hun and then press Ctrl+O to open the contact form.**

Check out the Notes window below the e-mail address field. You now see Attila T. Hun's Birthday and Attila T. Hun's Anniversary shortcut icons. Outlook automatically creates recurring events for these special days. Open the recurring event forms, to add information or set reminders, by double-clicking the shortcut icons.

So far you've done a great job, except for your selection of business associates — uncivilized, to say the least.

Notes:

Save and Close

Save and Close button

☑ Progress Check

If you can do the following, you've mastered this lesson:

- ❑ Open the personal information (Details) form.
- ❑ Fill out the Details form.
- ❑ Save your changes and return to the Contacts window.

Setting Journal Options

Lesson 8-4

Contact management does not stop with entering contact information in the database. As a matter of fact, that's just the beginning. Improved communications technology, increased competition, and an ever-shrinking globe cause you to process more information than ever before. To retain even a minimal amount of the data that you need to be productive requires an effective information-management system. Tracking and organizing your communications with a contact is an essential part of that system. Outlook enables you to keep track of e-mail messages, phone calls, documents, tasks, and other items related to contacts by recording each item as an entry in the Outlook Journal.

The Journal is a log book of contact-related activities, Outlook items, and Microsoft Office documents.

The first step in creating Journal entries is setting the global Journal entry options to meet your needs:

1. **Choose Tools➪Options from the menu bar to open Outlook Options.**
2. **Click the Journal tab to open the Journal options as seen in Figure 8-6.**

   The global options include:

   - **Automatically record these items:** A list of items which can be automatically recorded for selected contacts.
   - **For these contacts:** A list of all contacts in the database. Select the contacts for whom automatic journal entry recording is turned on.
   - **Also record files from:** Other Microsoft programs from which documents can be automatically recorded.
   - **Double-clicking a journal entry:** Determines whether the journal entry or the item (e-mail message, contact form, and so on) opens when you double-click the journal entry.
   - **AutoArchive Journal Entries:** AutoArchiving options for journal entries.
3. **Click E-mail message in the Automatically record these items section.**

   Outlook places a check mark next to each option you choose. Any items selected in this list will automatically be recorded for all contacts selected in the next option.
4. **Click Attila T. Hun in the For these contacts section.**

   Any items selected in the previous section will automatically be recorded for Attila, but not for Genghis.
5. **Click OK to save your changes and return to the Contacts window.**

   After you set the global options, you no longer need return to the Journal tab of the Options window to activate automatic journal entries for individual contacts. You can turn on automatic journal entry recording from within the contact form, which you will do in the following steps.
6. **Switch to Address Cards view, click on Khan, Genghis, and press Ctrl+O to open his contact form.**
7. **Click the Journal tab located above the Full Name text box to open the journal form.**
8. **Click to place a check mark in the check box labeled Automatically record journal entries for this contact box.**

   Identical to the For these contacts option on the Journal tab of the Options window, the Automatically record journal entries for this contact option activates the automatic recording of all items selected in the Options window's Journal Automatically record these items section.

☑ Progress Check

If you can do the following, you've mastered this lesson:

- ☐ Change global options for journal entries.
- ☐ Set journal entry options using the contact input form.

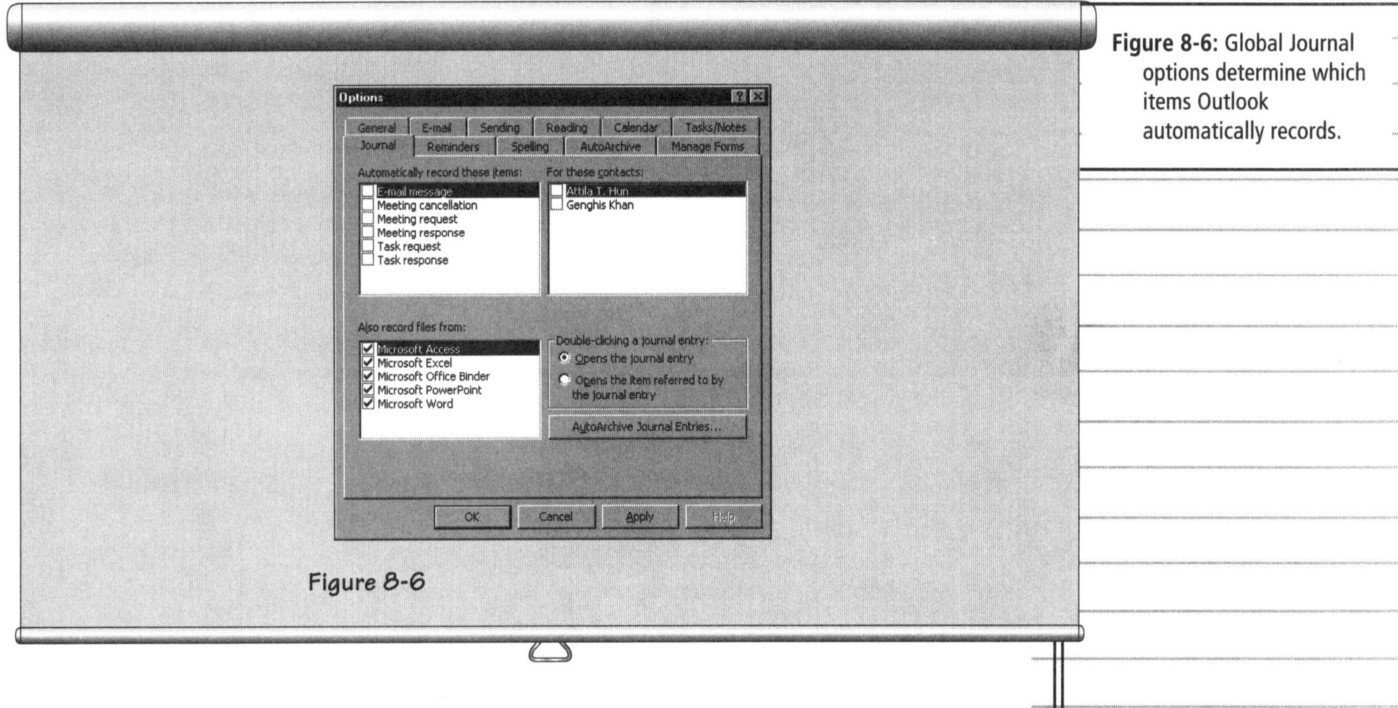

Figure 8-6: Global Journal options determine which items Outlook automatically records.

9. **Click the Save and Close button to return to the Contacts window.**

Now as you create new contacts, you can choose to automate the journal entry process on a case-by-case basis either through the global options or while creating the contact, by using the Journal tab of the contact input form.

Creating a Contact from an E-Mail — Lesson 8-5

Although filling out a new contact form is an effective way to include someone in your contact database, it's not always the most efficient way. A quicker method is to use an incoming e-mail message from the person you wish to add. Only the sender's name and e-mail address are copied into the new contact form, but it gives you a head start on filling in the necessary information. Choose an e-mail message from your Inbox and follow the steps below to add an individual to your contact database.

1. **Click the Inbox shortcut in the Outlook bar to open your Inbox.**
2. **Click an e-mail message from someone who is not already in your Contacts folder.**
3. **Press Ctrl+O to open the e-mail message.**
4. **Click the From address to highlight it.**

   You must click the From address itself directly, not the word From. Outlook highlights the address in dark gray.

Figure 8-7: Creating a contact from an e-mail is easy with Outlook.

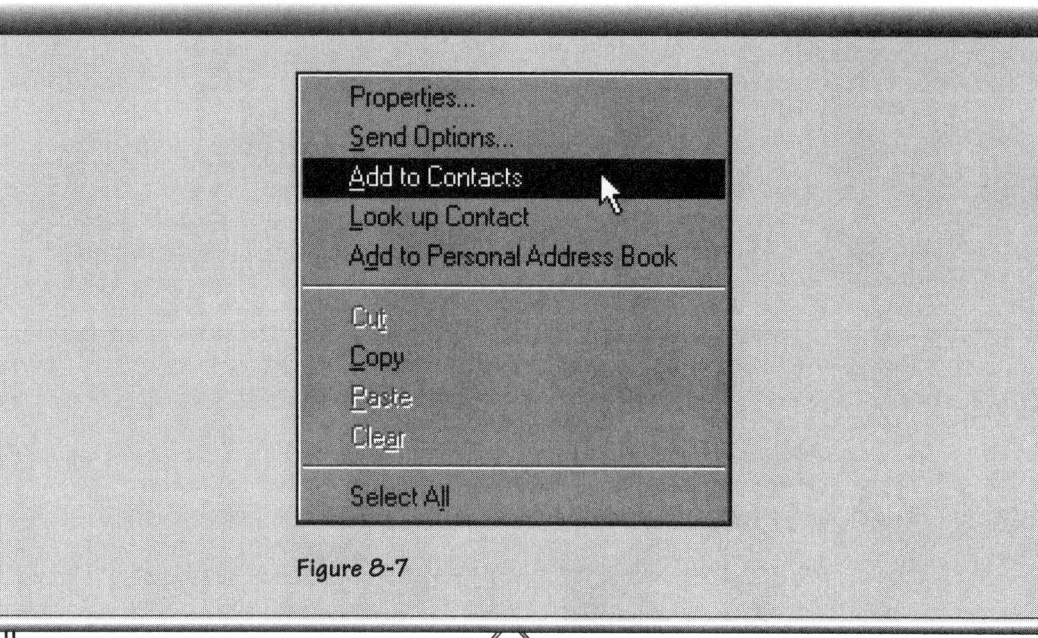

5. **Keep your mouse pointer over the address and right-click to open the pop-up menu, as shown in Figure 8-7.**

6. **Choose Add to Contacts from the pop-up menu.**

   A new contact form opens with the sender's e-mail name as the Full Name and as the File as name, and the sender's e-mail address is automatically entered in the E-mail field. Depending on the sender's e-mail program, you may have to edit the Full Name to reflect the sender's complete name as opposed to the e-mail name.

Save and Close

Contacts shortcut

7. **Fill out as much of the contact information as you require and then click Save and Close to return to the Inbox window.**

8. **Click the Contacts shortcut in the Outlook bar to return to the Contacts window.**

   You now have a new contact listed in the Address Cards view.

Recess

You're moving right along. Perhaps it's time to break, put your feet up on the desk, and pat yourself on the back for doing a great job. Take five and relax. You want to be fresh and alert for the remaining lessons. If there's going to be any sleeping in this class, we'll take care of it while you work.

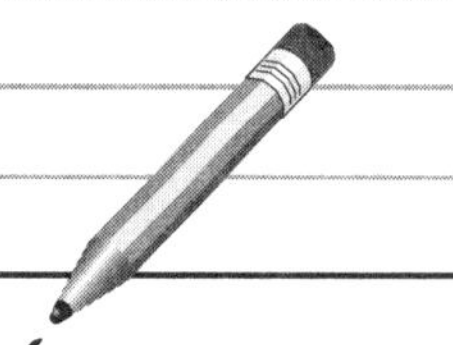

☑ Progress Check

If you can do the following, you've mastered this lesson:

- ❑ Switch to the Inbox and open an e-mail message.
- ❑ Create a contact entry from an e-mail message.

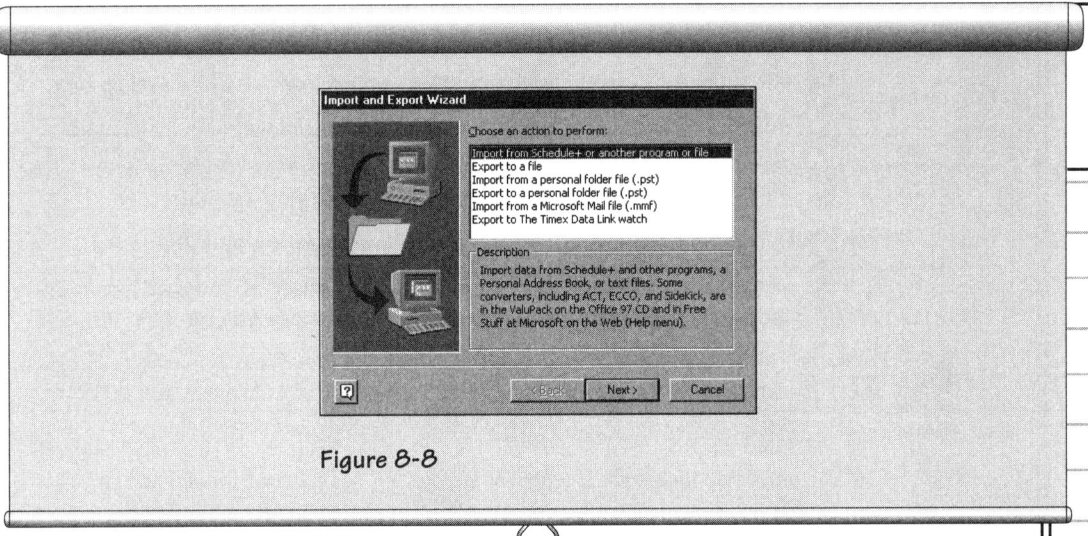

Figure 8-8

Figure 8-8: Outlook lets you import and export from a variety of programs and formats.

Notes:

Importing Your Personal Address Book

Lesson 8-6

Now that you have a contact manager at your disposal, it sure would be nice to have access to all the names in your Personal Address Book. This is especially true if you previously used Exchange and accumulated a large selection of names and e-mail addresses in that program. Outlook lets you do just that. Make sure you're in the Contacts window to proceed.

on the test

To import a Personal Address Book into the Contacts folder, follow these steps:

1. **Choose File⇨Import and Export from the menu bar to open the Import and Export wizard, as seen in Figure 8-8.**
2. **Click Import from Schedule+ or another program or file from the Choose an action to perform list.**

   The description box below the list of action choices provides information on the particular action you choose.
3. **Click the Next button to open the Import a File dialog box (see Figure 8-8).**
4. **Scroll down the Select file type to import from list and choose Personal Address Book.**

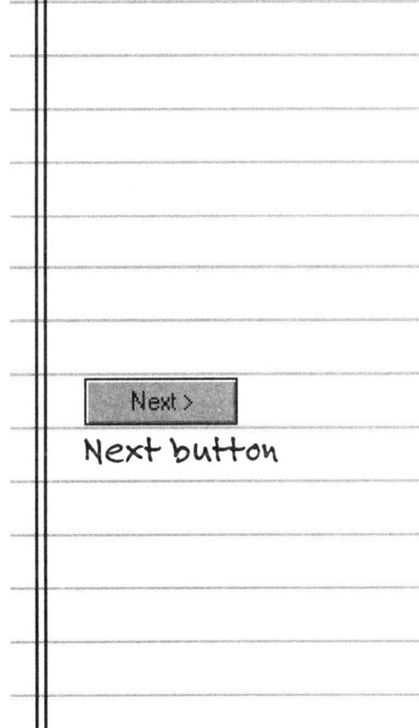

Next button

heads up

Outlook also provides a number of utilities for importing contact from various personal information managers such as Act, Ecco, Sidekick and others. They are covered in Lesson 8-7.

5 Click the Next button to open the second Import a File dialog box.

The new dialog box contains your current Outlook folders, with the Contacts folder highlighted.

6 Click the Contacts folder in the Select destination folder list.

7 Click the Next button to open the final Import a File dialog box.

8 If there is no check mark in the box to the left of "Import Personal Address Book into the Contac...", click the box to choose it.

heads up

This feature is very handy, but it does have one drawback. The import process can create duplicate entries. Unfortunately, this results in a new contact entry for all names on each Personal Distribution List in your Personal Address Book. Because Al Gore, William J. Clinton, and Newt Gingrich are individually entered in the address book and appear on the TopDogs Personal Distribution List, Outlook creates two contact records for each name when importing them into the Contacts folder. An individual who appears on five Personal Distribution Lists has six entries in the Contacts folder after importing. It's a pain, but you need to go through and delete any extra entries. We'll show you how later in this lesson.

Finish button

Progress Check

If you can do the following, you've mastered this lesson:

- ❑ Open the Import and Export wizard.
- ❑ Delete unwanted contacts.

9 Click the Finish button to convert the records.

on the test

10 If you have duplicate records as a result of Personal Distribution List entries, highlight each duplicate contact and press Ctrl+D to delete it.

Of course, you will have to enter any information not included in the address book for the new entries.

Lesson 8-7

Importing a Contact List from Another Program

Quite a few popular software programs enable you to keep track of contact lists. If you're currently using a contact manager or database program, switching to Outlook can be relatively painless, if you learn to import a contact list into the Outlook Contacts folder. Outlook imports information from the following programs: Act, Ecco, Access, Excel, dBase, and even text files.

on the CD

For this example, we use an Access contact database called Governor.mdb, which can be found on the CD included with this book. The database contains contact information for ten state governors. To import Governor.mdb follow these steps:

on the test

1. **Click the Contacts shortcut in the Outlook bar to make sure you are in the Contacts window.**
2. **Choose File⇨Import and Export to open the Import and Export wizard.**
3. **Click Import from Schedule+ or another program or file from the Choose an action to perform list.**
4. **Click the Next button to open the first Import a File dialog box.**
5. **Click Microsoft Access in the Select file type to import from list as seen in Figure 8-9.**
6. **Click Next to open the second Import a File dialog box (see Figure 8-10).**

   This box lets you choose the file to import and decide whether or not to permit the creation of duplicate records. Too bad Microsoft didn't include this option for importing your Personal Address Book.
7. **Click the Browse button to find the Governor.mdb database.**

   This opens the Browse dialog box, which lets you locate and select the file to import. Depending upon where you installed the CD files, you may have to click the Look in list box and change the drive and directory where the Governor.mdb file can be found.
8. **Click Do not import duplicate items in the Options section.**
9. **Click Next to open the third Import a File dialog box.**
10. **Highlight the Contacts folder in the Select destination folder list.**
11. **Click Next to move to the next Import a File dialog box.**

    Make sure that the box to the left of Import "Governor" into the "Contacts" folder contains a check mark.
12. **Click the Map Custom Fields button to open the Map Custom Fields dialog box.**

    To ensure that the information is transferred accurately from the file you're importing (the Access database, in this case) into your Outlook contact database, you must tell Outlook which import fields match up with the corresponding Outlook Contacts fields. While the whole thing sounds complicated, it's not. As a matter of fact, the most complicated thing about it is the jargon Outlook uses.

    The contact information that you're importing contains basic information such as name, address, phone number, and so on, as does the Outlook Contacts database. The only problem is Outlook and the other program don't necessarily call those fields of information by the same name. Mapping fields really means just letting Outlook know what you named a field in the file you're importing, so it can transfer the information from that field into the correct Outlook field. It's like a matching question on a test. You tell Outlook which field from the import file matches up with which Outlook field.

Notes:

Browse ...

Browse button

Map Custom Fields ...

Map Custom Fields button

Figure 8-9: Outlook provides a variety of import file options.

Figure 8-10: At last, an option to eliminate duplicates.

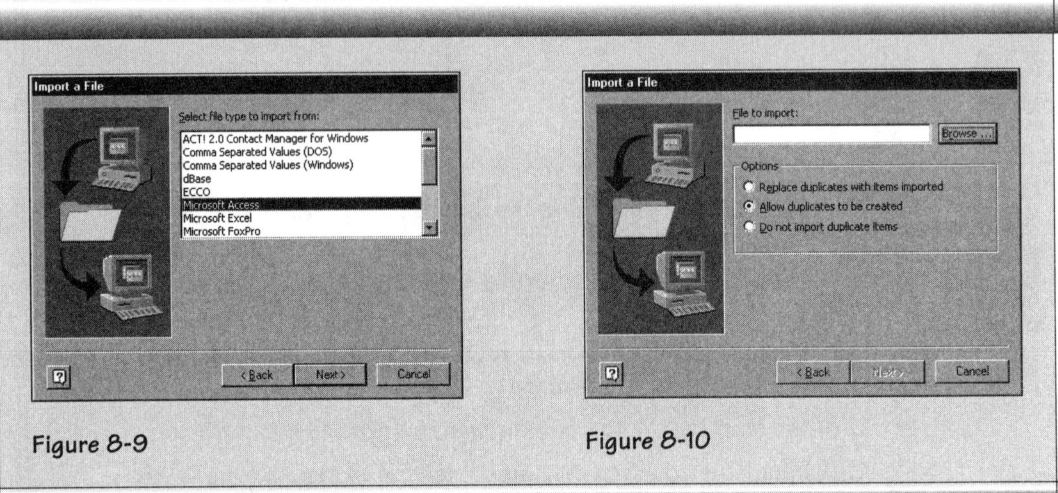

Figure 8-9

Figure 8-10

You must map the fields to complete the process. Complicated though it may seem, it's quite simple. All you do is drag the Governor field to the appropriate Contacts field and drop it.

13 **Click Full Name in the From window, hold down the left mouse button, drag Full Name to the right window, and drop it (let the left mouse button up) on Name.**

As you drag the Full Name field you can see its name moving along with your mouse pointer.

Continue to transfer the important fields from your database to their corresponding positions in your Outlook Contacts database. The following table shows you where each Access field belongs in the Outlook Contacts database:

Table 8-1

Access Field	*Outlook Contacts Database Field*
Address	Business Street
City	Business City
StateOrProvince	Business State
EmailAddress	E-mail
Web Page	Web Page

Hey, that was great! You got a lot of drag-and-drop practice. Now you're ready to import your Governor database into Outlook.

14 **Click OK to return to the last Import a File dialog box.**

15 **Click Finish to import the contact information.**

Now your Address Cards view contains entries for ten state governors. Open up a couple of the contacts and review the information to make sure that the import procedure placed the information in the correct fields. Note that not all of the governors had complete contact information, so some may be missing a phone or fax number or an e-mail address.

☑ Progress Check

If you can do the following, you've mastered this lesson:

- ❑ Import a file into Outlook.
- ❑ Drag and drop in Outlook.

Customizing the Address Cards View

Lesson 8-8

After you have imported the Governor.mdb file into the Contacts database, the Address Cards view probably appears somewhat deranged. Perhaps disarranged is a better word, and then again, perhaps not. Nevertheless, Outlook provides you with the tools to change the appearance of the Contacts views. This lesson takes you on a tour of those formatting options, including:

- **Best Fit:** Adjusts the column widths to use all the space available in the Information Viewer. This option is available only in Address Cards view and Detailed Address Cards view.
- **Show Empty Fields:** Shows all contact fields (addresses, phone numbers, and e-mail) whether or not the field contains data.
- **Format View:** Changes address card size, font style and size, and more.
- **Show Fields:** Lets you determine which fields show up in the Address Card view.

You want to begin by cleaning up the Address Cards view after importing the Governor.mdb file. Your Contacts window should look something like Figure 8-11, with a partial column showing.

If your Address Cards view does not show a partial column, we want you to create one so that you can follow along with this lesson. Position your mouse pointer over the vertical line separating the first and second columns until the pointer turns into a pair of parallel lines with horizontal arrows. When the mouse pointer changes, you can manually adjust the column width by dragging the vertical lines left or right. After the mouse pointer changes, hold down the left button and drag the vertical line to the right or left until the rightmost column is half hidden, and then let go of the mouse button. Your Address Card view should now resemble the one in Figure 8-11.

Follow these steps to turn your now topsy turvy Address Cards view into a neat and pretty sight your mother would be proud of:

1. **Move the mouse pointer to a blank area on the Address Cards view and right-click to open the pop-up menu.**

   Be sure that mouse pointer is an arrow, not a text I bar before right-clicking. If you get a pop-up menu that does not contain Best Fit, move the pointer to another blank spot and right-click again.

2. **Choose Best Fit from the pop-up menu to adjust the column widths automatically.**

   The Address Cards view changes to include whole columns only. To include more columns manually, drag a vertical column separator to the left until you have the desired number of columns showing, then use the Best Fit option to adjust the final view.

pop-up menu

Figure 8-11: There's nothing worse than a disorganized contact manager.

Figure 8-12: Change the font size and style with Format options.

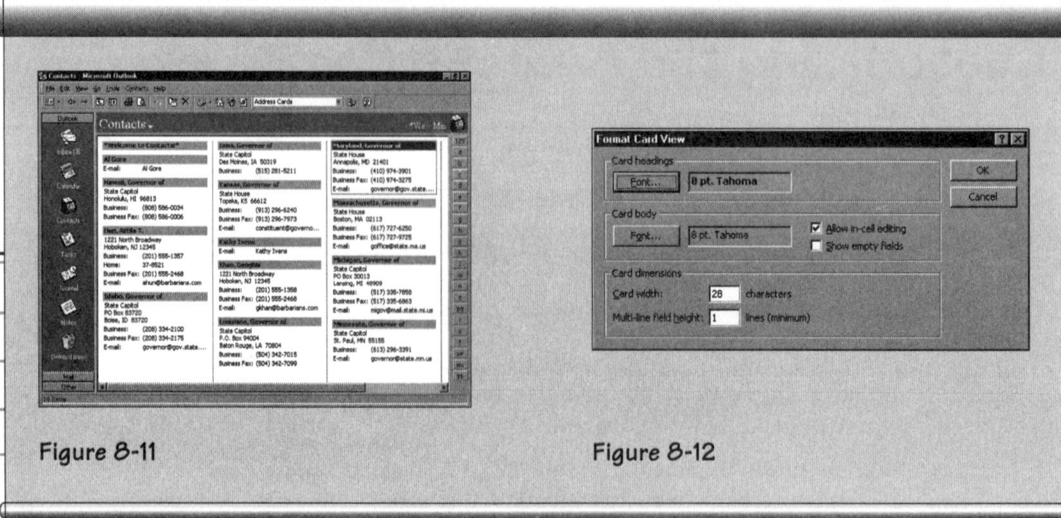

On that rare occasion when you find yourself with some spare time, you may want to update your contact information or add missing information. That's when the Show Empty Fields option comes in handy. By displaying fields without data, you can quickly determine the information required, and input it without opening each contact form.

3. **Move your mouse pointer to a blank area of the Address Cards view and right-click to open the pop-up menu again.**

4. **Choose Show Empty Fields to display contact data fields that contain no information.**

   Each of the address cards now shows all the contact fields (address, phone numbers, e-mail addresses) regardless of whether or not they contain information.

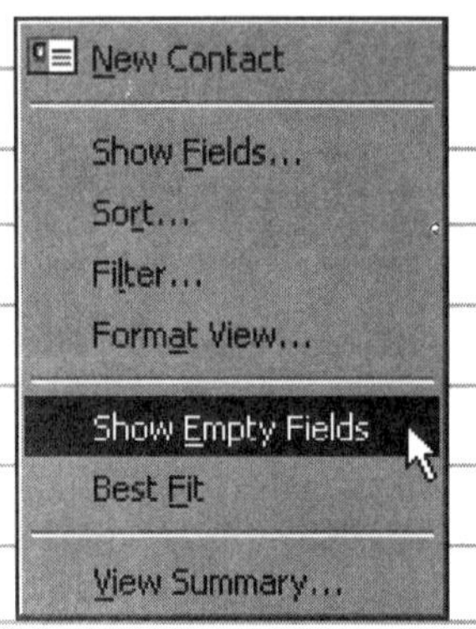

pop-up menu

5. **Move your mouse pointer to a blank area of the Address Cards view and right-click to open the pop-up menu again.**

   Notice that the Show Empty Fields selection now has a check mark to the left of it, indicating that the option is turned on.

6. **Choose Show Empty Fields to deselect the option.**

   The Address Cards view returns to normal, showing only those fields that contain data.

   Whether for practical (the old eyes are going) or aesthetic (that old 8-point Tahoma font is quite tedious) reasons, you occasionally need to change the design of the individual contact forms in the Address Cards view, no problem; go to Format View and tinker until you have it just the way you like it.

7. **Choose View⇨Format View from the menu bar to open the Format Card View dialog box (Figure 8-12).**

8. **Click the Card headings Font button to open the Font dialog box.**

9. **Choose 9 from the Size column and then click OK to return to the Format Card View dialog box.**

   The text box next to the Font button now says 9 pt. Tahoma.

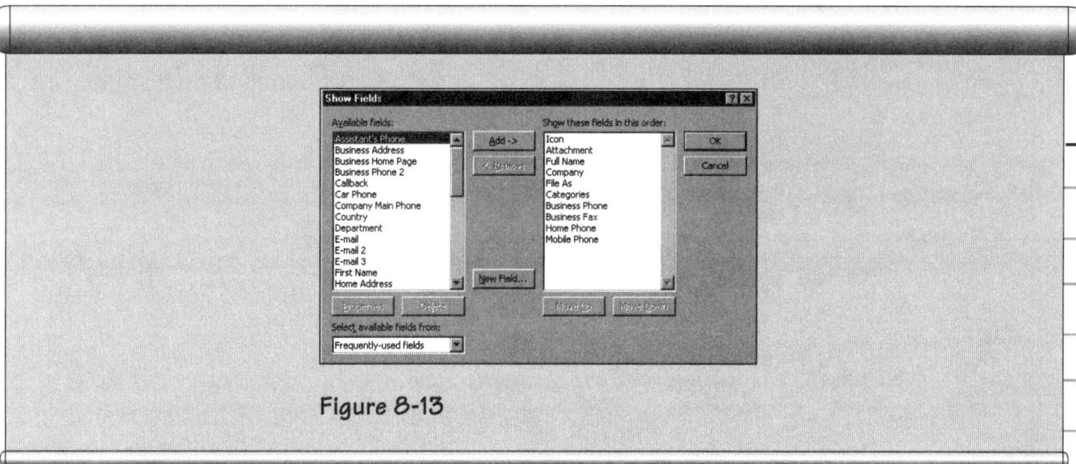

Figure 8-13: You decide what appears in the Address Cards view.

Notes:

10 **Click the Card body Font button to open the Font dialog box.**

11 **Scroll up the Font list and choose Arial.**

12 **Click OK to return to the Format Card View dialog box.**

Additional options in the Format Card View dialog box enable you to turn on or off in-cell editing and Show empty fields. In addition, you can change the size of the card with the Card dimensions options.

13 **Click OK to return to the Contacts window.**

The size of the card heading has increased to 9 point and the font for the body text of the cards is now Arial, not Tahoma.

Outlook is set up to appeal to a wide variety of users. That's great because it means that you probably don't have to make a ton of changes before you use it. However, because no two people are alike, there always comes a time when your needs and the majority's needs diverge.

on the test

Perhaps most of your communication is done via e-mail or telephone, which means you rarely use the mailing address information. However, you do spend a lot of time on the Internet, so you want to see if your contacts have their own Web pages. With a couple of mouse-clicks you can change the Address Cards view to eliminate the address information and include the Web page information.

14 **Choose View⇨Show Fields from the menu bar to open the Show Fields dialog box as seen in Figure 8-13.**

15 **Choose Mailing Address from the Show these fields in this order list on the right side of the dialog box.**

16 **Click the Remove button to eliminate it from the Address Cards view.**

<- Remove

Remove button

Removing the field from the Address Card view does not permanently delete it from the contact database, it merely removes it from view. The address information is still retained in the database and can be accessed by opening the individual contact forms.

17 **Scroll to the bottom of the Available fields list on the left side of the Show Fields dialog box and choose Web Page.**

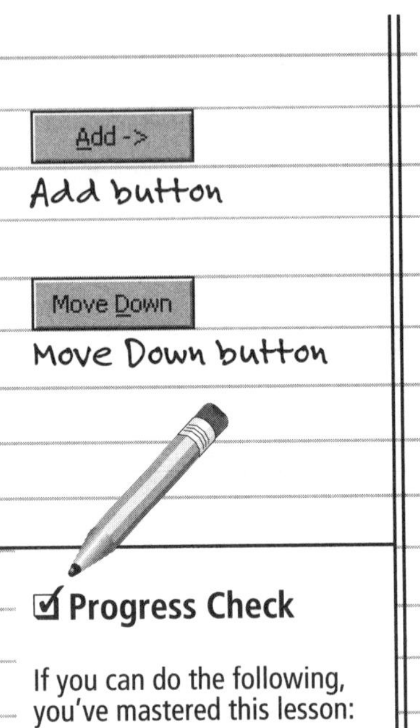

18 Click the Add button to include the Web Page field in the Address Cards view.

Notice that the Web Page field is now positioned between the Business Phone and the Company Main Phone fields. You want to put it at the bottom of the list.

19 With the Web Page field highlighted, click the Move Down button until the Web Page field appears at the bottom of the list, following E-mail 3.

20 Click OK to return to the Contacts window.

Now you can see that the Mailing Address field is missing from all cards and the Web Page field is visible for each contact that has a Web page.

The ability to mold the Contacts folder to suit your needs is one of the nice things about Outlook. Now you've got the tools to make it look and perform the way you want it to.

☑ Progress Check

If you can do the following, you've mastered this lesson:

- ❑ Automatically adjust column widths in the Address Cards view.
- ❑ Manually adjust column widths in the Address Cards view.
- ❑ Add and remove fields from the address cards.
- ❑ Change the font style and size of the address cards.

Unit 8 Quiz

1. **How do you add a new contact to the Contacts folder?**

   A. Use a calculator.

   B. Tear out the appropriate page from the phone book and toss it in the folder.

   C. Press Ctrl+N in the Contacts window and fill out a new contact form.

   D. Assign it as a task to someone else.

   E Sorry, that information is confidential.

2. **How do you enter additional contacts from the same company?**

   A. One at a time.

   B. You don't. Just enter the first contact, then call her and ask to be transferred to any of the others.

   C. Through the open slot in the back of the computer.

   D. You can't fool me — type 'em in!

   E. Enter the first contact and then choose Contacts➪New Contact from Same Company to enter each additional contact.

3. **How do you import a contact list from another program?**

   A. Get the proper State Department clearances and ship it in by freighter.

   B. Call Scottie and have him beam it up.

   C. Print the entire Personal Address Book and type the information into the contact database.

   D. Who's this Scottie guy?

   E. Choose File➪Import and Export and use the Import and Export wizard.

4. **Why is it a good idea to keep track of detailed contact information?**

   A. So you don't forget.

   B. Your boss threatened to fire you unless you do it.

   C. It gives you something to do while you're waiting for the lunch hour to arrive.

   D. So you can hunt the contact down if he skips town.

   E. It's a good business practice. It lets the contact know that you're interested enough to remember the small things.

5. **Where can you find the global journal options?**

   A. In the closet, behind the paper towels.

   B. On a world map.

   C. Try the blue coffee can out on the workbench.

   D. Choose Tools➪Options to open the Options dialog box and then click the Journal tab.

   E. Somewhere between Salt Lake City and Des Moines.

Notes:

Unit 8 Exercise

1. Enter contact information for three business associates who do not currently appear in your Contacts folder or Personal Address Book.
2. Set the Journal options for the new contacts using the global Options feature.
3. Create a contact from the last e-mail you received from someone not already in your contact database.
4. Change the Address Cards headings back to 8-point Tahoma bold and the card body text to 8-point Tahoma regular.
5. Use the Show Fields option to add the Mailing Address field to the Address Cards view and remove the Web Page field.

Unit 9

Using the Contact List

Objectives for This Unit

- ✓ Viewing contacts
- ✓ Modifying contact list views
- ✓ Using contacts to create e-mail messages
- ✓ Recording journal entries for contacts
- ✓ Sorting contacts
- ✓ Printing contacts
- ✓ Using the Contacts database with Word mail merge

Prerequisites

- Entering a new contact (Lesson 8-1)
- Setting journal options (Lesson 8-4)
- Creating an e-mail from a contact (Lesson 8-5)

- Tribute.doc

The previous unit provided you with the tools you need to set up and maintain a good contact-management system using Outlook. After you set up your system and build your Contacts database, you can put it to good use. This lesson gives you the hands-on experience you need to do just that.

Keeping track of names, addresses, and phone numbers is just the beginning of what you can accomplish with the Outlook Contacts database. You can create form letters, print labels, and create printouts to add a hardcopy of your contact information to many popular daily planners and organizers, just to name a few.

Viewing Contacts — Lesson 9-1

If the only thing you intend to do with your Contacts database is open it up, look for a name, and retrieve some basic contact information, you'll be wasting a powerful tool. Computers excel at manipulating data, and the Outlook Contacts database is a prime example.

use different views to see just the information you want to see

Very often you search for information using different criteria. When you use your Rolodex or paper address book, you are limited to viewing your contact information in one format only, regardless of your search criteria. Not so with Outlook. The Contacts folder offers several different standard views that give you a great deal of flexibility in viewing your contact information. We start off this unit by taking a tour of the different views available in the Contacts folder.

1 If you are not in the Contacts window, click the Contacts shortcut in the Outlook bar.

The default view for the Contacts folder is the Address Cards view. This view presents the basic address, phone, and e-mail information in the form of an address card for each contact. Double-clicking a card opens the contact form, where you enter or edit information as needed.

Also notice the Letter tab that runs down the length of the right side of the Contacts window (see Figure 9-1). This list of buttons enables you to move quickly to the first contact whose displayed name begins with the letter you click.

heads up

You see the Letter tab unless you sort the Contacts database by a nontext field, such as birthday or anniversary. To display the Letter tab, re-sort the contacts using a text field such as File As or Full Name. You can sort the Contacts database by choosing View⇨Sort from the menu bar and selecting a sort field from the Sort items by field of the Sort dialog box that appears. After you've made your selection, click OK to return to the Contacts window.

on the test

2 Choose View⇨Current View⇨Detailed Address Cards to open the Detailed Address Cards view.

The Contacts window retains the address card format, but provides additional information not found in the Address Cards view. Note that Full Name, Job Title, Department, Home information, and more now appear on the address cards. Of course, if you did not enter any information in the newly visible fields, no new information appears.

3 Choose View⇨Current View⇨Phone List to open the Phone List view.

Now the view has changed dramatically from an address card format to a table format. A table, as you can see, is a row-and-column format, not unlike a spreadsheet. Rows contain items, while columns contain specific information related to the items. Table views are great for creating lists and arranging them by various criteria, such as city or state, company, last name, first name, and so on. It's an excellent way to separate personal from business contacts if you keep them in the same database.

4 Choose View⇨Current View⇨By Category to open the By Category view.

The By Category view, like the Phone List view, is a table view. However, the By Category view groups the contacts by category. This view is extremely helpful if you assign your contacts to categories. If you do not use categories, it simply groups the contacts alphabetically under one category called *none*. Also note that the fields shown are different from those displayed in the Phone List view.

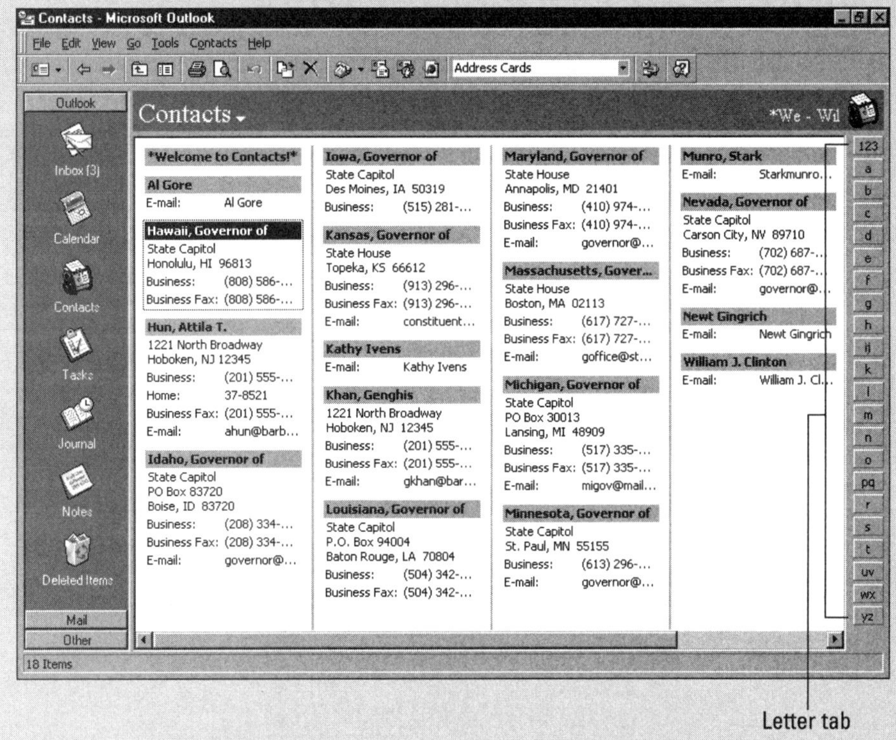

Letter tab

Figure 9-1

Figure 9-1: Use the Letter tab to find a contact quickly.

Notes:

5 Choose View⇨Current View⇨By Company to open the By Company view.

This table view assembles your contacts by the company name that you associate with each contact. There are times when you work on a project that involves different departments of the same company. It sure makes life simple if you can group all of the contacts from that company and make all your calls or send your e-mail messages one right after the other.

6 Choose View⇨Current View⇨By Location to open the By Location view.

Another table view, the By Location view comes in handy when you want to group your contacts by locale. The default group is country, but can be set to state, city, or zip code to refine the results even further. It's an ideal tool for a sales rep planning a trip through his or her territory.

heads up

When importing contact information from another program such as Access, dBase, or a personal information manager, Outlook occasionally fails to include some of the contact information in the table views, even though it appears in the contact form itself. If you find this happening to you, the only solution is to open the contact form and reenter the information manually.

Being able to view your contact information from different perspectives lets you squeeze the most value out of the effort you expend inputting the data.

☑ Progress Check

If you can do the following, you've mastered this lesson:

- ❑ Tell the difference between a table view and an address card view.
- ❑ Change views in the Contacts window.
- ❑ Use the letter tab to locate contacts in the Address Cards view.

Lesson 9-2 Modifying Contacts Table Views

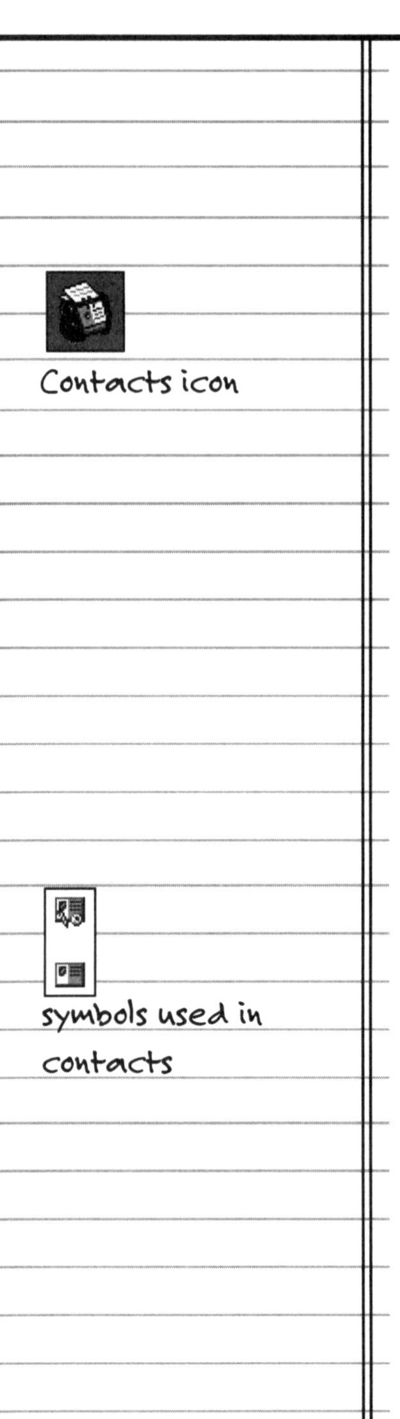

Outlook offers a number of standard views you can use to look at your contact information. The standard views, such as the views you saw in Lesson 9-1, are those that have the widest appeal. While these standard views may suffice for most users, you may encounter situations that require a view not provided by Outlook. Fortunately, you have all the tools you need to meet such an occasion when it arises. Outlook allows you to change the existing views and create new views of your own.

We covered modifying the Address Cards view in Lesson 8-8, therefore, we want to concentrate on changing table views in this lesson. Because any method used to make a change in one table view has the same results when applied to different table views, we will use the Phone List view to practice on.

To begin customizing the Phone List view, follow these steps:

1. **Choose View⇨Current View⇨Phone List to open the Phone List view as seen in Figure 9-2.**

   A couple of things to take note of before we begin:

   - The contacts that appear in your contact list may not match ours, but the layout should be the same.
   - The Symbol column indicates the status of the record (see symbols in margin notes) and the Attachment column indicates the presence (or absence) of an attachment.
   - The list is initially sorted by the File As column, not Full Name, the first text field. The *Welcome to Contacts!* entry (see Figure 9-1) appears first due to the leading asterisk, which is a special character and precedes letters and numbers in a sort.

   If you prefer that the File As column appears as the first text field in the view, and you want to reposition it between the attachments column and the Full Name column, no problem, just grab it and put it where you want it.

2. **Position your mouse pointer over the File As column header.**

3. **Press the left mouse button, hold it down, and drag the File As header to the left.**

   As you pick up the File As header and move it, two things happen. It leaves a File As depression behind indicating the header is gone. In addition, a pair of red arrows appear as you move to the left, indicating the new insertion point (see Figure 9-3).

   You can only move the header left or right along the column header plane. If you move above or below the column headers a large, black X appears on the header you are dragging, indicating that you are out of bounds and can't drop the header in that area.

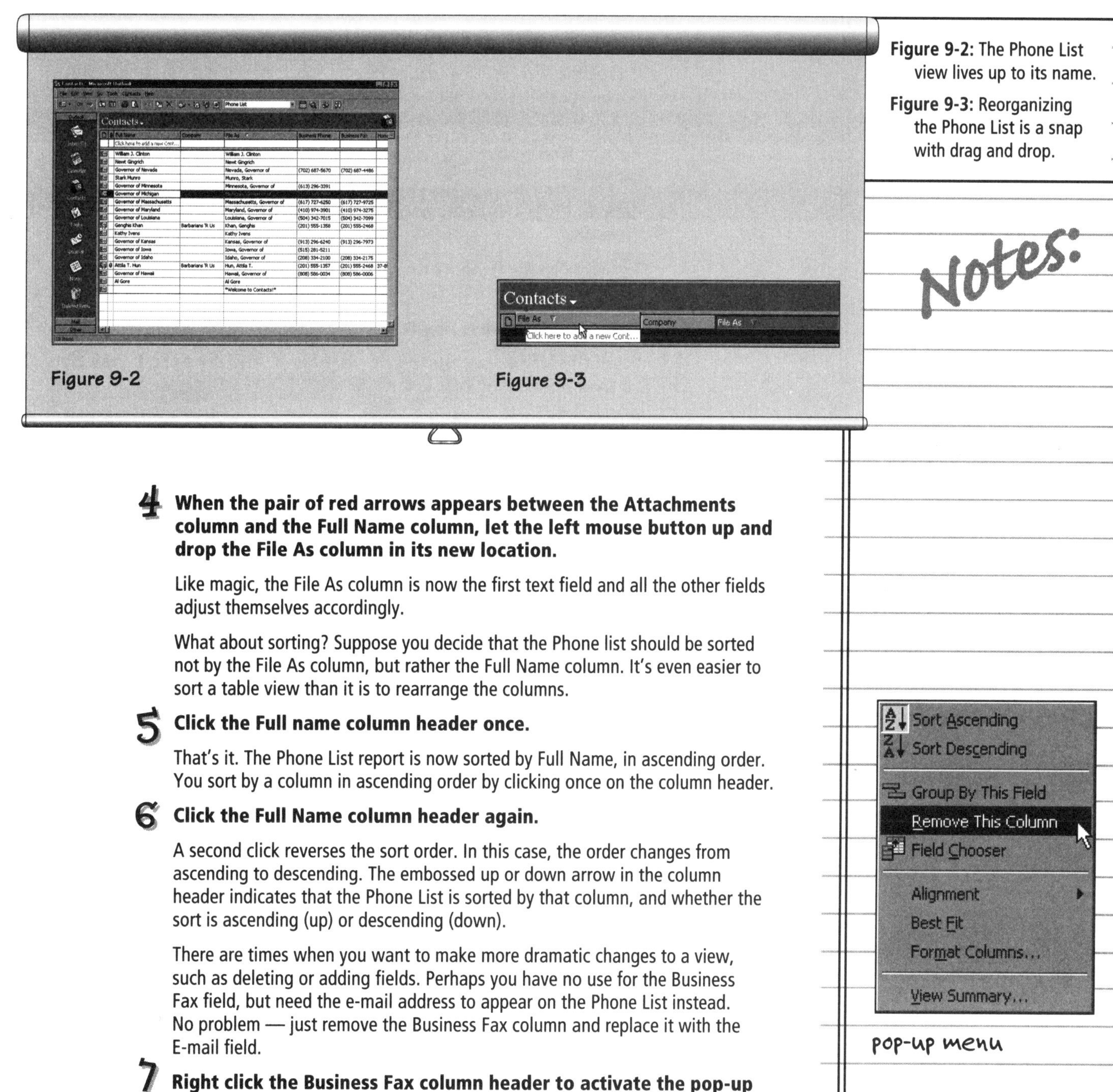

Figure 9-2: The Phone List view lives up to its name.

Figure 9-3: Reorganizing the Phone List is a snap with drag and drop.

4 When the pair of red arrows appears between the Attachments column and the Full Name column, let the left mouse button up and drop the File As column in its new location.

Like magic, the File As column is now the first text field and all the other fields adjust themselves accordingly.

What about sorting? Suppose you decide that the Phone list should be sorted not by the File As column, but rather the Full Name column. It's even easier to sort a table view than it is to rearrange the columns.

5 Click the Full name column header once.

That's it. The Phone List report is now sorted by Full Name, in ascending order. You sort by a column in ascending order by clicking once on the column header.

6 Click the Full Name column header again.

A second click reverses the sort order. In this case, the order changes from ascending to descending. The embossed up or down arrow in the column header indicates that the Phone List is sorted by that column, and whether the sort is ascending (up) or descending (down).

There are times when you want to make more dramatic changes to a view, such as deleting or adding fields. Perhaps you have no use for the Business Fax field, but need the e-mail address to appear on the Phone List instead. No problem — just remove the Business Fax column and replace it with the E-mail field.

7 Right click the Business Fax column header to activate the pop-up menu.

8 Choose Remove This Column to eliminate the Business Fax column from the Phone List.

Notes:

Sort Ascending
Sort Descending
Group By This Field
Remove This Column
Field Chooser
Alignment
Best Fit
Format Columns...
View Summary...

pop-up menu

In the blink of an eye, the column disappears. However, it is not permanently deleted, just removed from the Phone List until such time that you decide to re-add it. All the Business Fax data is still safe and sound in the Contacts database.

Now it's time to add the E-mail field to replace the Business Fax field we just removed.

9 **Choose View⇨Field Chooser from the menu bar to open the Field Chooser.**

The Field Chooser is exactly what it claims to be, a list of available fields from which to choose.

10 **Position your mouse pointer over the E-mail field.**

11 **Press the left mouse button down, hold it, and drag the E-mail field to the Phone List header bar.**

12 **Position the E-mail field between the Business Phone column and the Home Phone column (indicated by a pair of red arrows), let go of the left mouse button and drop the E-mail field.**

The Business Phone column and the Home Phone column cooperate by spreading apart and making room for the E-mail field. Note that the E-mail field is no longer available in the Field Chooser. Should you remove it from Phone List it reappears in the Field Chooser.

The new E-mail column is rather scrunched. Why don't you expand it a little and reduce the size of the File As column while you're at it?

13 **Position your mouse pointer over the vertical line dividing the E-mail column header and the Home Phone column header.**

14 **Click and hold the left mouse button when the mouse pointer turns into a cross consisting of a vertical bar with a double sided arrow; then drag the divider line to the right until the column is wide enough.**

You can make the column as wide or as narrow as you wish by dragging the sides left or right. Now reduce the size of the File As column.

15 **Using the same procedure, grab the divider line between the File As column header and the Full Name column header and move it to the left until the File As column reaches the desired width.**

Another way to adjust the width of a column is by using the Best Fit feature.

16 **Position your mouse pointer over the Business Phone column header and right click to open the pop-up menu.**

17 **Choose Best Fit to automatically adjust the width of the Business Phone column.**

The column is reduced to the exact width necessary to display the contents of the column.

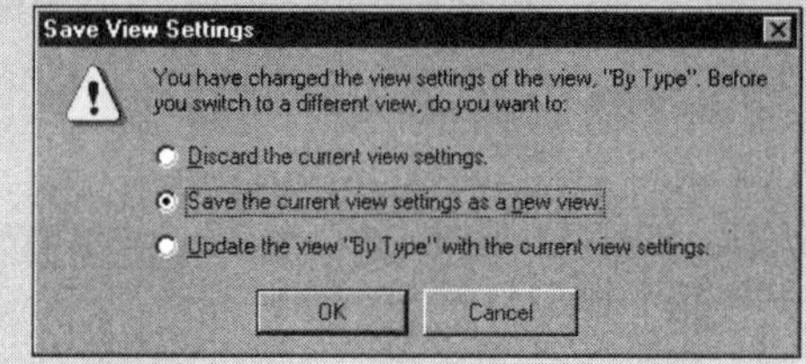

Save View Settings

You have changed the view settings of the view, "By Type". Before you switch to a different view, do you want to:

- Discard the current view settings.
- Save the current view settings as a new view.
- Update the view "By Type" with the current view settings.

OK Cancel

Figure 9-4

Figure 9-4: You can save or discard the changes you make to a view.

18 Choose View⇨Current View⇨Address Cards to return to the Address Cards view.

The Save View Settings dialog box appears and gives you three choices for dealing with the changes you've made to the Phone List view (see Figure 9-4).

19 Click the second choice, Save the current view settings as a new view, and then click OK.

The Copy View dialog box pops up and asks you to name the new view and determine which folders can use the new view.

20 Type Phone List 2 in the Name of new view text box and then click OK to save the new view and return to the Address Cards view.

21 Choose View⇨Current View to open the Current View menu.

The newly created Phone List 2 view now displays at the bottom of the menu as an additional choice.

22 Click anywhere on the Contacts window (except the open menus) to close the menus and return to the Contacts window.

In one short (well, relatively short) lesson, you've learned to move columns, sort columns, add and delete columns, change the size of columns and create a new table view. Not bad for a morning's work.

☑ Progress Check

If you can do the following, you've mastered this lesson:

- ❑ Reorganize a table view by moving the column headers.
- ❑ Sort a table view by a particular column.
- ❑ Adjust the width of columns in a table view.
- ❑ Create a new view by modifying an existing view.

Doing Real Work from the Contacts Database

Lesson 9-3

Because most of what you do in Outlook involves people who are likely to appear in your Contacts database, it stands to reason that you can perform many of the common Outlook tasks without leaving the Contacts window.

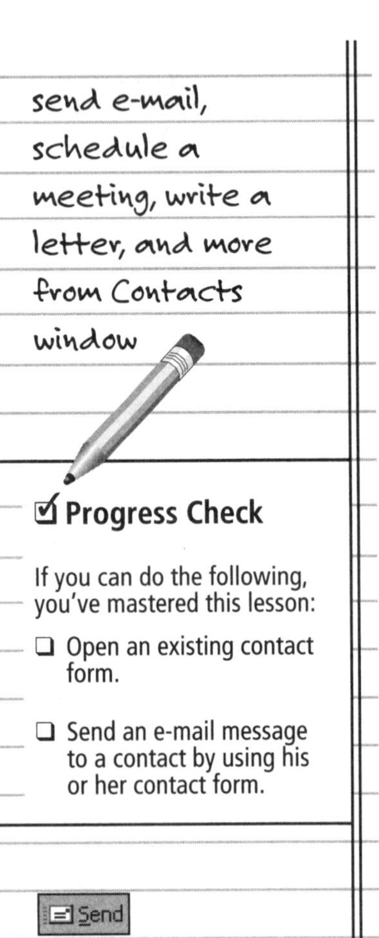

In fact, you never have to leave the Contacts window to create an e-mail, set up a meeting, assign a task, or compose a letter to any of the contacts listed in your database. Outlook makes it possible to perform all these functions from within the Contacts window.

All you need to do is highlight the desired contact, choose the action to perform from the Contacts menu, and complete the appropriate forms as they appear.

In this lesson, we show you how to send e-mail from the Contacts window. Performing other functions from the Contacts window is as simple as choosing the desired activity from the Contacts menu.

☑ Progress Check

If you can do the following, you've mastered this lesson:

- ❑ Open an existing contact form.
- ❑ Send an e-mail message to a contact by using his or her contact form.

Follow these steps to send an e-mail from within the Contacts database:

1. **In the Address Cards view, click Al Gore's address card to highlight it.**
2. **Choose Contacts⇨New Message to Contact from the menu bar to open a new message form for Al Gore.**

   A new e-mail message form appears with Mr. Gore's e-mail address inserted in the To field. Outlook automatically places the cursor in the Subject field.
3. **Type** My Opinion **in the Subject field and then Tab to the message body.**
4. **Type a brief message to the vice president voicing your opinion on an issue of importance to you.**
5. **Click the Send button to send the message.**

   Refer to Unit 2 if you need a refresher on sending e-mail from Outlook.

Send

Send button

The Contacts database provides a prime example of how the various components in Outlook can work together to make your life easier.

Lesson 9-4 Recording Automatic Journal Entries

Outlook can automatically track e-mail related information for a contact

One of the primary reasons for maintaining a Contacts database is to keep a record of your dealings with business associates. Unless you have a photographic memory, chances are you can't recall the details of conversations you had two weeks ago or last month's team meeting. Taking notes on paper is an excellent idea. Unfortunately, trying to find those notes when you need them the most is a feat worthy of a master magician. Tracking all of the bits and pieces of communication with your contacts is one of the major strengths of the Contacts feature. A direct link between the Contacts folder and the Journal folder is the secret of successful contact management. Recording journal entries for each contact stores a particular bit of information so that it is directly associated with the contact.

As discussed in Unit 8, you can record some journal entries automatically, while you must enter others manually. The only items that you can record automatically are e-mail messages, meeting requests, and task assignments, all of which involve e-mail.

To see how automatic journal entries work, send an e-mail message to President Clinton. However, before you send the e-mail, you must first turn on automatic journal entry recording for Mr. Clinton:

1. **If you are not in Address Cards view choose View⇨Current View⇨Address Cards and open it now.**
2. **In Address Cards view, click William J. Clinton's address card to highlight it.**
3. **Press Ctrl+O to open Mr. Clinton's contact form.**
4. **Click the Journal tab to open the contact journal entries form.**
5. **Click Automatically record journal entries for this contact to place a check mark in the box to the left and enable automatic journal entry recording for the president.**
6. **Click the Save and Close button to save the changes and return to the Contacts window.**

   When you return to the Contacts window, William J. Clinton's address card should still be highlighted. If it is not highlighted, click Mr. Clinton's address card to select it before moving on to the next step.

heads up

7. **Choose Contacts⇨New Message to Contact from the menu bar to open a new message form for William J. Clinton.**

   A new e-mail message form appears with Mr. Clinton's e-mail address inserted in the To field. The cursor is automatically placed in the Subject field.
8. **Type** My Opinion **in the Subject text box and Tab to the message body.**
9. **Pick a current topic and let the president know how you feel about it in a short note.**
10. **Press the Send button to close the form and send the e-mail.**

    An automatic journal entry for an e-mail is not recorded until the e-mail is sent. Depending upon the e-mail system to which you are connected, hitting the Send button may or may not actually send your e-mail. If you are on a network, your e-mail is most likely sent to the network post office as soon as you click the Send button, and therefore is considered sent. However, if you use a modem and log onto an Internet service provider (ISP) to send your e-mail, clicking the Send button places your e-mail in the Outbox until you connect to your ISP and complete the transfer. The bottom line here is that until the e-mail appears in your Sent folder, it does not show up as an automatic journal entry.

heads up

11. **After your e-mail is sent, click William J. Clinton's address card and press Ctrl+O to open the contact form.**
12. **Click the Journal tab to see the automatic entry, which should look like the entry in Figure 9-5.**

Notes:

Save and Close

Save and Close button

Send

Send button

send e-mail for Outlook to record an entry

Type	Start	Subject
E-mail message	Wed 2/26/97 9:10 AM	My Opinion (sent)

Figure 9-5

Figure 9-5: Keep tabs on all your contacts with journal entries.

Notes:

13 **Double-click the My Opinion journal entry to open it.**

The My Opinion journal entry form opens, providing the subject, type, contact, and time of the journal entry. In the display window at the bottom is a shortcut to the e-mail message itself.

14 **Double-click the My Opinion shortcut in the display window.**

A copy of the original e-mail message opens for your review.

15 **Press Alt+F4 to close the message, then press Alt+F4 again to close the My Opinion journal entry, and then press Alt+F4 a third time to close William J. Clinton's contact form.**

Before moving on, take a quick look at the Journal folder and see where the new journal entry is located.

Journal shortcut

16 **Click the Journal shortcut in the Outlook bar to open the Journal window.**

17 **Choose View⇨Current View⇨By Contact to open the By Contact view.**

18 **Click the + button next to Contact: William J. Clinton to see the journal entries for Mr. Clinton.**

The journal entry is positioned according to the time line at the top of the Journal information viewer to reflect the date and time at which the entry was recorded.

19 **Click the Contacts icon in the Outlook bar to return to the Contacts window.**

You are now well on your way to becoming an accomplished Outlook user. Keep this up and you may even find that you can leave the office at a reasonable hour and spend some time with the family or friends.

☑ Progress Check

If you can do the following, you've mastered this lesson:

- ❑ Set automatic journal entry options for a contact.
- ❑ View journal entries in the Journal window.
- ❑ Delete a journal entry for a contact.
- ❑ Restore a deleted journal entry for a contact.

Recess

You've made tremendous progress and may consider taking a break at this point. Not only have you earned it, but you'll be better prepared to tackle the rest of this unit after you relax and refresh your mental faculties.

Recording Manual Journal Entries

Lesson 9-5

Outlook puts a limit on which items you can record automatically, making it necessary to enter some journal entries manually. All non–e-mail items, including phone calls, letters, conversations, and documents, fall into the manual entry category. The basic manual entry procedure involves creating a journal entry and inserting the particular item into the newly created journal entry.

non-e-mail related information must be entered manually

Entering documents in the journal

In this lesson, you create a manual entry for a recent letter sent to Genghis concerning his demand for the payment of tribute. You can find the letter, called Tribute.doc, on the CD included with this book.

1. **In the Address Cards view of the Contacts window, highlight Genghis Khan's card and press Ctrl+O to open his contact form.**
2. **Click the Journal tab to open the journal entries form.**

on the test

3. **Click the New Journal Entry button to open a new journal entry form as seen in Figure 9-6.**

New Journal Entry...

New Journal Entry button

4. **Press Alt+U to move the cursor to the Subject text box.**
5. **Delete Genghis Khan using the Delete key.**
6. **Type** Demand for Tribute **in the Subject text box.**
7. **Click the down arrow at the end of the Entry type field to open the drop-down list.**
8. **Choose Letter from the drop-down list.**
9. **Choose Insert⇨File from the entry form menu bar to open the Insert File dialog box.**

   on the CD

   The Insert File dialog box enables you to locate and select the file to insert. Depending upon where you installed the CD files you may have to click the Look in list box and change the drive and directory where the Tribute.doc file can be found.
10. **After you've found and selected the Tribute.doc file, click OK to return to the journal entry form.**

   Notice that the file has been inserted in the notes window at the bottom of the journal entry window next to the shortcut to the Genghis Khan contact form. Clicking the Tribute.doc icon opens the letter in Microsoft Word.

Figure 9-6: The new journal entry form provides for all your manual journal-entry needs.

Figure 9-7: An Outlook note resembles an electronic sticky note.

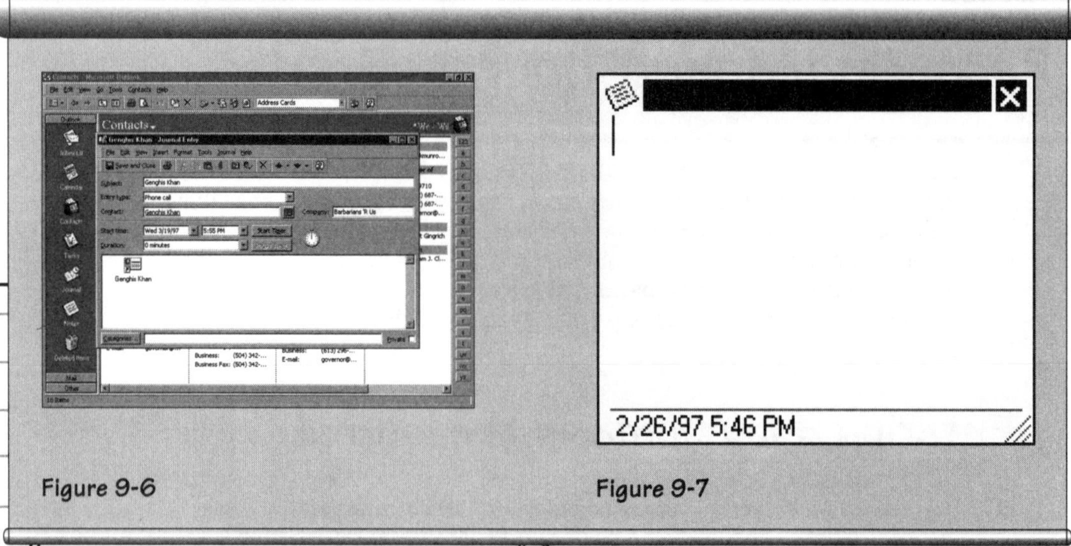

11 **Click the Save and Close button to save the new journal entry and return to Genghis Khan's contact form.**

The Demand for Tribute letter now appears in the journal entries window. To see the contents of a journal entry, double-click to open it.

12 **Click Save and Close to return to the Contacts window.**

Entering other Outlook items in the journal

Save and Close button

Manual journal entries can also include Outlook items such as notes, appointments, e-mail messages from a contact, and so on. To see how the inclusion of an Outlook item differs from a document or letter, we want you to jot down a quick note about Attila T. Hun and create a new journal entry for the note. Notes in Outlook are the electronic equivalent of the sticky notes you probably have plastered all over your monitor. They even look like little yellow sticky notes when you create them. You can jot down, ideas, information, questions, or anything else you want.

Notes shortcut

1. **Click the Notes shortcut in the Outlook bar to open the Notes window.**
2. **Press Ctrl+N to open a new notes form as seen in Figure 9-7.**
3. **Type** Attila's Hobbies: burning villages, stampeding livestock, collecting stamps **and then press Alt+F4 to close the note.**
4. **Click the Contacts shortcut in the Outlook bar to return to the Contacts window.**

Contacts shortcut

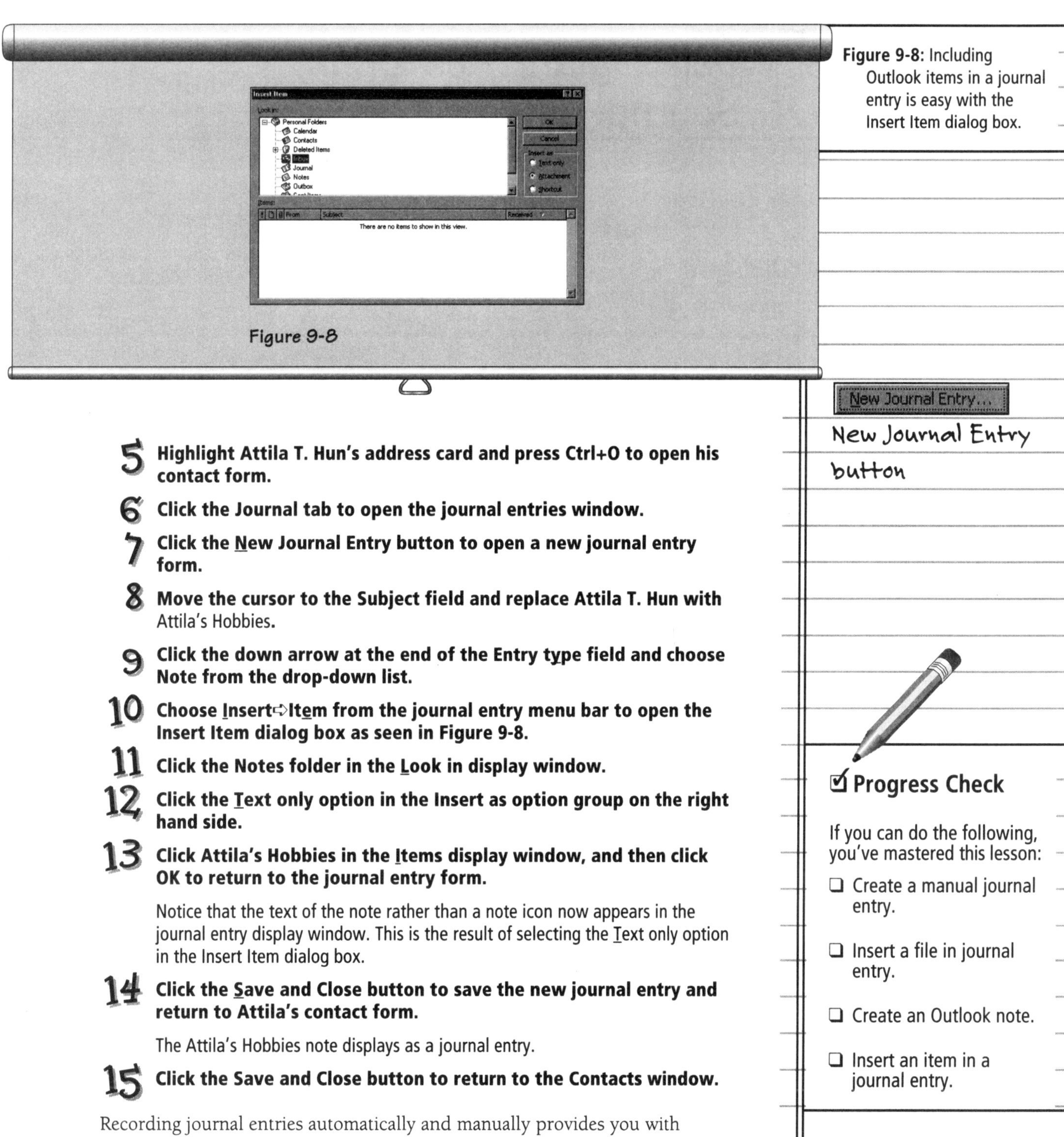

Figure 9-8: Including Outlook items in a journal entry is easy with the Insert Item dialog box.

New Journal Entry...

New Journal Entry button

5 **Highlight Attila T. Hun's address card and press Ctrl+O to open his contact form.**

6 **Click the Journal tab to open the journal entries window.**

7 **Click the New Journal Entry button to open a new journal entry form.**

8 **Move the cursor to the Subject field and replace Attila T. Hun with** Attila's Hobbies.

9 **Click the down arrow at the end of the Entry type field and choose Note from the drop-down list.**

10 **Choose Insert⇨Item from the journal entry menu bar to open the Insert Item dialog box as seen in Figure 9-8.**

11 **Click the Notes folder in the Look in display window.**

12 **Click the Text only option in the Insert as option group on the right hand side.**

13 **Click Attila's Hobbies in the Items display window, and then click OK to return to the journal entry form.**

Notice that the text of the note rather than a note icon now appears in the journal entry display window. This is the result of selecting the Text only option in the Insert Item dialog box.

14 **Click the Save and Close button to save the new journal entry and return to Attila's contact form.**

The Attila's Hobbies note displays as a journal entry.

15 **Click the Save and Close button to return to the Contacts window.**

Recording journal entries automatically and manually provides you with instant access to all your important communication and correspondence with each contact.

☑ Progress Check

If you can do the following, you've mastered this lesson:

- ❑ Create a manual journal entry.
- ❑ Insert a file in journal entry.
- ❑ Create an Outlook note.
- ❑ Insert an item in a journal entry.

Lesson 9-6

Deleting and Restoring Journal Entries

There is, of course, a downside to automatic journal entry recording: the fact that it is automatic. As a result, everything you send to the contact is recorded regardless of its importance or value. Even with manual journal entry recording, you sometimes record items that you later wish to remove. Fortunately, there's a simple solution. It's called the Delete Journal Entry button and it resides on the Journal tab of the contact form.

To delete a journal entry from a contact form follow these steps:

1. **Click William J. Clinton's address card and press Ctrl+O to open the contact form.**
2. **Click the Journal tab to open the journal entries tab.**
3. **Highlight the My Opinion e-mail entry by clicking it.**
4. **Click the Delete Journal Entry button to delete the My Opinion entry.**

   Once again, Outlook does your bidding, and the journal entry disappears. Ah, but what if you delete the wrong entry? Is there a way to retrieve it? Fortunately, the answer is yes. Just follow the steps below.

Delete Journal Entry button

5. **Press Alt+F4 to close the contact form and return to the Contacts window.**

   If you're thinking that exiting without clicking the Save and Close button will do the trick, you're in for a disappointment. It's a good idea and shows that you are starting to think like a computer whiz. Unfortunately, Outlook deletes a journal entry as soon as you click the Delete Journal Entry button.

Deleted Items shortcut

on the test

6. **Click the Deleted Items shortcut in the Outlook bar to open the Deleted Items folder.**

   The very first item on the list of Deleted Items is the My Opinion journal entry.

7. **Choose View⇨Folder List from the menu bar to open the Folder list.**
8. **Position your mouse pointer over the deleted My Opinion journal entry.**
9. **Click, hold the left mouse button down, drag the My Opinion journal entry into the Folder list, and drop it on the Journal folder.**
10. **Choose View⇨Folder List from the menu bar to close the Folder list.**
11. **Click the Contacts shortcut in the Outlook bar to return to the Contacts window.**
12. **Click William J. Clinton's address card and press Ctrl+O to open it.**
13. **Click the Journal tab.**

    Like magic, the My Opinion journal entry is back.

The ability to delete and restore journal entries lets you easily manage your contact information without fear of losing important data. You can feel free to include too much information, just to be on the safe side, and later cull out the unnecessary data at your convenience.

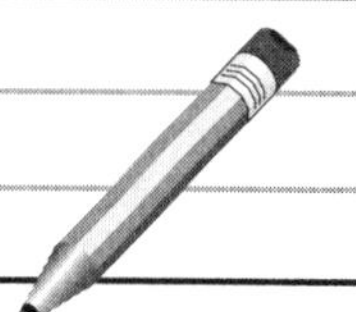

☑ Progress Check

If you can do the following, you've mastered this lesson:

- ❑ Delete a journal entry from a contact form.
- ❑ Restore a deleted journal entry from the Deleted Items folder.

Filtering the Contacts Database

Lesson 9-7

Filters are an electronic means of limiting the information that any given view displays by temporarily hiding (filtering) items that you select. Say that you are a sales rep planning a business trip to New York. Rather than go through your entire contact list searching for New York customers to call and make appointments with, you can filter out all contacts except those in the state of New York. From that point it's an easy process to go down the list and make the necessary calls.

Although a filter can be applied in a card view or a table view, you are more apt to use a filter in a table view. The results of a filter are more readily seen and utilized in a table view. Because the procedure is identical for either view, we want you to apply filters to the Phone List for this lesson.

Start by filtering out all contacts in the Phone List except the ten state governors we imported in Unit 8:

Contacts shortcut

1. **If you are not in the Contacts window, click the Contacts shortcut to open the Contacts window now.**
2. **Choose View⇨Current View⇨Phone List to open the Phone List view.**

on the test

3. **Choose View⇨Filter to access the Filter dialog box as seen in Figure 9-9.**

   The Filter dialog has three tabs. The first tab reflects the current folder, which in this case is Contacts. If you were in the Task folder, the first tab would be Tasks, and so on. The next two tabs, More Choices and Advanced, are the same regardless of which folder you're working in.

4. **Type** governor **in the Search for the word(s) text box and then Tab to the next field.**
5. **Click the down arrow at the end of the In field to open the drop-down list.**
6. **Select name fields only from the drop-down list.**
7. **Click OK to return to the Phone List view and apply the filter.**

   Now the only records that appear in the Phone List view are the ten state governors that you imported, and any other contacts already in your Contacts database containing the word *governor* in a name field. Also notice that (Filter Applied) appears at the right side of the Contacts name banner, indicating that a filter has been activated.

   This is an example of a very basic search in Outlook. But sometimes you need to narrow the search down to a more specific level. In the case of the governors' filter, say that you want to send e-mail to the governors. Therefore, you're not interested in any governor who does not have an e-mail address.

advanced filters narrow your search

8. **Choose View⇨Filter to open the Filter dialog box.**

   Note that your original filter criteria remain in place.

9. **Click the Advanced tab to open the advanced filter options.**

   The advanced options enable you to narrow your search by defining multiple search criteria based on the contents of various Contacts database fields.

Figure 9-9: Create filters as simple or complex as your needs dictate.

Notes:

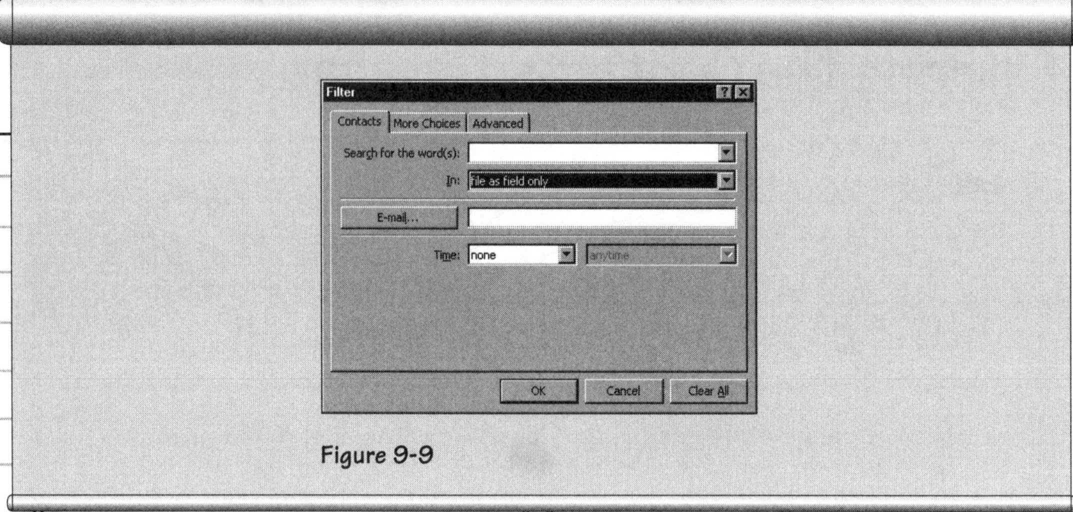

Figure 9-9

Field button

10 **Click the Field button to open the drop-down list of available fields.**

11 **Choose E-mail fields⇨E-mail to select the e-mail field as the basis for the new search criteria.**

12 **Click the down arrow at the right side of the Condition field to open the Condition drop-down list.**

13 **Choose is not empty as the Condition.**

The quickest way to find governors with an e-mail address is to filter out those without an e-mail address.

Add to List button

14 **Click the Add to List button to add the new search parameters to the filter search criteria list at the top of the Advanced tab.**

15 **Click OK to return to the Phone List view and apply the new filter.**

The number of governors appearing on the Phone List drops to seven. These are the only seven of the original ten who have e-mail addresses. Note that the Governor of Minnesota does not have a business fax number. You can narrow the search down even further by limiting it only to governors who possess both an e-mail address and a fax number.

16 **Choose View⇨Filter to open the Filter dialog box.**

17 **Click the Advanced tab to open the advanced filter options.**

Field button

18 **Click the Field button to open the drop-down list of available fields.**

19 **Choose Fax/other number fields⇨Business Fax to select the Business Fax field to add to the existing search criteria and create a new filter.**

20 **Click the down arrow at the right side of the Condition field to open the Condition drop-down list.**

21 **Choose is not empty from the Condition drop-down list.**

22 Click Add to List to add the new criteria to the Advanced tab search criteria display list.

Now both E-mail is not empty and Business Fax is not empty appear in the display list, indicating both conditions must be met before a contact is included in the filtered view.

23 Click OK to return to the Phone List view and apply the new filter.

Now the list is down to six governors. The Governor of Minnesota is no longer on the list because he does not have a business fax number.

Outlook filters enable you to fine-tune your viewing options to a very precise level. The larger your database gets, the more handy the filtering options become.

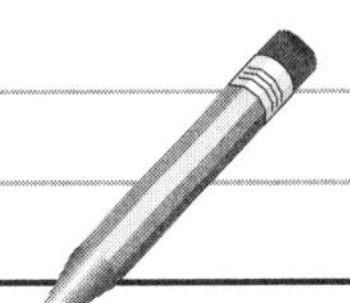

☑ Progress Check

If you can do the following, you've mastered this lesson:

- ❑ Perform a basic filter of your contacts
- ❑ Perform an advanced filter of your contacts.

Printing Contacts

Lesson 9-8

No matter how electronically advanced we get, we still need the security of having some information on paper, whether to make it real, portable, or just plain easier to read. Whatever the reasons, there are times when you want to print a hard copy of your contact information. When those times come, you'll be prepared if you complete this lesson.

Outlook provides you with several different formats for printing contact information. These formats are called *print styles* and number five in all. They include:

- **Card style:** Prints contacts as they appear in the Address Cards view, with identical headers and body text.
- **Small Booklet style:** Displays contacts in the address card format. However, the print size is reduced and a special page setup facilitates cutting and folding the printout into a small booklet.
- **Medium Booklet style:** The same as Small Booklet style, only larger.
- **Memo style:** Displays one contact per page, set up in a format similar to what you'd use for an interoffice memo.
- **Phone Directory style:** Organizes contacts alphabetically by the File as field. This view contains the File as name and all phone numbers only.

Let's do a sample print run from the Address Cards view. To ensure that it's a short print job, we'll filter out all contacts except the governors. To print your contact information follow these steps:

1 If you're not in the Contacts window, click the Contacts shortcut in the Outlook bar to open the Contacts window.

Contacts shortcut

2 Choose View⇨Filter from the menu bar to open the Filter dialog box.

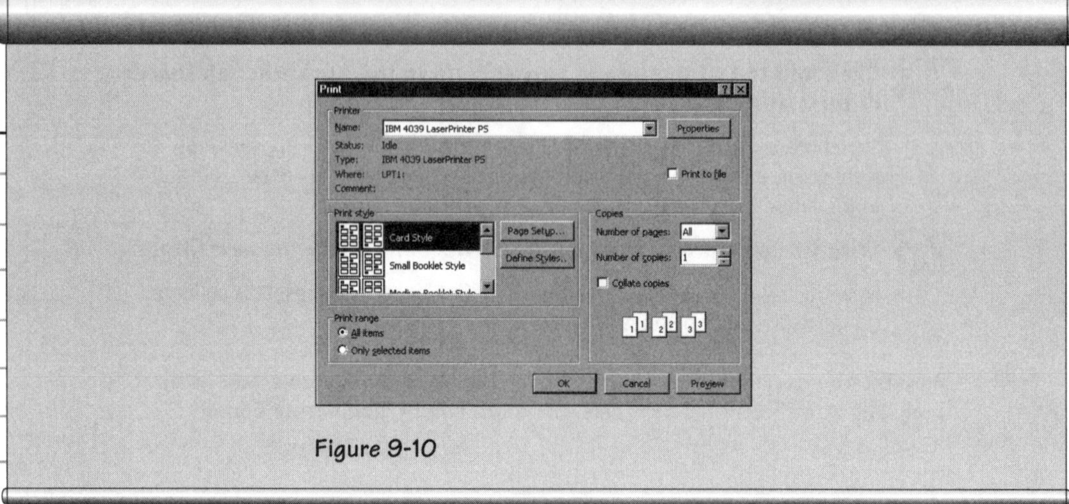

Figure 9-10: Print options put you in command of the print job.

Notes:

3. **Type** governor **in the Search for the word(s) text box.**
4. **Click OK to return to the Address Cards view and apply the filter.**

   The Address Cards view now contains only those contacts with the word *governor* in the File as field.

5. **Press Ctrl+P or choose File⇨Print to open the Print dialog box as seen in Figure 9-10.**
6. **Your default printer should appear in Printer options in the Name field. To switch printers, click the down arrow at the end of the Name field and select the desired printer from the drop-down list.**
7. **Move to the Print style options, scroll down the list, and choose Phone Directory Style.**
8. **Click the Preview button to see what the printed list will look like.**

   Note that your mouse pointer turns into a magnifying glass with a plus sign in it. This means that you can enlarge an area of the preview screen by clicking it.

9. **Click one of the listings on the preview to get a better look.**

   Now the magnifying glass pointer has a minus sign (–), indicating that a click returns the screen to its original size.

10. **Click the screen anywhere to return the document preview to its original size.**

    heads up: Before printing a document, it's always a good idea to make sure that the printer is turned on and is *online* (ready to print). So take a minute and verify that the printer is ready to go.

11. **Click the Print button to begin the print job.**

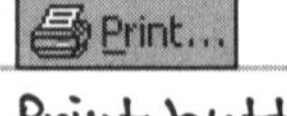

Print button

☑ Progress Check

If you can do the following, you've mastered this lesson:

- ❑ Filter your contacts.
- ❑ Print your contacts.

That's all it takes. A few mouse-clicks and you've got yourself a personalized phone list to hang on the wall next to the phone. At work, you can print out a list with business associates only. At home, a list of friends, family, and emergency numbers is great for everyone, but especially the kids. Any time they're home alone they have quick and easy access to important phone numbers in the event of an emergency.

Creating an Outlook Address Book

Lesson 9-9

on the test

Having all of your contact information in the Contacts database is extremely useful. At times, however, it would be nice to have that same contact information available as an Outlook Address Book as well. If you're in the habit of using your Address Book to address e-mail, or if you do any amount of mail merging with Word, creating an Outlook Address Book is essential, because the only way Word can use Outlook contact information as mail merge data source is in the form of an Address Book.

To create an Outlook Address Book using your Contacts database follow these steps:

1. **Choose Tools⇨Services to open the Services dialog box as seen in Figure 9-11.**
2. **Click the Add button to open the Add Service to Profile dialog box (Figure 9-12).**
3. **Click Outlook Address Book to include an Address Book as a new information service.**

heads up

4. **Click OK to return to the Services dialog box.**

   As soon as you click OK, another dialog box pops up informing you that your new service (Outlook Address Book) will not start until you exit and log off of Outlook and restart the program. This is a must.

5. **Click OK to close the informational dialog box.**

   You return to the Services dialog box, where you can see that the Outlook Address Book has been added to the list of information services available for this profile.

6. **Click OK to return to the Contacts window.**
7. **Choose File⇨Exit and Log Off to close Outlook.**

   Remember that to activate the Outlook Address Book, you have to exit and restart Outlook.

heads up

8. **Move your mouse pointer to the bottom of your screen to activate your task bar.**

   Some people prefer to position the task bar to the right or left of the screen. If your task bar does not appear at the bottom of the screen, try the left or right side.

9. **Click the Start button to open the Start menu.**
10. **Choose Programs⇨Microsoft Outlook to reopen Outlook.**
11. **Click the Contacts shortcut in the Outlook bar to open the Contacts window.**

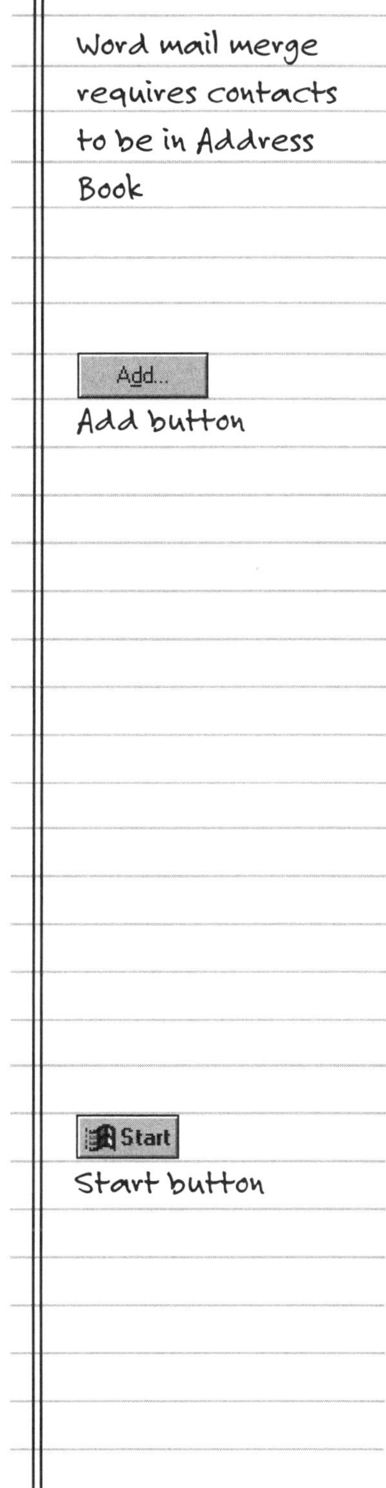

Figure 9-11: Information services allow you to control how Outlook handles e-mail.

Figure 9-12: Outlook provides a number of information service choices.

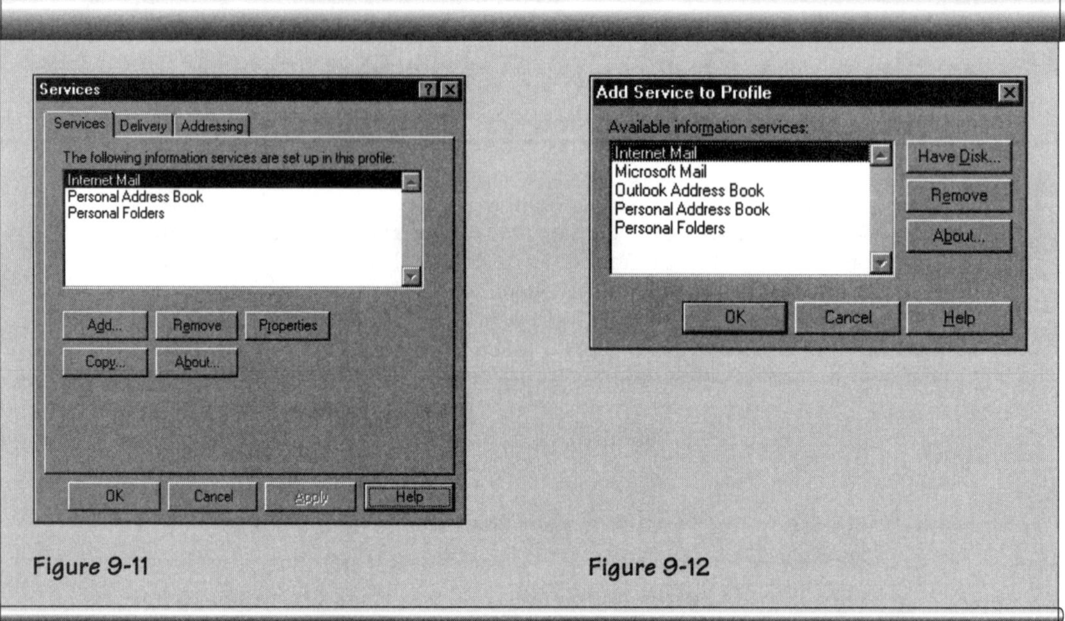

Figure 9-11

Figure 9-12

Contacts shortcut

12. **Position your mouse pointer over the Contacts shortcut in the Outlook bar and right-click to activate the pop-up menu.**
13. **Choose Properties from the menu to open the Contacts Properties dialog box as seen in Figure 9-13.**
14. **Click the Outlook Address Book tab to open the property sheet for the Outlook Address Book.**
15. **Click the Show this folder as an e-mail Address Book field to place a check mark in the box and enable the option.**
16. **Click OK to return to the Contacts window.**
17. **Press Ctrl+Shift+B to open the Address Book.**
18. **Click the down arrow at the end of the Show Names from the field to open the drop-down list.**
19. **Choose Contacts, which appears as a subset of Outlook Address Book.**

    That's all there is to it. All your contacts now appear as the Contacts Outlook Address Book. You can access the Outlook Address Book any time you want by opening the Address Book and selecting the Outlook Address Book called Contacts.
20. **Press Alt+F4 to return to the Contacts window.**

If you've made it this far, you're practically an Outlook expert. Finish up the rest of Unit 9, do the reviews and quizzes, and everyone at the office will be knocking on your door asking for help with Outlook.

☑ Progress Check

If you can do the following, you've mastered this lesson:

- ❑ Turn your Contacts database into an Outlook Address Book.
- ❑ Impress your friends with your knowledge of Outlook.

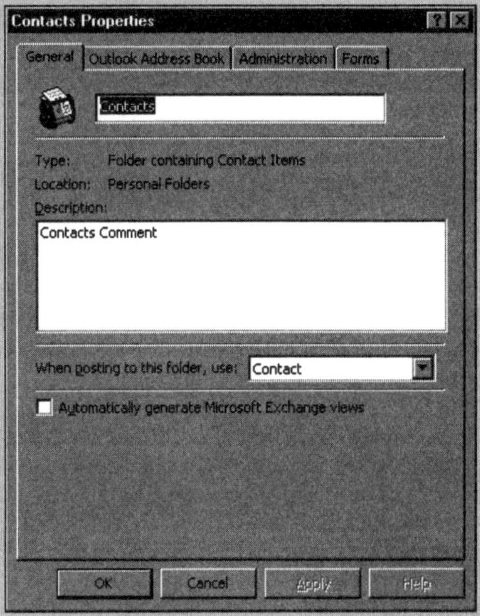

Figure 9-13

Figure 9-13: The Contacts Properties dialog box lets you set contact options, including the Outlook Address Book options.

Notes:

Using Word Mail Merge with the Contacts Database

Lesson 9-10

One of the reasons we love (when we're not hating) our computers is that they are so good at automating tedious, repetitive tasks that used to drive us crazy. One of those chores that seemed overwhelming before the advent of the PC is the creation of form letters. Thankfully, we now have word processor programs such as Microsoft Word that provide us with mail merge features that turn form letters, labels, and other such documents into child's play. Now, if only we could get Outlook to work with Word and create mail merge documents for all the people in our Contacts database.

The truth of the matter is, you can. Now that you've added the Outlook Address Book to the information services available in Outlook, you've got all you need to merge your Contacts database with Word documents. The first step is to open Microsoft Word and design a mail merge document to use with the Outlook Address Book. Follow the steps below to get started.

1. **Move your mouse pointer to the bottom of your screen to bring up the task bar.**

2. **Click the Start button to open the Start menu and choose Programs⇨Microsoft Word to open Word.**

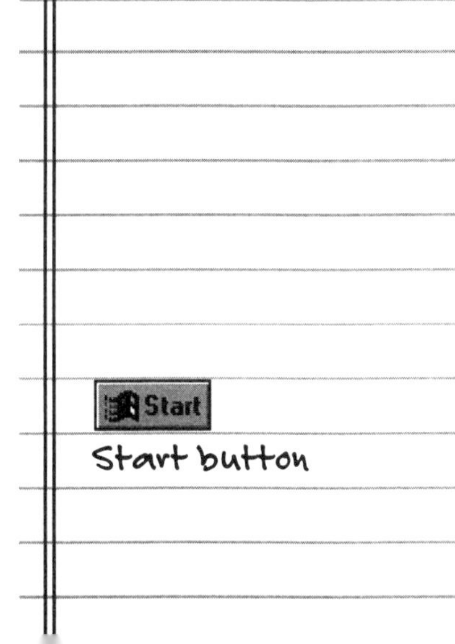

Start button

Figure 9-14: The Mail Merge Helper walks you through the mail merge process.

Figure 9-15: The first step is to choose the size, font, bar code, and printing options for your main document.

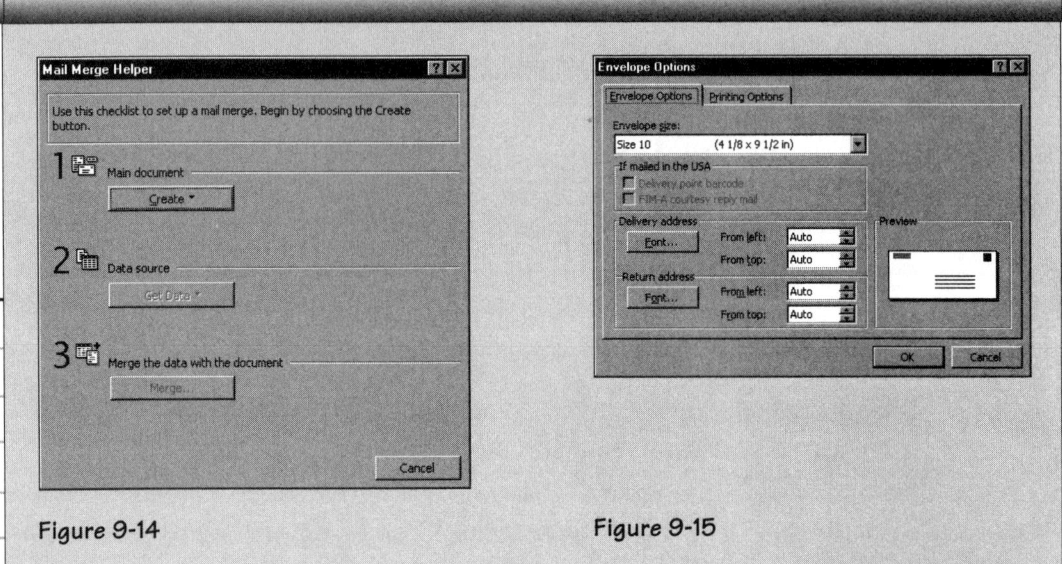

Figure 9-14

Figure 9-15

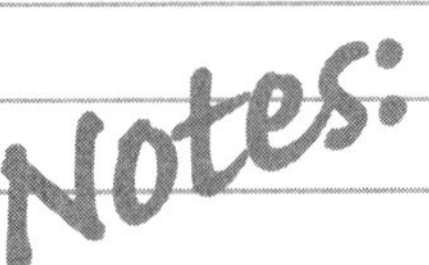

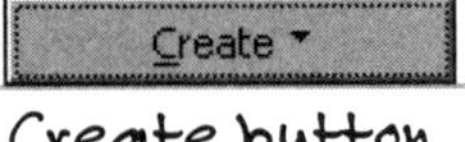

Create button

Get Data

Get Data button

3 **Choose Tools⇨Mail Merge to open the Mail Merge Helper (see Figure 9-14).**

4 **Click the Create button for choice number 1, Main document, to open the drop-down list of document types.**

5 **Click Envelopes to create envelopes using your Outlook Address Book contact information.**

A dialog box appears asking if you want to use the active (currently in use) Word document or if you want to create a new Word document to use for the envelopes. Because your active document is blank, you want to use it. If, however, you had a letter or some other document that you were working on, you would select a new document.

6 **Click Active Window to return to the Mail Merge Helper.**

Notice that choice number 2, Data source, is now available.

7 **Click the Get Data button and choose Use Address Book from the drop-down list.**

The Use Address Book dialog box displays the available Address Books.

8 **Choose Outlook Address Book from the Use Address Book dialog box and click OK to confirm your selection and continue the mail merge process.**

Because you never set up your envelopes document, a Word dialog box appears informing you that you must now complete the main document setup before proceeding any further.

9 **Click the Set Up Main Document button to open the Envelope Options dialog box as seen in Figure 9-15 and then click OK to proceed.**

The default options in the Envelope Options dialog box are adequate for this example.

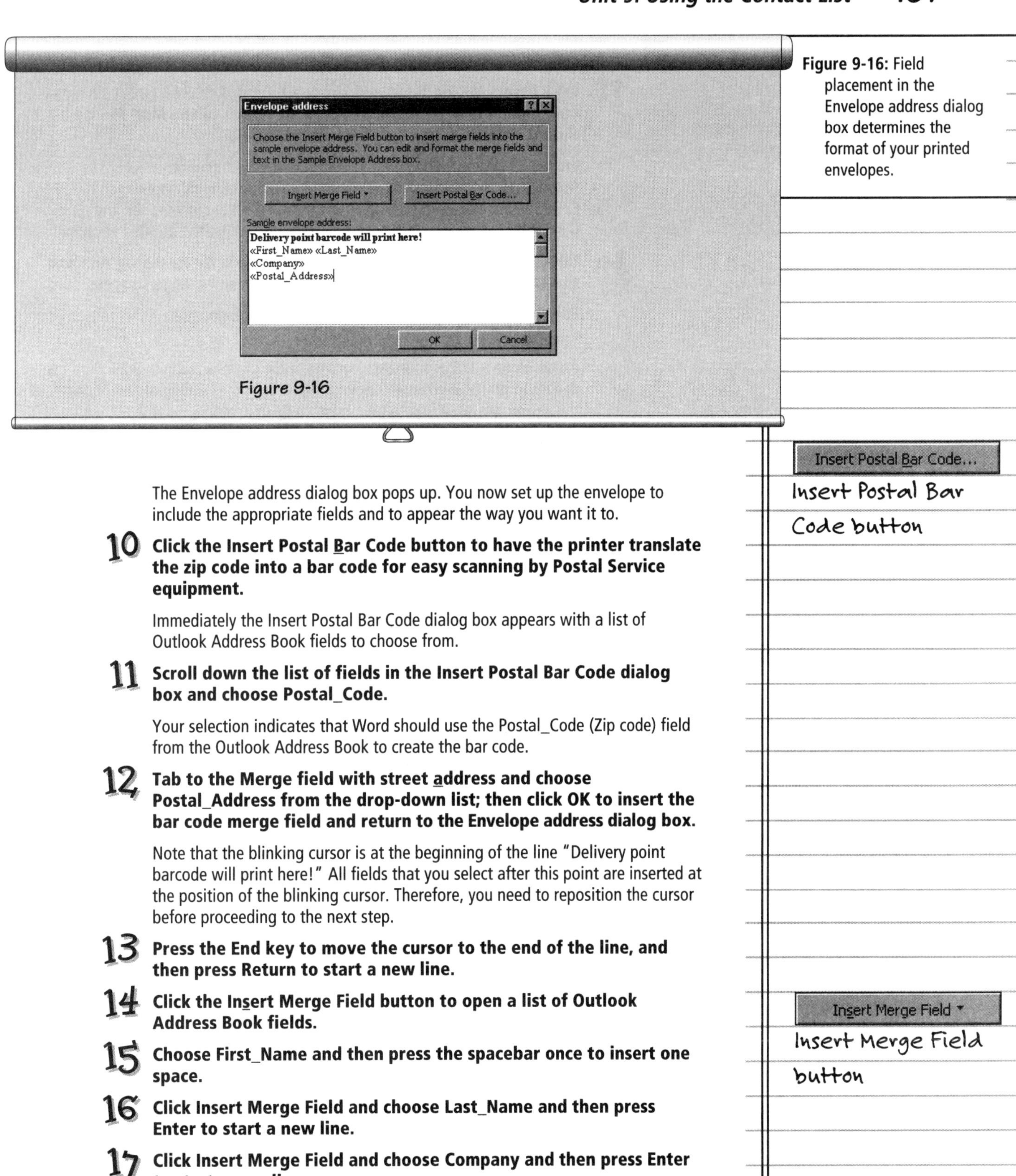

Figure 9-16

Figure 9-16: Field placement in the Envelope address dialog box determines the format of your printed envelopes.

The Envelope address dialog box pops up. You now set up the envelope to include the appropriate fields and to appear the way you want it to.

10 **Click the Insert Postal Bar Code button to have the printer translate the zip code into a bar code for easy scanning by Postal Service equipment.**

Immediately the Insert Postal Bar Code dialog box appears with a list of Outlook Address Book fields to choose from.

Insert Postal Bar Code...

Insert Postal Bar Code button

11 **Scroll down the list of fields in the Insert Postal Bar Code dialog box and choose Postal_Code.**

Your selection indicates that Word should use the Postal_Code (Zip code) field from the Outlook Address Book to create the bar code.

12 **Tab to the Merge field with street address and choose Postal_Address from the drop-down list; then click OK to insert the bar code merge field and return to the Envelope address dialog box.**

Note that the blinking cursor is at the beginning of the line "Delivery point barcode will print here!" All fields that you select after this point are inserted at the position of the blinking cursor. Therefore, you need to reposition the cursor before proceeding to the next step.

13 **Press the End key to move the cursor to the end of the line, and then press Return to start a new line.**

14 **Click the Insert Merge Field button to open a list of Outlook Address Book fields.**

Insert Merge Field

Insert Merge Field button

15 **Choose First_Name and then press the spacebar once to insert one space.**

16 **Click Insert Merge Field and choose Last_Name and then press Enter to start a new line.**

17 **Click Insert Merge Field and choose Company and then press Enter to start a new line.**

Merge...

Merge button

18 Click Insert Merge Field and choose Postal_Address, press Enter to start a new line, and then click OK to return to the Mail Merge Helper.

Word automatically allocates the correct number of lines required by the Postal_Address. Your Envelope address dialog box should now match the Envelope address dialog box in Figure 9-16. Everything is now set. The only thing left to do is complete the mail merge and create the finished envelopes.

19 Click the Merge button to open the Merge options dialog box and then click the Merge button to begin the mail merge process.

The Merge options dialog box appears with appropriate default settings for our example.

An envelope is created for each contact in the Outlook Address Book. You can choose to print the envelopes now, or save them for printing at another time. In this lesson, we want you to save them and exit Word.

20 Press Alt+F4 to exit Word 97 and click Yes to save the envelopes document.

Because you created two new documents (the mail merge document and the envelopes document), a dialog box appears asking if you want to save the first of the two documents. After you click Yes, the Save As dialog box opens, letting you name and select the location for the new file.

21 Choose a folder from the Save in drop-down list and tab to the File name field.

22 Type envelope **in the File name text box and then click Save.**

A new dialog box appears, asking if you want to save the Outlook Address Book that is being used as the data source.

23 Click No (because the Outlook Address Book is not an independent data source that requires saving).

Another dialog box pops up asking if you want to save the mail merge document (the one with the merge fields inserted). You should save a merge document that you may use again in the future. It saves you the hassle of creating it again when you need it.

24 Click Yes to save the mail merge document.

25 Choose a folder from the Save in drop-down list and then tab to the File name field.

26 Type EnvMerge **in the File name text box and then click Save to save the document.**

A final dialog box appears asking if you want to save changes to the temporary data source file that was created. After you finish the mail merge there is no need to keep the temporary file.

27 Click No to exit Word and return to Outlook.

Congratulations! You've reached the end of your long and hopefully fruitful journey through Outlook. With the addition of Word mail merge using an Outlook Address Book, you now possess the foundation skills necessary to use Outlook effectively and organize your personal and business information.

☑ Progress Check

If you can do the following, you've mastered this lesson:

- ❑ Sort and filter the Outlook Contacts database.
- ❑ Create a Word mail merge document using the Outlook Address Book.

Unit 9 Quiz

Notes:

1. **How do you switch between Outlook views?**
   A. Move to a different computer.
   B. Turn the monitor on its side.
   C. Choose View➪Current View and select the desired view.
   D. Move your chair.
   E. What's wrong with this view?
2. **How do you create a manual journal entry?**
   A. That's easy, use the manual.
   B. Come up with a design first, then build a working model, then create the journal entry.
   C. Two parts gin, one part carrot juice.
   D. Open a contact, click the Journal Tab, click the New Journal Entry button, and fill out the new journal entry form.
   E. Put your hand in the journal.
3. **How do you restore a deleted Journal entry?**
   A. With care and patience.
   B. Use all original materials.
   C. Open the Deleted Items folder, select the journal entry to restore, and then drag the journal entry to the Outlook bar and drop it on the Journal shortcut.
   D. In a dust-free environment.
   E. Don't delete it in the first place!
4. **How do you apply a filter to an Outlook Contacts database?**
   A. With a trowel and some mortar.
   B. Hold a piece of cheesecloth over the monitor and press Enter.
   C. If you're careful, you can use Superglue.
   D. Choose View➪Filter and enter the search criteria in the Filter dialog box.
   E. Spread it over the entire surface of the database and let it dry for 24 hours.

5. **What can you do with the Outlook Address Book other than create e-mail messages?**

   A. Paint it black and pretend you're a swinger.

   B. Leave it on the coffee table as a conversation piece.

   C. Create mail merge documents with Microsoft Word.

   D. Wedge it under the short desk leg to stop the rocking that occurs every time you lean on the desk.

   E. Place it in a time capsule for posterity.

Unit 9 Exercise

1. Switch to the By Category view and sort it by Business Phone.
2. Create an e-mail using a contact.
3. Filter your contact list so that only contacts with Web pages show.
4. Print a phone list of your business contacts.
5. Create address labels for all of your personal contacts using the Word mail merge feature.

Part III Review

Unit 8 Summary

- **Opening the Contacts window:** Click the Contacts shortcut in the Outlook bar.
- **Adding a name to the Outlook Contacts database:** Open a new contact form by pressing Ctrl+N in the Contacts window and then fill in the information.
- **Adding multiple contacts from the same company:** To avoid retyping the information common to each contact, use the New Contact from Same Company feature found on the Contacts menu.
- **Recording personal information about a contact:** Use the Details tab of the contact form to record personal information about a contact, such as the birthday, anniversary, and nickname.
- **Saving changes you make to an existing contact:** Press Ctrl+S.
- **Setting global Journal options:** Choose Tools➪Options to open the Options dialog box and make the appropriate changes.
- **Adding a name to the Contacts database from an e-mail:** Open the e-mail, right-click the From e-mail address, and choose Add to Contacts from the pop-up menu.
- **Importing a Personal Address Book or a contact list from another program:** Choose File➪Import and Export from the menu bar.
- **Displaying fields in the Address view even when they contain no data:** Choose View➪Format View from the menu bar and then select the Show Empty Fields option.

Unit 9 Summary

- **Switching views in the Contacts window:** Choose View➪Current View and select the desired view.
- **Tables and card views:** Tables view presents information in rows and columns where the rows represent individual records and the columns represent different fields within the records. A card view displays contact information in a format similar to that of a rolodex card or a paper address book entry.
- **Moving quickly to the group of contacts beginning with a specific letter:** Click the appropriate letter on the Letter tab, which runs down the right side of the Address Cards view.
- **Rearranging fields in a table view:** Drag the field and drop it in a new location on the field header bar. Outlook uses a pair of red arrows to indicate location insert points on the field header bar.
- **Sorting a table view:** Click a column header to sort a table view by the selected field (column). If the embossed arrow that appears in a sort field points up, the sort is ascending (from A to Z); if the arrow points down, the sort is descending (from Z to A).
- **Creating an e-mail message from a contact record:** Highlight the contact and choose Contacts➪New Message to Contact from the menu bar.
- **Automatically recording journal entries for a contact:** Open the contact form, click the Journal tab, and select the Automatically record journal entries for this contact option.
- **Creating a manual journal entry for a contact:** Open the contact form, click the Journal tab, and then click the New Journal Entry button.

Part III Review

- **Including an Outlook item in a journal entry:** Use the Insert Item feature available from the journal entry form menu bar.
- **Deleting a journal entry open the contact form:** Click the Journal tab, highlight the entry to delete, and click the Delete Journal Entry button.
- **Restoring a deleted journal entry:** Open the Deleted Items folder, drag the entry you want to restore to the Outlook bar, and drop it on the Journal shortcut.
- **Creating an Outlook Address Book:** First add Outlook Address Book to Outlook Services by choosing Tools⇨Services. Then, after closing Outlook and reopening it to update the Services, open the Contacts Properties dialog box and select the Show this folder as an e-mail Address Book option.
- **Creating a mail merge document using names in your Contacts database:** Start a mail merge document in Word and choose Outlook Address Book as the data source.

Part III Test

The following test questions correspond to all material covered in Units 8 and 9 of Part III. You can find the answers to these questions in Appendix A.

True False

T F 1. If you enter partial information in the Full Name text box of a new contact form, the Check Full Name dialog box appears.

T F 2. You must retype all information for each contact even if the contacts are from the same company.

T F 3. Automatic journal entries can include e-mail messages, Outlook notes, and Word documents.

T F 4. The Outlook Import and Export Wizard allows you to import contact files from either a Personal Address Book or third party programs.

T F 5. To adjust the column width of the Address Cards view automatically, use the Show Fields feature.

T F 6. The Detailed Address Cards view shows records that contain information on the Details tab of the contact form.

T F 7. You can add fields to a table view by opening the Field Chooser and dragging a field name to the column header and dropping it.

T F 8. An automatic journal entry for an e-mail message is recorded as soon as you write the message.

T F 9. You can print your Outlook contact information in more than one format.

T F 10. To create form letters using Outlook contact information, you should create an Outlook Address Book.

Part III Test

Multiple Choice

Circle the letter of the statement(s) that best answers the question (some questions may offer more than one correct answer).

11. To enable automatic journal entries for a contact you must:

A. Press Ctrl+J and then choose the Auto option.

B. Enable the Automatically record journal entries for this contact option in the Journal tab of the contact form.

C. Click the Journal shortcut to open the Journal window, right-click the Timeline, and select Automatically record journal entries from the pop-up menu.

D. Double click the contact in the Address Cards view.

E. Select Automatic journal entry from the drop-down list on the Contacts window toolbar.

12. Address Cards View formatting options include:

A. Changing Address Cards font colors.

B. Best Fit, which automatically adjusts column widths.

C. Show Empty Fields, which shows all contact fields regardless of their content (or lack thereof).

D. Line spacing and indentation.

E. Format View, which allows you to change the font style and size.

13. The Letter tab in the Address Cards view does not appear when:

A. The moon is in the seventh house.

B. You sort the Contacts database by a nontext field such as birthday or anniversary.

C. You disable the Letter tab option.

D. You apply a filter to the Contacts database.

E. All the contact records begin with the same letter.

14. If you drag a field header above or below the column header plane in a table view, the following happens:

A. Outlook crashes and you get a General Protection Fault error.

B. The field header that you are dragging returns to its original position.

C. A large black X appears on the field header, indicating that you can't drop the header at this location.

D. The view automatically resorts itself based on the field represented by the column header.

E. The column is removed from the view.

15. To delete a journal entry do the following:

A. Delete the contact associated with the journal entry.

B. Call your system administrator to get the required password.

C. Deselect the Automatically record journal entries for this contact option on the Journal tab of the contact form.

D. Open the journal entry and erase all the information.

E. Highlight the journal entry on the Journal tab of the contact form and click the Delete Journal Entry button.

Part III Test

Matching

Draw a line from the item in the left column to the closest match in the right column.

16. Match the following shortcut keys to the actions they trigger.

A. Ctrl+N	1. Open an existing contact form.
B. Ctrl+O	2. Save the open form or item.
C. Ctrl+Shift+B	3. Open the Print dialog box.
D. Ctrl+P	4. Open the Address Book.
E. Ctrl+S	5. Open a new contact form.

Part III Lab Assignment

Are you ready for some practical application? We hope so, because the following lab assignment provides some hands-on experience. The object of this assignment is to create a new contact and apply the skills you learned in Unit 8 and Unit 9 to managing information for the new contact.

Step 1: Adding Attila's brother, Bleda the Hun, to your Contacts database

Move to the Contacts window and open a new contact form for Bleda. Remember, he also works for Barbarians "R" Us, so make it easy on yourself and let Outlook fill in the company information for you. Fill in Bleda's General information and Details information using your imagination.

Step 2: Setting the journal options for Bleda the Hun

Start with the Journal tab of the global Options dialog box. Select all items for automatic journal entry. When you're through, close the Options dialog box and open Bleda's contact form. From the Journal tab, enable automatic journal entry recording for Bleda.

Part III Lab Assignment

Step 3: Recording journal entries for Bleda

Manually record a phone call with Bleda that took place today, lasted for ten minutes, and covered the planned activities for the Barbarians "R" Us annual company picnic. Insert in the journal entry the activities list (Activity.doc) which is located on the CD.

Step 4: Creating an e-mail from the contact form

Use Bleda's contact form to create an e-mail message informing him that you will have to get a permit from the local fire department to allow the village razing contest to take place. After you send the message, check to see if the message was automatically recorded.

Part IV

Appendixes

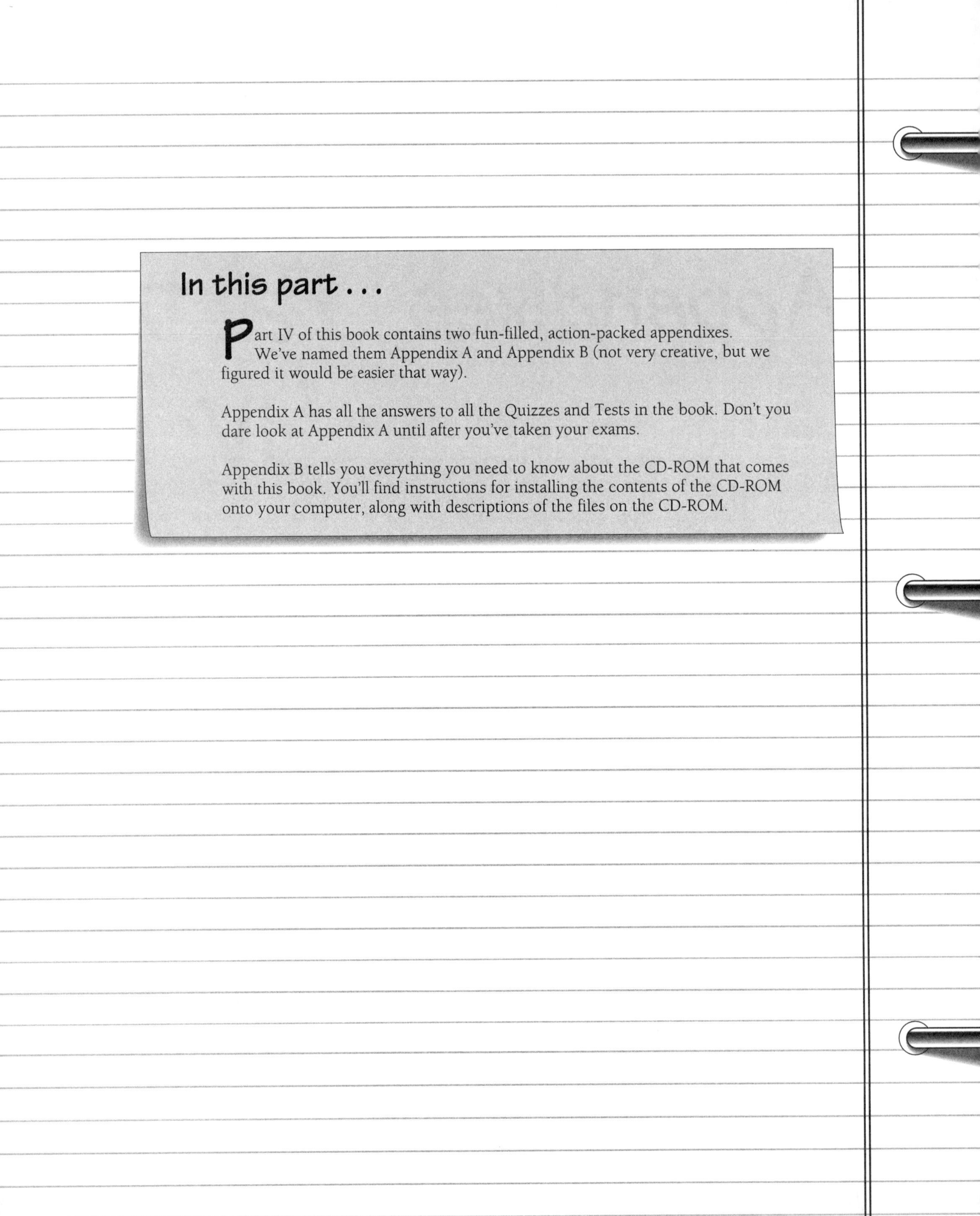

In this part . . .

Part IV of this book contains two fun-filled, action-packed appendixes. We've named them Appendix A and Appendix B (not very creative, but we figured it would be easier that way).

Appendix A has all the answers to all the Quizzes and Tests in the book. Don't you dare look at Appendix A until after you've taken your exams.

Appendix B tells you everything you need to know about the CD-ROM that comes with this book. You'll find instructions for installing the contents of the CD-ROM onto your computer, along with descriptions of the files on the CD-ROM.

Appendix A

Answers to the Quizzes and Tests

Unit 1 Quiz Answers

Question	Answer	
1.	B	Double-clicking a program shortcut opens the program.
2.	C	The shortcut icons on the Outlook bar represent Outlook folders.
3.	D	The window for each part of Outlook is the Information Viewer for that Outlook feature.
4.	C	The Inbox automatically receives messages.

Unit 2 Quiz Answers

Question	Answer	
1.	C	When the Address Book opens, choose File⇨New Entry.
2.	D	You are asked to confirm the deletion, click Yes to delete.
3.	C	Choose the distribution list as a recipient to send a message to the entire group.
4.	B	The color choices appear in a dialog box; click the color you want.
5.	C	Choose the file from the dialog box that appears.

Unit 3 Quiz Answers

Question	Answer	
1.	C	Only unread messages present previews.
2.	A	You can configure the flag for specific types of action.
3.	C	Click the flag button on the toolbar to mark a message high priority.
4.	C	Click the Reply to All button on the toolbar.
5.	C	The associated software opens, and then it opens the attachment.

Unit 4 Quiz Answers

Question	Answer	
1.	C	Click the Folder List button again to remove the folder list from the display.
2.	D	When the pointer turns into a double arrow, click the left mouse button and drag the bar to the right.
3.	B	Choose the appropriate folder from the list.
4.	A	The folder appears indented so that you know it's in the parent folder.
5.	E	Click the plus sign (+) on the box to display the list of messages in the group.

Part I Test Answers

Question	Answer	If You Missed It, Try This
1.	F	Remember that Sly Stallone will also be ready to retire and unable to fight.
2.	T	Review Lesson 2-3.
3.	T	Review Lesson 2-8.
4.	T	Review Lesson 2-2.
5.	F	Review Lesson 4-4.
6.	F	Review Lesson 4-2.
7.	T	Review Lesson 3-3.
8.	F	Watch John Wayne movies more carefully.

9.	T	Review Lesson 3-1.
10.	T	Review Lesson 3-2.
11.	B	Review Lesson 1-2.
12.	A	Review Lesson 2-3.
13.	C	Review Lesson 1-3.
14.	D	Review Lesson 4-3.
15.	A	Review Lesson 2-5.
16.	A: 5	Review Lessons 2-5, 4-3, 3-2, 2-4, 2-1.
	B: 4	
	C: 1	
	D: 2	
	E: 3	
17.	A: 5	Watch more television.
	B: 1	
	C: 2	
	D: 3	
	E: 4	

Unit 5 Quiz Answers

Question	Answer	
1.	C	Fill in the information and then click the Save and Close button.
2.	B	The Reminder field is in the Appointment window.
3.	D	Events do not block specific times in your calendar.
4.	B	The Date Navigator is not displayed in the Month view.
5.	D	Any calendar view will permit you to view your schedule.

Unit 6 Quiz Answers

Question	Answer	
1.	D	Click the Find Items button on the toolbar.
2.	D	To get to the Deleted Items folder, click its icon on the Outlook bar.

3.	C	Drag the appointment from the old date to the new date.
4.	C	Choose File⇨Archive from the menu bar.
5.	C	You can also choose File⇨Print from the menu bar.

Unit 7 Quiz Answers

Question	Answer	
1.	B	Click any icon on the Outlook bar to move to that Outlook feature.
2.	A	The Reminder field is in the Task's dialog box.
3.	D	Click the Recurrence button on the toolbar to make a task a recurring task.
4.	A	Choose By Category from the Current View drop-down list.
5.	D	You can view the task by going to the Deleted Items folder.

Part II Test Answers

Question	Answer	If You Missed It, Try This
1.	T	Review Lesson 6-2.
2.	T	Review Lesson 5-1.
3.	F	Review Lesson 5-2.
4.	F	Review Lesson 5-3.
5.	F	Review Lesson 5-6.
6.	F	Review Lesson 6-1.
7.	T	Review Lesson 6-2.
8.	T	Review Lesson 6-3.
9.	F	Review Lesson 7-1.
10.	T	Review Lesson 7-7.
11.	B, D	Review Lesson 5-2.
12.	C	Review Lesson 5-1.
13.	B, D	Review Lesson 6-2.
14.	C	Review Lesson 5-6.
15.	D	Review Lesson 7-7.

16.	A: 3	Review Lessons 5-3, 6-1, 7-7.
	B: 2	
	C: 5	
	D: 1	
	E: 4	
17.	A: 5	Review Lessons 5-1, 5-2, 5-3.
	B: 4	
	C: 2	
	D: 3	
	E: 1	

Unit 8 Quiz Answers

1.	C	You can also click the New Contact button on the toolbar.
2.	E	You can edit any information in any field when you use this shortcut.
3.	E	Follow the steps given by the Wizard to complete the process.
4.	E	Entering additional information in the Contact file can be helpful in maintaining a relationship with a contact.
5.	D	Click OK when you are finished making changes.

Unit 9 Quiz Answers

1.	C	You can also use the Current View drop-down list on the toolbar.
2.	D	You can also press Ctrl+J to create a new journal entry.
3.	C	If you change the default settings for the Deleted Items folder, you may lose all deleted items each time you close Outlook.
4.	D	Advanced filter options allow you to enter multiple filter criteria.
5.	C	You can create form letters, labels, envelopes, and more.

Part III Test Answers

Question	Answer	If You Missed It, Try This
1.	T	Review Lesson 8-1.
2.	F	Review Lesson 8-2.
3.	F	Review Lesson 8-4.
4.	T	Review Lesson 8-6.
5.	F	Review Lesson 8-8.
6.	F	Review Lesson 9-1.
7.	T	Review Lesson 9-2.
8.	F	Review Lesson 9-4.
9.	T	Review Lesson 9-8.
10.	T	Review Lesson 9-10.
11.	B	Review Lesson 8-4.
12.	B, C, D	Review Lesson 8-8.
13.	B	Review Lesson 9-1.
14.	C	Review Lesson 9-2.
15.	E	Review Lesson 9-6.
16.	A: 5	Review Lessons 8-1, 8-3, 9-8, 9-9.
	B: 1	
	C: 4	
	D: 3	
	E: 2	

Appendix B

Using the CD-ROM

This appendix tells you how to install and use the programs and other files on the CD-ROM that comes with this book. Specifically, the CD contains the following:

- **AT&T WorldNet Service:** AT&T WorldNet signup software. If you don't have access to e-mail, you can sign up for an Internet account with AT&T WorldNet Service, which includes Internet e-mail. (Part I of this book discusses the e-mail features available in Outlook. In order to utilize these e-mail features, you must have access to e-mail, either through your company's network or from an Internet account.)
- **WinZip:** A shareware program that compresses and decompresses files. We discuss the advantages of using WinZip in Unit 3.
- **Exercise Files:** You use these files as you perform the exercises in this book. As you go through the steps of some exercises, you'll be asked to use a file from this CD-ROM.

Before we discuss the installation, we want to take a moment for a commercial. Well, it's actually more of a public service announcement. Installing shareware, such as WinZip, on your computer carries a few responsibilities you should be aware of.

Shareware programs are not free. You can use a shareware program without paying for it in order to decide whether you like it enough to use it in the future. This is called an *evaluation period*, and you don't have to pay for this evaluation period.

After you've evaluated the software and the way it works, decide whether you want to keep it. If you decide you don't need it or don't like it, you should delete it from your computer. If you decide you do like it, you must register your copy of the software. You can find instructions for registering shareware software, including the registration fee, in the shareware software files. Payment for shareware programs is based on the honor system. Incidentally, besides making you an honorable person, registering the software entitles you to upgrades, information, and other goodies from the software company.

System Requirements

Before you install the CD, make sure that your system meets the following system requirements. If your computer doesn't meet the minimum requirements, you may have trouble using the practice files and computer programs on the CD.

- A 486 or Pentium-equipped PC with CD-ROM drive
- Microsoft Office 97 installed on your computer
- Microsoft Windows 95 installed on your computer
- At least 8MB of RAM installed on your computer
- At least 15MB of free hard-disk space available if you want to install just the exercise files; at least 33MB if you want to install all the programs
- A high-speed modem — at least 14,400 bps (if you intend to send e-mail with Outlook)

Putting the CD Files on Your Hard Drive

The CD contains exercise files that you need to follow along with the lessons in the book. You need to put these files on your hard drive before you can use them. After you read this book, you can easily remove the files.

After the CD installer appears, you can install the exercise files, and finally, you can install WinZip or AT&T WorldNet Service, if you desire.

If you have problems with the installation process, you can call the IDG Books Worldwide, Inc., Customer Support number: 800-762-2974 (outside the U.S.: 317-596-5261).

Using the CD

With Windows 95 up and running, follow these steps:

1. **Insert the Dummies 101 CD (label side up) into your computer's CD drive and wait about 30 seconds to see whether AutoPlay starts the CD for you.**

   Be careful to touch only the edges of the CD. The CD drive is the one that pops out with a circular drawer.

   If your computer has the Windows CD AutoPlay feature, the CD installer should begin automatically. If nothing seems to happen after a minute or so, go to Step 2. If you see the CD installer window (it looks like a piece of notebook paper with the book's title), go to "Installing the exercise files" in this appendix.

2. **If the installation program doesn't start automatically, click the Start button and click Run.**
3. **In the dialog box that appears, type** d:\seticon.exe **(if your CD drive is not drive D, substitute the appropriate letter for D) and click OK.**

   A message informs you that the program is about to install the icons.
4. **Click OK in the message window.**

   After a moment, a program group called Dummies 101 appears on the Start menu, along with an icon that runs the CD installer. Then another message appears, asking whether you want to use the CD now.
5. **Click Yes to use the CD now, or click No if you want to use the CD later.**

   If you click No, you can use the CD simply by clicking the Dummies 101 - Outlook 97 For Windows CD icon in the Dummies 101 program group (on the Start menu).

(Re)Starting the CD

If you closed the CD installer, restart the CD by double-clicking the My Computer icon and then double-clicking the CD-ROM icon. This works only if your CD-ROM drive automatically starts the CD installer when you pop it in your CD-ROM drive.

If you had to follow Step 2 in "Using the CD," you can restart the CD by clicking the Start button, clicking Dummies 101, and clicking Dummies 101 - Outlook 97 For Windows CD.

Installing the exercise files

Click the Install Exercise Files button in the CD's window and follow the instructions that appear on-screen to install the exercise (sometimes known as *practice*) files on your computer.

To make the installation and the exercises in this book as simple as possible, let the installer place the exercise files in the recommended location. If you really want to put the files somewhere else, you can change the location by following the on-screen instructions (make sure that you remember where you put them if you customize the location).

Unless you change the location, the exercise files are installed to C:\Outlook101.

You don't have to do anything with the files yet — we tell you when you need to open the first file. The files are meant to accompany the book's lessons. If you open a file prematurely, you may accidentally make changes to the file, which may prevent you from following along with the steps in the lessons. So please don't try to open or view a file until you've reached the point in the lessons where we explain how to open the file.

heads up

If at some point you accidentally modify an exercise file and want to reinstall the original version, just run the CD again and click on Install Exercise Files once more. If you want to save your modified versions of files, either move the files to another folder before reinstalling the originals, or tell the exercise file installer to place the new replacement file in a different folder.

Removing the exercise files and icons

After you finish with the lessons in the book, you may want to delete the exercise files. If you installed an icon to run the CD installer as shown in Step 2 in the section, "Using the CD," you may want to get rid of the icon for the CD as well.

Deleting the exercise files is easy. Just follow these steps:

1. **Double-click the My Computer icon.**
2. **Double-click the Drive C icon.**
3. **Click the Outlook101 folder.**

   We assume that you let the CD installer copy the files to the folder it recommended. If you decided to change the recommended location for the exercise files, you may need to open additional folders to find where you saved the exercise file folder.

4. **Choose File⇨Delete.**

   Depending on your Windows 95 settings, you may see a message asking if you really want to delete these items. Click the appropriate button to indicate Yes.

heads up

Caution: As soon as you delete the exercise files, they are as good as gone, and the only way to get them back is to run the CD and choose Install Exercise Files again. (This won't bring back your changes to the files; they disappeared with the modified file.) If you want to keep any of the installed files, move them to a different folder *before* you delete the exercise file's folder.

If you installed an icon to your Start button to run the CD installer, follow these steps to remove it:

1. **Click the Start button and choose Settings⇨Taskbar.**
2. **Click the Start Menu Programs tab at the top of the window.**
3. **Click the Remove button.**

   A window appears that shows all the items on your Start menu.

4. **In the window, click the tiny plus sign next to the Dummies 101 folder.**

   If this is the only Dummies 101 CD you've used, you'll find only the Dummies 101 - Outlook 97 CD icon. If you've used other Dummies 101 CDs, you'll see a few more icons here for those CDs. Your goal here is to remove only the Dummies 101 - Outlook 97 icon.

5. **Click on the Dummies 101 - Outlook 97 CD icon.**
6. **Click the Remove button and then click the Close button.**

   If the Dummies 101 program group doesn't have any other icons in it, you can delete that as well by repeating the steps and selecting the Dummies 101 folder for removal.

Removing programs installed from the CD

You may decide to uninstall the programs available from the Choose Software section of the CD. Most software designed for Windows 95 has some sort of uninstall feature that you can use to remove the program. The key word is "most." Not all Windows programs make it easy to remove a program.

To remove a program, look in these locations for the items you may need to uninstall the program:

- Click the Start button and then choose Programs. Here you may find the name of the program or the name of the company that made it. Open that program group and choose the icon named Uninstall or Remove.
- Click the Start button, choose Settings⇨Control Panel, and double-click the icon Add/Remove Programs. Listed on the Install/Uninstall tab of the window are any programs that Windows 95 can remove for you.

If these two options don't work, you have two more options:

- Drop by your computer store and pick up a program designed to uninstall programs from your computer, such as CleanSweep, Uninstaller, and RemoveIt. These programs are also great for cleaning up the old files that build up on your computer over time.
- Locate the folder in Windows that contains the software for the program and delete the folder, and then delete the program's icons from the Start menu.

heads up

Deleting the program's folder is usually enough for some programs, but sometimes your computer may still have other information about the program that can't be removed in this way. Also, there is a chance that you could delete files that are shared by other programs you still use. Never delete anything from the Windows folder unless you know *exactly* what you are doing. Be careful!

Installing the AT&T WorldNet Software

If you don't have access to e-mail, you may want to consider AT&T WorldNet Service, a pay-per-use Internet service, which provides e-mail and Internet access.

To install the AT&T WorldNet software, click the Choose Software button in the CD program window. Next, click the AT&T WorldNet Service button and then, in the next window that appears, click the Install AT&T WorldNet Service button. Read the description that appears for any important information. If you want to install the program, then click Continue. Click OK in the confirmation dialog box that appears. Note: If users want to change the destination directory, they can do so in the confirmation dialog box. The CD copies files to your hard disk and launches the AT&T WorldNet installer. Follow the on-screen prompts to finish the installation.

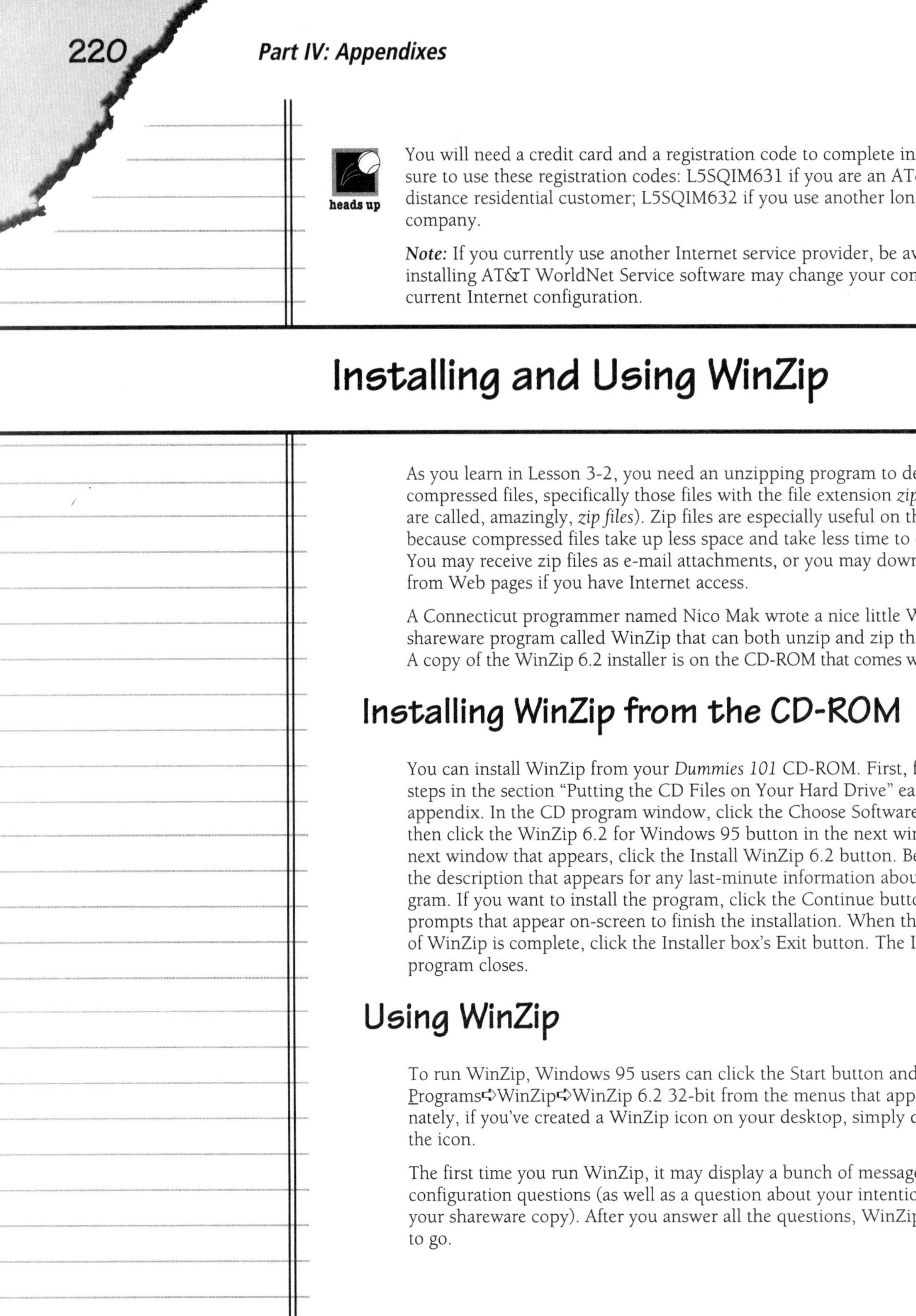

heads up

You will need a credit card and a registration code to complete installation. Be sure to use these registration codes: L5SQIM631 if you are an AT&T long-distance residential customer; L5SQIM632 if you use another long-distance company.

Note: If you currently use another Internet service provider, be aware that installing AT&T WorldNet Service software may change your computer's current Internet configuration.

Installing and Using WinZip

As you learn in Lesson 3-2, you need an unzipping program to deal with compressed files, specifically those files with the file extension *zip* (these files are called, amazingly, *zip files*). Zip files are especially useful on the Internet, because compressed files take up less space and take less time to download. You may receive zip files as e-mail attachments, or you may download them from Web pages if you have Internet access.

A Connecticut programmer named Nico Mak wrote a nice little Windows shareware program called WinZip that can both unzip and zip things for you. A copy of the WinZip 6.2 installer is on the CD-ROM that comes with this book.

Installing WinZip from the CD-ROM

You can install WinZip from your *Dummies 101* CD-ROM. First, follow the steps in the section "Putting the CD Files on Your Hard Drive" earlier in this appendix. In the CD program window, click the Choose Software button, and then click the WinZip 6.2 for Windows 95 button in the next window. In the next window that appears, click the Install WinZip 6.2 button. Be sure to read the description that appears for any last-minute information about the program. If you want to install the program, click the Continue button. Follow the prompts that appear on-screen to finish the installation. When the installation of WinZip is complete, click the Installer box's Exit button. The Installer program closes.

Using WinZip

To run WinZip, Windows 95 users can click the Start button and choose Programs➪WinZip➪WinZip 6.2 32-bit from the menus that appear. Alternately, if you've created a WinZip icon on your desktop, simply double-click the icon.

The first time you run WinZip, it may display a bunch of messages and configuration questions (as well as a question about your intention to register your shareware copy). After you answer all the questions, WinZip is ready to go.

Viewing the contents of a zip file

To open a zip file and view the files it contains, follow these steps:

1. **Click the Open button on the WinZip Toolbar, press Ctrl+O, or choose File➪Open Archive from the menu bar.**

   You see an Open Archive dialog box. (The WinZip folks also call zip files *archives.*)

2. **Move to the drive and folder that holds your file and then double-click the name of the zip file you want.**

   WinZip opens the zip file and displays information about the files it contains. For each file, you see the filename, date, time, size when decompressed, and how much WinZip was able to compress the file.

Extracting the contents of a zip file

After you open a zip file, you can copy decompressed versions of its files to any folder you specify. The zip file itself remains unchanged.

To extract the files from a zip file and make them useable, follow these steps:

1. **Open the zip file you want to work with (see "Viewing the contents of a zip file").**

   The files in the zip file should be displayed in the WinZip window.

2. **To select one file to decompress, simply click its name. To select more than one file, click each file's name while holding down the Ctrl key. To select all the listed files, choose Actions➪Select All from the menu bar.**

   Each file you select is highlighted.

3. **Click the Extract button on the Toolbar.**

   An Extract dialog box appears. Notice that the Extract To box is selected, as indicated by a text cursor blinking in it. This box lets you specify where you want to store the decompressed files.

4. **In the Extract To box, type the name of the folder you want to use to store the extracted files.**

   For example, if you want to store the decompressed files in a folder named MyData on drive C, you type **C:\MyData**. Your text replaces the highlighted text in the Extract To box.

5. **Press Enter or click Extract.**

   The files you selected are decompressed and copied to the folder you specified, and the zip file remains unchanged.

Note: If you ever decide that you don't want to use WinZip, you can uninstall it from your system, a process that deletes all its program and data files. To remove WinZip, Windows 95 users click the Start button on the Taskbar and then choose Programs➪WinZip➪Uninstall WinZip.

heads up

To learn more about WinZip's features while the program is running, press the F1 key or click Help from the program's menu bar and click one of the options that appear. Alternately, Windows 95 users can click the Start button and then choose Programs⇨WinZip⇨Online Manual to get detailed information about using WinZip.

Registering WinZip

Now that you know how to use WinZip, we think you'll probably want to register and keep the program. To order your own legal copy, choose Help⇨Ordering Information from the WinZip menu. Go ahead and register the shareware programs you use — doing so entitles you to upgrades and the great feeling of doing the right thing.

AT&T WorldNet℠ Service

A World of Possibilities…

Thank you for selecting AT&T WorldNet Service — it's the Internet as only AT&T can bring it to you. With AT&T WorldNet Service, a world of infinite possibilities is now within your reach. Research virtually any subject. Stay abreast of current events. Participate in online newsgroups. Purchase merchandise from leading retailers. Send and receive electronic mail.

AT&T WorldNet Service is rapidly becoming the preferred way of accessing the Internet. It was recently awarded one of the most highly coveted awards in the computer industry, *PC Computing*'s 1996 MVP Award for Best Internet Service Provider. Now, more than ever, it's the best way to stay in touch with the people, ideas, and information that are important to you.

You need a computer with a mouse, a modem, a phone line, and the enclosed software. That's all. We've taken care of the rest.

If You Can Point and Click, You're There

With AT&T WorldNet Service, finding the information you want on the Internet is easier than you ever imagined it could be. You can surf the Net within minutes. And find almost anything you want to know — from the weather in Paris, Texas — to the cost of a ticket to Paris, France. You're just a point and click away. It's that easy.

AT&T WorldNet Service features specially customized, industry-leading browsers, integrated with advanced Internet directories and search engines. The result is an Internet service that sets a new standard for ease of use — virtually everywhere you want to go is a point and click away, making it a snap to navigate the Internet.

When you go online with AT&T WorldNet Service, you'll benefit from being connected to the Internet by the world leader in networking. We offer you fast access of up to 28.8 Kbps in more than 215 cities throughout the U.S. that will make going online as easy as picking up your phone.

Online Help and Advice 24 Hours a Day, 7 Days a Week

Before you begin exploring the Internet, you may want to take a moment to check two useful sources of information.

If you're new to the Internet, from the AT&T WorldNet Service home page at `www.worldnet.att.net`, click on the Net Tutorial hyperlink for a quick explanation of unfamiliar terms and useful advice about exploring the Internet.

Another useful source of information is the HELP icon. The area contains pertinent, time saving, information-intensive reference tips, and topics such as Accounts & Billing, Trouble Reporting, Downloads & Upgrades, Security Tips, Network Hot Spots, Newsgroups, Special Announcements, etc.

Whether online or off-line, 24 hours a day, seven days a week, we will provide World Class technical expertise and fast, reliable responses to your questions. To reach AT&T WorldNet Customer Care, call **1-800-400-1447**.

Nothing is more important to us than making sure that your Internet experience is a truly enriching and satisfying one.

Safeguard Your Online Purchases

AT&T WorldNet Service is committed to making the Internet a safe and convenient way to transact business. By registering and continuing to charge your AT&T WorldNet Service to your AT&T Universal Card, you'll enjoy peace of mind whenever you shop the Internet. Should your account number be compromised on the Net, you won't be liable for any online transactions charged to your AT&T Universal Card by a person who is not an authorized user.*

*Today, cardmembers may be liable for the first $50 of charges made by a person who is not an authorized user, which will not be imposed under this program as long as the cardmember notifies AT&T Universal Card of the loss within 24 hours and otherwise complies with the Cardmember Agreement. Refer to Cardmember Agreement for definition of authorized user.

Minimum System Requirements

IBM-Compatible Personal Computer Users:

- IBM-compatible personal computer with 486SX or higher processor
- 8MB of RAM (or more for better performance)
- 15–36MB of available hard disk space to install software, depending on platform (14–21MB to use service after installation, depending on platform)
- Graphics system capable of displaying 256 colors
- 14,400 bps modem connected to an outside phone line and not a LAN or ISDN line
- Microsoft Windows 3.1*x* or Windows 95

Macintosh Users:

- Macintosh 68030 or higher (including 68LC0X0 models and all Power Macintosh models)
- System 7.5.3 Revision 2 or higher for PCI Power Macintosh models: System 7.1 or higher for all 680X0 and non-PCI Power Macintosh models
- Mac TCP 2.0.6 or Open Transport 1.1 or higher

- 8MB of RAM (minimum) with Virtual Memory turned on or RAM Doubler; 16MB recommended for Power Macintosh users
- 12MB of available hard disk space (15MB recommended)
- 14,400 bps modem connected to an outside phone line and not a LAN or ISDN line
- Color or 256 grayscale monitor
- Apple Guide 1.2 or higher (if you want to view online help)

  If you are uncertain of the configuration of your Macintosh computer, consult your Macintosh User's guide or call Apple at 1-800-767-2775.

Installation Tips and Instructions

- If you have other Web browsers or online software, please consider uninstalling them according to the vendor's instructions.
- If you are installing AT&T WorldNet Service on a computer with Local Area Networking, please contact your LAN administrator for setup instructions.
- At the end of installation, you may be asked to restart your computer. Don't attempt the registration process until you have done so.

IBM-compatible PC users:

- Insert the CD-ROM into the CD-ROM drive on your computer.
- Select ***File/Run*** (for Windows 3.1*x*) or ***Start/Run*** (for Windows 95 if setup did not start automatically).
- Type ***D:\setup.exe*** (or change the "D" if your CD-ROM is another drive).
- Click ***OK***.
- Follow the onscreen instructions to install and register.

Macintosh users:

- Disable all extensions except the Apple CD-ROM and Foreign Files Access extensions.
- Restart computer.
- Insert the CD-ROM into the CD-ROM drive on your computer.
- Double-click the *Install AT&T WorldNet Service* icon.
- Follow the onscreen instructions to install. (Upon restarting your Macintosh, AT&T WorldNet Service Account Setup automatically starts.)
- Follow the onscreen instructions to register.

Registering with AT&T WorldNet Service

After you have connected with AT&T WorldNet online registration service, you will be presented with a series of screens that confirm billing information and prompt you for additional account set-up data.

The following is a list of registration tips and comments that will help you during the registration process.

I. Use one of the following registration codes, which can also be found in Appendix B of *Dummies 101: Microsoft Outlook 97 For Windows*. Use L5SQIM631 if you are an AT&T long-distance residential customer or L5SQIM632 if you use another long-distance phone company.

II. During registration, you will need to supply your name, address, and valid credit card number, and choose an account information security word, e-mail name, and e-mail password. You will also be requested to select your preferred price plan at this time. (We advise that you use all lowercase letters when assigning an e-mail ID and security code, since they are easier to remember.)

III. If you make a mistake and exit or get disconnected during the registration process prematurely, simply click on "Create New Account." Do not click on "Edit Existing Account."

IV. When choosing your local access telephone number, you will be given several options. Please choose the one nearest to you. Please note that calling a number within your area does not guarantee that the call is free.

Connecting to AT&T WorldNet Service

When you have finished installing and registering with AT&T WorldNet Service, you are ready to access the Internet. Make sure your modem and phone line are available before attempting to connect to the service.

For Windows 95 users:

- Double-click on the ***Connect to AT&T WorldNet Service*** icon on your desktop.

  OR
- Select ***Start, Programs, AT&T WorldNet Software, Connect to AT&T WorldNet Service.***

For Windows 3.*x* users:

- Double-click on the ***Connect to AT&T WorldNet Service*** icon located in the AT&T WorldNet Service group.

For Macintosh users:

- Double-click on the ***AT&T WorldNet Service*** icon in the AT&T WorldNet Service folder.

Choose the Plan That's Right for You

The Internet is for everyone, whether at home or at work. In addition to making the time you spend online productive and fun, we're also committed to making it affordable. Choose one of two price plans: unlimited usage access or hourly usage access. The latest pricing information can be obtained during online registration. No matter which plan you use, we're confident that after you take advantage of everything AT&T WorldNet Service has to offer, you'll wonder how you got along without it.

AT&T

Explore our AT&T WorldNet Service site at `http://www.att.com/worldnet`.

Index

Symbols

A

B

C

(continued)

D

E

F

G

H

I

J

L

M

N

O

P

Q

R

S

T

U

V

W

X

Z

Notes

Notes

Notes

Notes

Notes

Notes

Notes

Notes

Notes

Notes

Notes

Notes

Notes

Notes

IDG BOOKS WORLDWIDE, INC.

END-USER LICENSE AGREEMENT

Read This. You should carefully read these terms and conditions before opening the software packet(s) included with this book ("Book"). This is a license agreement ("Agreement") between you and IDG Books Worldwide, Inc. ("IDGB"). By opening the accompanying software packet(s), you acknowledge that you have read and accept the following terms and conditions. If you do not agree and do not want to be bound by such terms and conditions, promptly return the Book and the unopened software packet(s) to the place you obtained them for a full refund.

1. **License Grant**. IDGB grants to you (either an individual or entity) a nonexclusive license to use one copy of the enclosed software program(s) (collectively, the "Software") solely for your own personal or business purposes on a single computer (whether a standard computer or a workstation component of a multiuser network). The Software is in use on a computer when it is loaded into temporary memory (i.e., RAM) or installed into permanent memory (e.g., hard disk, CD-ROM, or other storage device). IDGB reserves all rights not expressly granted herein.

2. **Ownership**. IDGB is the owner of all right, title, and interest, including copyright, in and to the compilation of the Software recorded on the CD-ROM. Copyright to the individual programs on the CD-ROM is owned by the author or other authorized copyright owner of each program. Ownership of the Software and all proprietary rights relating thereto remain with IDGB and its licensors.

3. **Restrictions on Use and Transfer**.

   (a) You may only (i) make one copy of the Software for backup or archival purposes, or (ii) transfer the Software to a single hard disk, provided that you keep the original for backup or archival purposes. You may not (i) rent or lease the Software, (ii) copy or reproduce the Software through a LAN or other network system or through any computer subscriber system or bulletin-board system, or (iii) modify, adapt, or create derivative works based on the Software.

   (b) You may not reverse engineer, decompile, or disassemble the Software. You may transfer the Software and user documentation on a permanent basis, provided that the transferee agrees to accept the terms and conditions of this Agreement and you retain no copies. If the Software is an update or has been updated, any transfer must include the most recent update and all prior versions.

4. **Restrictions on Use of Individual Programs**. You must follow the individual requirements and restrictions detailed for each individual program in Appendix B of this Book. These limitations are contained in the individual license agreements recorded on the CD-ROM. These restrictions may include a requirement that after using the program for the period of time specified in its text, the user must pay a registration

fee or discontinue use. By opening the Software packet(s), you will be agreeing to abide by the licenses and restrictions for these individual programs. None of the material on this disc or listed in this Book may ever be distributed, in original or modified form, for commercial purposes.

5. Limited Warranty.

   (a) IDGB warrants that the Software and CD-ROM are free from defects in materials and workmanship under normal use for a period of sixty (60) days from the date of purchase of this Book. If IDGB receives notification within the warranty period of defects in materials or workmanship, IDGB will replace the defective CD-ROM.

   (b) **IDGB AND THE AUTHORS OF THE BOOK DISCLAIM ALL OTHER WARRANTIES, EXPRESS OR IMPLIED, INCLUDING WITHOUT LIMITATION IMPLIED WARRANTIES OF MERCHANTABILITY AND FITNESS FOR A PARTICULAR PURPOSE, WITH RESPECT TO THE SOFTWARE, THE PROGRAMS, THE SOURCE CODE CONTAINED THEREIN, AND/OR THE TECHNIQUES DESCRIBED IN THIS BOOK. IDGB DOES NOT WARRANT THAT THE FUNCTIONS CONTAINED IN THE SOFTWARE WILL MEET YOUR REQUIREMENTS OR THAT THE OPERATION OF THE SOFTWARE WILL BE ERROR FREE.**

   (c) This limited warranty gives you specific legal rights, and you may have other rights which vary from jurisdiction to jurisdiction.

6. Remedies.

   (a) IDGB's entire liability and your exclusive remedy for defects in materials and workmanship shall be limited to replacement of the Software, which may be returned to IDGB with a copy of your receipt at the following address: Disk Fulfillment Department, Attn: Dummies 101: Microsoft Outlook 97 For Windows, IDG Books Worldwide, Inc., 7260 Shadeland Station, Ste. 100, Indianapolis, IN 46256, or call 1-800-762-2974. Please allow 3–4 weeks for delivery. This Limited Warranty is void if failure of the Software has resulted from accident, abuse, or misapplication. Any replacement Software will be warranted for the remainder of the original warranty period or thirty (30) days, whichever is longer.

   (b) In no event shall IDGB or the author be liable for any damages whatsoever (including without limitation damages for loss of business profits, business interruption, loss of business information, or any other pecuniary loss) arising from the use of or inability to use the Book or the Software, even if IDGB has been advised of the possibility of such damages.

   (c) Because some jurisdictions do not allow the exclusion or limitation of liability for consequential or incidental damages, the above limitation or exclusion may not apply to you.

7. **U.S. Government Restricted Rights.** Use, duplication, or disclosure of the Software by the U.S. Government is subject to restrictions stated in paragraph (c) (1) (ii) of the Rights in Technical Data and Computer Software clause of DFARS 252.227-7013, and in subparagraphs (a) through (d) of the Commercial Computer — Restricted Rights clause at FAR 52.227-19, and in similar clauses in the NASA FAR supplement, when applicable.

8. **General.** This Agreement constitutes the entire understanding of the parties and revokes and supersedes all prior agreements, oral or written, between them and may not be modified or amended except in a writing signed by both parties hereto which specifically refers to this Agreement. This Agreement shall take precedence over any other documents that may be in conflict herewith. If any one or more provisions contained in this Agreement are held by any court or tribunal to be invalid, illegal, or otherwise unenforceable, each and every other provision shall remain in full force and effect.

Dummies 101 CD-ROM Installation Instructions

The CD that comes with this book contains exercise files that you need to follow along with the lessons in the book. You need to put these files on your hard drive before you can use them. After you read this book, you can easily remove the files.

After the CD installer appears, you can install the exercise files and software. See Appendix B for the details on installing the files from the CD.

With Windows 95 up and running, follow these steps:

1. **Insert the Dummies 101 CD (label side up) into your computer's CD drive and wait about 30 seconds to see whether AutoPlay starts the CD for you.**

   Be careful to touch only the edges of the CD. The CD drive is the one that pops out with a circular drawer.

   If your computer has the Windows CD AutoPlay feature, the CD installer should begin automatically. If you see the CD installer window (it looks like a piece of notebook paper with the book's title), see "Installing the exercise files" in Appendix B to install the files.

   If nothing happens after a minute or so, go to Step 2.

2. **If the installation program doesn't start automatically, click the Start button and click Run.**

3. **In the dialog box that appears, type** d:\seticon.exe **(if your CD drive is not drive D, substitute the appropriate letter for D) and click OK.**

   A message informs you that the program is about to install the icons.

4. **Click OK in the message window.**

   After a moment, a program group called Dummies 101 appears on the Start menu, along with an icon that runs the CD installer. Then another message appears, asking whether you want to use the CD now.

5. **Click Yes to use the CD now or click No if you want to use the CD later.**

   If you click No, you can start the CD later simply by clicking the Dummies 101 - Outlook 97 For Windows CD icon in the Dummies 101 program group (on the Start button).

You don't have to do anything to the files yet. We tell you when you need to open a file from the CD.

heads up

Remember that you need to have Outlook 97 and Windows 95 installed on your computer in order to work through the lessons in this book.

If you have problems with the installation process, you can call the IDG Books Worldwide, Inc. Customer Support number: 800-762-2974 (outside the U.S.: 317-596-5261).

IDG BOOKS WORLDWIDE REGISTRATION CARD

RETURN THIS REGISTRATION CARD FOR FREE CATALOG

Title of this book: Dummies 101®: Microsoft® Outlook™ 97 For Windows®

My overall rating of this book: ❑ Very good [1] ❑ Good [2] ❑ Satisfactory [3] ❑ Fair [4] ❑ Poor [5]

How I first heard about this book:

❑ Found in bookstore; name: [6] ______ ❑ Book review: [7] ______

❑ Advertisement: [8] ______ ❑ Catalog: [9] ______

❑ Word of mouth; heard about book from friend, co-worker, etc.: [10] ______ ❑ Other: [11] ______

What I liked most about this book: ______

What I would change, add, delete, etc., in future editions of this book: ______

Other comments: ______

Number of computer books I purchase in a year: ❑ 1 [12] ❑ 2-5 [13] ❑ 6-10 [14] ❑ More than 10 [15]

I would characterize my computer skills as: ❑ Beginner [16] ❑ Intermediate [17] ❑ Advanced [18] ❑ Professional [19]

I use ❑ DOS [20] ❑ Windows [21] ❑ OS/2 [22] ❑ Unix [23] ❑ Macintosh [24] ❑ Other: [25] ______ (please specify)

I would be interested in new books on the following subjects:
(please check all that apply, and use the spaces provided to identify specific software)

❑ Word processing: [26] ______ ❑ Spreadsheets: [27] ______

❑ Data bases: [28] ______ ❑ Desktop publishing: [29] ______

❑ File Utilities: [30] ______ ❑ Money management: [31] ______

❑ Networking: [32] ______ ❑ Programming languages: [33] ______

❑ Other: [34] ______

I use a PC at (please check all that apply): ❑ home [35] ❑ work [36] ❑ school [37] ❑ other: [38] ______

The disks I prefer to use are ❑ 5.25 [39] ❑ 3.5 [40] ❑ other: [41] ______

I have a CD ROM: ❑ yes [42] ❑ no [43]

I plan to buy or upgrade computer hardware this year: ❑ yes [44] ❑ no [45]

I plan to buy or upgrade computer software this year: ❑ yes [46] ❑ no [47]

Name: ______ Business title: [48] ______ Type of Business: [49] ______

Address (❑ home [50] ❑ work [51]/Company name: ______)

Street/Suite# ______

City [52]/State [53]/Zipcode [54]: ______ Country [55] ______

❑ **I liked this book!** You may quote me by name in future IDG Books Worldwide promotional materials.

My daytime phone number is ______

IDG BOOKS

THE WORLD OF COMPUTER KNOWLEDGE

Please keep me informed about IDG's World of Computer Knowledge.
Send me the latest IDG Books catalog.

NO POSTAGE
NECESSARY
IF MAILED
IN THE
UNITED STATES

BUSINESS REPLY MAIL

FIRST CLASS MAIL PERMIT NO. 2605 FOSTER CITY, CALIFORNIA

IDG Books Worldwide
919 E Hillsdale Blvd, STE 400
Foster City, CA 94404-9691